The Aesthetics of History

This book offers an understanding and analysis of the aesthetics of historying through the specific concepts and process of the *factional, factitious, fabricated, factious, factitive, factive, factualist, fictitious, fictive,* and *figurative*. These concepts create the(ir) connection(s) between 'the past' and 'history' hitherto to rethink the nature of 'the historical past'. There are many different available 'forms' of histories that shape the minds of historians when they deploy their historical imaginations through 'the past(s) via their preferred history creations'. For every historian and every history reader, there is a different experience of 'the history past aesthetic'.

Alun Munslow is Professor Emeritus of History and Historical Theory at Staffordshire University and has held various professorial chairs.

Routledge Approaches to History

Cowrie Shells and Cowrie Money
A Global History
Bin Yang

A Personalist Philosophy of History
Bennett Gilbert

Historical Parallels, Commemoration and Icons
Edited by Andreas Leutzsch

Historians Without Borders
New Studies in Multidisciplinary History
Edited by Lawrence Abrams and Kaleb Knoblauch

Leopold von Ranke
A Biography
Andreas D. Boldt

Teleology and Modernity
Edited by Dan O'Brien, Marius Turda, David Ohana and William Gibson

Historia Ludens
The Playing Historian
Edited by Alexander von Lünen, Katherine J. Lewis, Benjamin Litherland and Pat Cullum

The Aesthetics of History
Alun Munslow

For more information about this series, please visit: https://www.routledge.com/Routledge-Approaches-to-History/book-series/RSHISTHRY

The Aesthetics of History

Alun Munslow

NEW YORK AND LONDON

First published 2020
by Routledge
52 Vanderbilt Avenue, New York, NY 10017

and by Routledge
2 Park Square, Milton Park, Abingdon, Oxon, OX14 4RN

Routledge is an imprint of the Taylor & Francis Group, an informa business

© 2020 Taylor & Francis

The right of Alun Munslow to be identified as author of this work has been asserted in accordance with sections 77 and 78 of the Copyright, Designs and Patents Act 1988.

All rights reserved. No part of this book may be reprinted or reproduced or utilised in any form or by any electronic, mechanical, or other means, now known or hereafter invented, including photocopying and recording, or in any information storage or retrieval system, without permission in writing from the publishers.

Trademark notice: Product or corporate names may be trademarks or registered trademarks, and are used only for identification and explanation without intent to infringe.

Library of Congress Cataloging-in-Publication Data
Names: Munslow, Alun, 1947– author.
Title: The aesthetics of history / Alun Munslow.
Description: New York : Routledge Taylor & Francis Group, 2019. | Series: Routledge approaches to history ; 31 | Includes index.
Identifiers: LCCN 2019032630 (print) | LCCN 2019032631 (ebook) | ISBN 9780367272739 (hardback) | ISBN 9780429295911 (ebook) | ISBN 9781000734058 (adobe pdf) | ISBN 9781000734126 (mobi) | ISBN 9781000734195 (epub)
Subjects: LCSH: History—Philosophy. | Historiography.
Classification: LCC D13 .M844 2019 (print) | LCC D13 (ebook) | DDC 901—dc23
LC record available at https://lccn.loc.gov/2019032630
LC ebook record available at https://lccn.loc.gov/2019032631

ISBN: 978-0-367-27273-9 (hbk)
ISBN: 978-0-429-29591-1 (ebk)

Typeset in Sabon
by Apex CoVantage, LLC

For Jane, as always

Contents

	Introduction	1
1	Factional	14
2	Factitious	30
3	Fabricated	47
4	Factious	64
5	Factitive	81
6	Factive	97
7	Factualist	115
8	Fictitious	132
9	Fictive	148
10	Figurative	164
	Conclusion	180
	Index	192

Introduction

Over a number of years, I have increasingly thought of history not as a deconstruction of the past, as I had previously thought, but as a complex (usually a very complex) authorial creation. This is not to claim that the past is what historians (variously) want to believe about the reality of the past. No, to be clear, the past is the time before our perpetual present, and what I have long designated as 'the-past-*as*-history' is not the same as 'the history of the past'. Plainly, the past is accessible only in the form of those narrative(s) we choose to create about it. This is not to endorse the notion that we can invent the past as it suits us. The past was the past and obviously there is no point in denying the reality of the past. Only meretricious fools deny the reality of the past. The past is what the past was.

Nevertheless and unavoidably engaging with the past can be delivered in a variety of forms. These include the 'written' and/or 'spoken' and/or 'danced' and/or 'built' and/or many other forms that can legitimately claim to be a (re)presentation of 'the past'. Almost regardless of its 'presentational form', no one, and obviously including historians, can claim that the past can be resurrected or resuscitated or revived as it actually was. It does no harm to accept that the supreme irony in doing history, then, is that 'the history' can only be a substitute for a past. For every historian there is always a preferred history. History then is not the past. History is a substitute for the past authored in whatever 'form and content' the historian wants. The historian's narrative creation of the past, even if it is claimed to be 'the past as it actually was', remains to be a form of imitation or simulation. Hence, no history can legitimately be regarded as a substitute for the past. Of course, on balance historians can know what 'really happened in the past'. Nevertheless, interpreting the available range of sensible possible meanings and explanations that historians contrive and create means that all histories almost invariably fail to produce 'the history of . . .'.

So, historians always end up striving to 'recreate and reconstitute' the nature, meaning, and explanation of the contents of the past by organising, classifying, and systemising what happened in the past. Now, it is hardly news (I have noted it before) that historians 'process' the 'ontic' and the 'epistemic' nature of the past. Those two terms are not as awkward as they sound. The concept of 'the ontic' simply refers to 'the empirical stuff' defined by historians. Thus, historians collate as 'the facts' the descriptions which they create/created about the past. The epistemic then refers to 'the theory' of how historians come to know what happened in respect of 'the knowledge of the past'. And there is plenty of 'the past' available that can be usefully turned into the historian's preferred 'history'.

Historians, like everyone else, deploy the simple mechanism of 'shaping the past' by turning it into 'a (hi)story'. The past, obviously, is just 'mush' until it is 'processed' into a history. However, turning the past into a description of what the historian believes to be previous reality—the past *as* it was—requires that the reality of the past can be adequately offered as a truthful description of the past. Obviously, the past is not history and history is not the past. You can have one or the other. So, historians along with everyone else have to define their preferred topics and events in the past with the aim of 'discovering' what they choose to believe is 'the history'. For every historian there is always a history to be discovered 'back there and then'. To discover the reality of the past historians (like everyone else) are required to 'shape and form' past reality through 'the(ir) authorial mechanism'. This process involves deploying 'concepts', 'theories', 'themes', and 'leitmotivs'. Moreover, the past has to be fashioned and formed by concepts such as gender, culture, class, regions, war, peace, ideology, the rise and fall of industrial processes, art and aesthetics, cities, and so forth. The past is particularly unhelpful for historians because 'the past' is and remains just 'stuff' until the historian claims to have discovered 'the explanation and meaning of the nature of the past'. But, obviously, the reality of the past—which cannot be sensibly denied given the available 'data and reference'—still has to be processed 'back into' what it was.

Unavoidably, engaging with the past can be delivered in a variety of forms. These include the 'written' and/or 'spoken' and/or 'danced' and/or 'built' and/or 'dug up' and many other forms that can legitimately claim to be a (re)presentation of 'the past'. Almost regardless of its 'presentational form' no one, and obviously including historians, can claim that the past can be resurrected or resuscitated or revived as it actually was. It does no harm to accept that the supreme irony in doing history, then, is that 'the history' can only be a substitute for a past. For every historian there is always a preferred history. History then is not the past. History is a substitute for the past authored in whatever 'form and content' the historian wants. The historian's narrative creation of the past and even if it is claimed to be 'the past as it actually was', remains to be a form of imitation or simulation. Hence, no history can legitimately be regarded as a substitute for the past. Of course, on balance historians can know what 'really happened in the past'. Nevertheless, interpreting the available range of sensible possible meanings and explanations that historians contrive and create means that all histories almost invariably fail to produce 'the history of . . .'.

So, historians always end up striving to 'recreate and reconstitute' the nature, meaning, and explanation of the contents of the past by organising, classifying, and systemising what happened in the past. Now, it is hardly news (I have noted it before) that historians 'process' the 'ontic' and the 'epistemic' nature of the past. Those two terms are not as awkward as they sound. The concept of 'the ontic' simply refers to 'the empirical stuff' defined by historians. Thus, historians collate as 'the facts' descriptions which they create/created about the past. The epistemic then refers to 'the theory' of how historians come to know what happened in respect of 'the knowledge of the past'. And there is plenty of 'the past' available that can be usefully turned into the historian's preferred 'history'.

Historians, like everyone else, deploy the simple mechanism of 'shaping the past' by turning it into 'a (hi)story'. The past, obviously, is just 'mush' until it is 'processed' into a history. However, turning the past into a description of what the historian believes to be previous reality—the past *as* it was—requires that the reality of the past can be adequately offered as a truthful description of the past. Obviously, the past is not history and history is not the past. You can have one or the other. So, historians along with everyone else have to define their preferred topics and events in the past with the aim of 'discovering' what they choose to believe is 'the history'. For every historian there is always a history to be discovered 'back there and then'. To discover the reality of the past historians (like everyone else) are required to 'shape and form' past reality through 'the(ir) authorial mechanism'. This process involves deploying 'concepts', 'theories', 'themes', and 'leitmotivs'. Moreover, the past has to be fashioned and formed by concepts such as gender, culture, class, regions, war, peace, ideology, the rise and fall of industrial processes, art and aesthetics, cities, and so forth. The past, then, is particularly unhelpful for historians because 'the past' is and remains just 'stuff' until the historian claims to have discovered 'the explanation and meaning of the nature of the past'. But, and obviously, the reality of the past, which cannot be sensibly denied given the available 'data and reference', still has to be processed back into what the historian believes it was.

Now, for most historians and probably also everyone else, it makes common sense to believe that the past is history and history is the past. However, that common sense makes no sense of any kind. Knowing what happened in the past is hardly difficult to 'discover' and 'figure out' its most likely meaning. And, even though it is difficult, the past can be infused (aka discovered) with meaning. Unhappily and awkwardly, the past has no inherent meaning until it is 'historied' by historians and also anybody else. Regardless of this, most historians, along with everybody else, will insist on conflating 'the past' with 'history' and vice versa. Thus, the 'now' inaccessible past is relocated into a variety of forms such as books, journal articles, lectures, seminars, news reports, or history.

There is very little doubt (in my view) that the past was once what it was. Awkwardly, 'the time before our constant present' is, of course, inaccessible even though we may have experienced it in our perpetual present (which is, of course, no longer present). And so, it is hardly news that engaging with the reality of the past can only be constituted through the production and processing of an unavoidable aesthetic truth. For historians (and everyone else) accepting an aesthetic truth in terms of what describing actually happened in the past means we cannot relate the reality of the past as it actually was and what it meant. The nature of the past, then, is entirely subject to the unavoidable aestheticisation and discursive imaginative disclosure of the historian and hence this book.

Plainly, then, there is no single given history of the past as far as we can 'tell' and that is why there are so many different 'historical pasts'. Now, basic and simple common sense suggests that we ought to believe that the past is the past because surely there can only be one (f)actual history? Unhappily, that makes no sense. Apart from denying past reality which, of course, is an example of meretricious stupidity, historians work very hard to uncover and 'write up' their 'history findings' of what they believe was (is?) the most likely narrative reality of the past. Now, this also makes no sense of course. Along with everyone else, historians invest in common sense notions such as 'historical facts', which unhappily are never more than events under a description.

Historians, of course, do not invent the past trained, as they are to discover the most likely history of the past. Historians are trained to acknowledge that the past has turned out to be the (hi)story which is that which they have authored. However, and regrettably, that makes no sense of any kind. This is because 'the past' is not simply awaiting discovery through its history. Hence, the past can only be accessed and processed through a history and/or histories. All histories, then, are fusions of the disparate authorial descriptions by people in the past as understood, well, by historians. Now, getting the (hi)story straight is foundational to our culture. Hence, it is important to know, discover and determine what actually happened in the past, which, of course, is not the same as history.

So, I want to be very clear, the historian's engagement with the past is the time which the historian has historied into existence. Now, it is acknowledged among historians that getting the (hi)story straight is simply their preferred narrative for the(ir) past. The notion of seeking out the most likely reality and truth of the past is, of course, the foundational aim of the historian. But the past is, of course, no longer the real thing once it is historied. This is obvious of course and to get round this awkward situation, there are two foundational beliefs that most historians adhere to: that there is always a narrative history in the past and that it can be discovered and/or uncovered and/or recovered and/or revealed. Hence, historians insist that histories exist in the past and with due diligence can be dug up, revealed, discovered, exposed, and so forth.

The necessary corollary to this processing is for the historian to reject the notion of the 'inventive' and 'creative' in discovering the most likely past. Unhappily, getting the (hi)story straight is a very odd belief among most historians because there is no (hi)story to discover and get straight in the past. Knowing what happened in the past is an absolute building block of our culture and denying past reality has very little to do with the process of 'doing history'. Knowing what actually happened in the past is not the same as discovering the history of the past. Hence, all that historians (and every other human being) can do is determine the master narrative that they chose to believe must be back there in the past. Happily, for historians (and everyone else) the past is never allowed to be 'just one thing after another'. In the absence of the most likely narrative, the historian will discover and provide it. This means that the past can have its history and history must be the past. When this process collapses (when a new interpretation turns up), historians eventually reconstitute/recreate the history of the past.

The past, then, is the time before now and history is assumed to exist in 'the past', awaiting discovery and delivery. Unhappily, what happened in 'the past' is not necessarily going to turn out to be 'the most likely history' and all those months and years in the archive the history investigators efforts come to naught. Of course, 'the-past-*as*-history' eventually always wears out. So, is it really possible and/or feasible and/or likely that 'the-past-*as*-history' once existed? Well, no, given that the past is not history and history is not the past. So, what next? Can we rely on the reality of the past? Well, of course we can but only if we apply due diligence. Unfortunately, the snag in this is that the past is not only what it was but also what it might have been and meant.

In this book, then, I address five twinned concepts, which might help us in making sense of our engagement with the past, which no longer exists. I began my efforts in this endeavour with my book *A History of History* (2012), which has turned out to be an early effort at understanding our (and my) aesthetic experience of the past. Now, in that book I argued that historians might usefully deploy six key concepts that I suggested shaped and formed the nature of the history of the past. These concepts were those of the *fabricated*, *factious*, *factual(ist/ism)*, *fictive*, and *figurative*. After further considerable and substantial thought on my part, I have now extended my analysis in this book.

My analysis in this book has turned out to be an extended range of concepts. The list has been now extended to the *factional, factitious, fabricated, factious, factitive, factive, factualist, fictitious, fictive,* and *figurative*. Now, what prompted me to do this half a decade later was my judgment that engaging with the past—ironically—can only be achieved by continuously authoring and re-authoring the past into varieties histories through the mechanism of the historian's engagement with their historical imagination. This is not to suggest that historians are unaware that they create the(ir) connection(s) between 'the past' and 'history'. Plainly, there are available 'forms' of histories in the minds of historians which constitute their historical imaginations by construing and construing the past(s) via their aesthetic 'history creations'. What I suggest this means is that for every historian and reader there is a different experience of the past and in order to make sense of this experience of the past, there is an unavoidable 'history aesthetic experience'.

So, doing history means that 'the-past-*as*-history' can only be construed and interpreted through the historian's personal and individual historical aesthetic experience. Like every author, then, historians are able to bring forth that which is not directly accessed by the empirical, observable, and presumed real. In this book, then, I extend several multiple notions that shape and form 'the historical imagination' rather than directly engage with the past. Now, knowing what happened in the past seems to summarize what historians do. But, while knowing what happened in the attested past is obviously foundational to understanding the nature of the past as it actually was, it tells us nothing about 'doing history'. Unfortunately and regrettably, then, the foundational problem of doing history is the historian's 'forming of the past' in accord with their preferred interpretation as to what it all meant. Somewhat awkwardly, then, the past is what the past was and it can only be accessed through the veiled intermediary of a history. The past is not history and history is not the past.

Knowing the content of the past does not constitute a history. To access the past, historians have to shape and form their authorial decisions in respect of their belief as to the nature of past reality. Now, the reality of the past can only be offered through varieties of (re)presentations. The past, then, can only be engaged once it is authored into a description of, well, the past. As the American history theorist Hayden White argued in 1973, all historians and everyone else have to accept that knowing what happened in the past is not simply a discovery of what happened in the past. Unfortunately, the past is not history and history is not the past even if the historian insists they have conflated them. The past is the past and history is a history.

This book, then, is awkward (very awkward) for those who insist the past and the history are conflated. Now, like everyone else, historians recognize that they produce histories of *a* past that is no longer available except when they historicize it. Plainly, then, the past is not history and history is not the past. To resolve this problem historians have to deploy their historical imagination. I am as dim as most historians (and every other human being), which means and necessitates our creation of our preferred 'historical interpretation' that eventually (hopefully and optimistically) turns into a convenient and useful historical meaning. Historians, then, test possible cause and effect relationships in the past and if they remain unsure as to their meaning they will go back to the sources and rethink their previous cause and effect connections. Now, the notion of the 'discovery of the history' is alternatively known as the 'historical interpretation' and/or 'the historical imagination'. This process is a very simple demonstration of the capacity of the historian (and everyone else) to construct and deconstruct the scholarship of the 'history past'.

This process is (obviously) a 'figurative language procedure' that permits the historian along with every other literate human being to connect different areas and kinds of explaining, understanding, imagining, and drawing inferences. Plainly, even this simple process makes no sense of any sort because historians are invariably unable to visualise and/or figure out the range of possibilities of historical explanations and meanings that are available in the past. There is no absolute knowledge of past reality. This means that to gain an understanding of the past, historians must deploy their narrative-authorial processing skills. Put simply, like every other human being, the historian has to create meanings and explanations based on the sources and this, of course, demands figurative or metaphorical uses of words and linguistic expressions. Now, historians (like every other human being) cannot avoid connecting events, incidents, movements, and myriad discoveries, and so on. It is all too easy, then, for the historian to forget that history is just another act of writing about something that does not exist. And which can never 'come alive'.

So, in constituting 'the-past-*as*-history', all histories unavoidably end up as events under a description. The truth of the past—obviously—is subject to figurative and creative writing acts, which all historians deploy along with everybody else. Obviously, to offer a historical explanation there is always an assumption that—of course—a 'realistic correspondence' between the content of the form of the history and that which is referred to i.e., what, happened in the past. Happily, deploying symbolic language (as humans do) we can continuously create fresh relationships and invent and deploy innovative concepts that lead to additional historical knowledge that may or may not be useful. This is where the historical imagination becomes useful. Weak though it always is.

The (infamous) theorist Hayden White sensibly argued that the historian's choice of figurative styles as 'rhetorical models for historical representations' suggested that form is as significant as any other feature of studying the past (as history). Symbolism, ironically then, is the only mechanism through which humans can reproduce past reality by deploying words, sentences, paragraphs, analogies, and so forth that characterise and shape narrative emplotments. Now, historians tend to figure out 'what happened' and 'why' and 'when' in the past through their preferred emplotments (tragedy, comedy, satire, and so forth) whether they know it or not. Unavoidably, then as author's historians create or believe they have found 'the most likely explanation'. Unfortunately, explanatory history narratives remain what they are—explanatory history narratives that are prefigured through its author's preferred emplotments and/or arguments and/or ideological positions.

The infamous and brief 1970s/1980s postmodern 'metahistorical' wave has now declined and historians have now restored the 'practical historical imagination', which is simply and adequately sustained by truth-conditions, inference, and attested factualism. The instructive proposition remains through the singular descriptive statement and the classic inference or judgment of testable results of hypotheses, probabilities, plausibility, and contextualisation. 'Doing history' now has returned to the literal rendition of the past as it actually was. Language is now returned to its primal status of 'telling it like it was'. Today academic historians have sought (f)actual and fair interpretations of the past without worrying about deploying metaphor and/or simile and insist that the past is once again 'deeply contextual'. Most historians today regard the argument, that while metaphorical, figurative, emblematic, and illustrative statements cannot be literally true, it is always best to tell it like it was and assume that anything else is almost certainly untrue. Obviously, then, how can an assertion of past reality need a metaphor or a simile? Obviously, historians, today (and for a while now), have gone back to understanding that the (hi)stories they author are most likely accurate word pictures of past reality. But that is nonsense of course. A description is not that which is described.

Unfortunately, far too many historians have gratefully returned to the peculiar and, frankly, silly supposition that the past is a 'thing' or 'event' that is entirely independent of the descriptive discourse through which it is adopted. Again at best, history is either a reconstruction even though it remains an obvious nonsense, or a construction which can be clever thinking about the past but which is still nonsense, or history can be delivered as a deconstruction, which cannot possibly have any sense attached to it at all. Obviously, today, the historian is (more than happily) involved in the writing up of the history narrative that surely must be back there. However, today the historian is not allowed to interfere with the 'factualism' of the real past. Unfortunately, in engaging with the reality of the past, historians still have to lean on a perpetual present, which (and unavoidably) leans on the perpetual presence of the past.

Incongruously, historians are trained to believe that the(ir) 'historical imagination' is a self-justifying undertaking. The reason for this rather odd belief is that they are taught and obliged to connect the past with what assuredly must be its history given the sources they have found and deployed. Unhappily, there remains the impermeable obstacle between the universe of language and everything else. Historians always try to control language in their effort to regulate both 'the meaning' and 'the explanation' by insisting that the past must be history and history must be the past. This makes no sense of course, and so they always end up with an unresolvable real problem. To be fair, all human beings have the same problem because there is no 'figurative truth'. That is obviously a desperate nonsense. Nevertheless and consequently, the past is never more than an unmanageable figurative intellectual space that will ultimately collapse into itself and which unhappily at some point will morph into a different nonsense. So, the inescapable and impervious barrier between the linguistic and aesthetic worlds of history means all we end up with is a rhetorical past. Yes, the past is a rhetorical contrivance. Hence, in this book, obviously, my claim is that history is not the past because it is a description about the past.

The presence of the past, then, can only 'exist' thanks to that universal symbolic representation called 'history' which is a cognitive instrument for the characterisation and adornment of a past historical narrative that some groups of historians construe. Happily, none of this is complex thinking. Hence, all that historians can do is author(ise) what they believe is the truth of the past, as they believe it is in accord with the evidence of what once happened in the past (or the evidence they chose). Now, for the historian, 'authorialism' is not a mismatch with the truth of the past because today's historians have to cast the past figuratively simply because they are human beings. By using and adopting the image metaphor, historians imbue and construe and thereby establish the(ir) historically imagined narratives. The notion of cross-examining the past through the available evidence as if it were in the witness box thus remains. Regrettably the author(ity) of the past is itself construed, interpreted, and understood by historians through their envisaging relationships between nominated, chosen, and listed fixed points, which are the assumed evidences of the sources. Understandably, and poignantly, this is not the past speaking to the historian. The-past-*as*-history is no more than ventriloquising the past in the hope the(ir) history is likely (given the historian's selected evidence) that 'history exists back there' and which has simply been awaiting discovery.

Admittedly, in my experience, whether they are hardcore social scientists who joyfully deploy statistical regression analysis and coefficients of elasticity and other obscure mechanisms (as I did with my Ph.D.), or those who just aim to the get the story straight, the historical imagination remains what it is—an imagining and imaginative undertaking. Historians (like everyone else then) posit what might have happened in the past and what it probably could have meant. To get at the most likely (hi)story and whether they are aware of anything like my nomenclature or not, I suggest that no historian can escape the concepts I have noted. Well, it is my book. In my judgment and whether they know it or not every historian (yes, every single one of them) is in some way or another engaged in a process that is shaped by the concepts I have noted before and now again expand upon. In my view then (and plainly it is only my judgment) all histories are *factional, factitious, fabricated, factious, factitive, factive, factualist, fictitious, fictive,* and *figurative*.

Now, this terminology is an extended invention of my thinking about what is history and how it is undertaken and what it achieves. Paradoxically, in what is another Collingwoodian metaphor his 'web of imaginative construction' was the simple deployment of contextualisation and verification. Not surprisingly, then, Collingwood noted the striking similarity between what the historian did as with any author. All histories, like all authored texts, are plainly self-standing, self-explanatory, self-justifying, and self-directed. The only difference, but one that is significant, is the requirement of historical narrative's that they produce a (re) presentation of things as they 'really were' and events as they 'really happened' (Collingwood 1994 [1946]). But this must exist in tandem with the situation that every generation must, surely, and will rewrite history. If anything is uncertain it is history. So, what is there in the contrivances of the historical narrative (as the product of the historical imagination) that inclines us all toward one reading rather than another to fix the statements about the past in one way or another.

To illustrate how the historical imagination works, I will take one of the most famous interpretations of American history. This is Frederick Jackson Turner's 'The Significance of the Frontier in American History' (1893). I choose this because I was a one time American historian and Turner was writing at a time—in the 1890s—when America was undergoing a cultural crisis which was brought on by disruptive industrialisation, mass immigration, wholesale political corruption, progressivism, metropolitanisation, the emergence of class conflict, and the 1890 Bureau of the Census declaring that the movement of the West was now over. It was also the era of Progressivism and the crusade for social justice. How did Turner's historical imagination work at such a time?

In the single most significant historical descriptive statement in American history, in 1893 Turner said, 'The existence of an area of free land, its continuous recession and the advance of American settlement westward explain American national development'. Without the deployment of (t)his metonymic figure of speech ('free land'), both the history and the future of America would never have been directly connected with or to the 'frontier' (and 'free land') of America. But, in some of the most austerely referential metonymic sentences written by Turner, he emplotted a historical metonymic narrative that, in a single statement, created the American historical narrative itself.

I speculate and suspect that Turner's objective in his fixing of the role of free land in the pushing back of the frontier was his desire for a unified American national identity. This, in turn, was reliant on the epistemic knowledge of what America was to both Turner and his readers in the 1890s. Turner's history was in harmony with a contemporary popular consensus that constituted the surety and unique character of the

American identity, which was demonstrated in the evidence of a substantial nationalist literature. This, of course, shaped the American frontier as Frederick Jackson Turner wanted. By insisting that the self-styled men of capital and enterprise moved westward, Turner's imaginative narrative of unstoppable nation-building emerged. The narrative of the movement west demonstrates, then, how the *fictive* narrative became so convincing.

In his search for a relevant past upon which to build the new American nation's culture, Turner deployed a magniloquent vision of America as an exceptional historical creation. In the 1890s America needed a useful history that was non-European and which could and would produce Turner's 'new American history' through his belief that America was a new 'free land'. By not imposing a class analysis on the new frontier, the demands of the up-and-coming and rapidly dominant industrial bourgeoisie required Turner's reconfigured 'free land', which created and enabled the American narrative. That narrative is now recast, of course, to meet contemporary cultural and epistemic demands for class unity. However, because the past has no in-built history, it is plainly the function of the historian to deploy the(ir) historical imagination.

Historians, subsequently, while I do not know whether Turner's history is the truth about American history, however, the rhetorical creation of the historical imaginations of American historians allows them to fashion many different pasts for the new nation. Dependent on how they selected the(ir) evidence, American historians have broadened the forms through which they constructed and deconstructed their historical knowledge in order to define the(ir) frontier culture. Given they are human beings, of course, American historians constantly then and still do today suffer from the seriously debilitating problem of 'the time before now'. The problem of creating America was rapidly resolved by endorsing a very odd belief in the experience of the frontier past. That very odd belief is that 'the-past-*as*-history', as endorsed by Turner's 'figurations', 'metaphors', and 'images', demonstrated what he could do with the new American history. This, of course, produced a considerable ontic and epistemic mistake that has blighted American history subsequently. However, like all nations American history became just another contemporary national literature 'about' the past. All national histories eventually decline. Knowing 'what happened in the past' is, of course, what happened in the past, but the past is never discovered for what it was. At best, then, the past looks like what the historian wants.

So, historians endure in a universe of figuration and symbolic representation with heavy dashes of nationalism, until at some point they believe they have finally accessed and perceived the reality of the(ir) past. Unhappily (or happily depending on how you think about it), all histories always fail because the(ir) access to the past is simply just another nonliteral narrative explication. Getting the data and/or story 'straight' is never more than an erstwhile effort at the reconstruction of a convenient (or inconvenient) past. *The* past, then, which is hardly surprising, is always eventually traded-in for 'a new history', which, of course, just becomes another (new, newer, newish) authorial construction that eventually slides down the continuous and unremitting deconstruction of the past. It is hardly surprising, then, that historians (along with everyone else), have to accept that the time before our perpetual present is merely the historian's hectoring historying of the(ir) description of the past.

Now, it might be that the mechanics of doing history is embarrassingly simple. Through its nature as a series of narrative reconstructions and constructions (and a few experimental deconstructions) the meaning and explanations of the past are understood through a number of historical concepts and historical categories. Simply, then, if you don't like the past, rewrite it. For historians and those who read them the short and simple version of 'doing history' is that the past has to be connected to the historian's preferred history. Histories are never discovered. Historians, by and large, insist that what they say is in accord with their archival discoveries and also engage with other historians who may or may not agree with them. The past, however, is what it is as 'historied' by historians.

Understandably then, the past is always 'revealed *as* a new history'. This does not mean historians invent, redesign, and contrive the past even if they might want to. However, historians can create many different forms of assignations with 'what probably happened in the past' as generated by 'the sources the historian has chosen' and obviously and understandably the result of this is that 'what the past meant' is never fixed. The past changes like the present. This is hardly surprising of course, because history can only be established through the form created by the historian. Consequently, there is no significance or importance in the past until historians turn it into 'the history'. Gloomily, far too often historians support the crude realist naïve belief that the past is always back there to be revealed for what it was. Unfortunately, there is no 'telling the history' until historians (re)present it in our perpetual present.

For most historians, doing history is meant to be a surgical undertaking. Unfortunately, doing history is an artless creation, which insists that the past is what it was in accord with the empirical data. Not surprisingly, however, historians constituting what they believe is the truth can only be sustained through the(ir) evidence and ultimately they designate their history narrative(s) as *the* most likely (hi)story. The consequence of this low-grade unpretentious reasoning is that the past is reachable through its assumed and/or presumed history. Regrettably, the past is not accessible *as* history. We can know what happened in the past (obviously) but what it meant or what it might have meant is never fixed (fortunately). The time before our perpetual present (aka now), history is not manageable and comprehensible for what it was. And that is why we have to replace histories regularly. To summarise the problem with 'doing history' then, is the flow of constant new data, new explanations, and/or, revising old data and old explanations.

Revising and (pro)visioning their preferred 'past-*as*-history' historians try very hard to create/recreate a range of authorial narratives which, of course, are based on the(ir) chosen evidence and the publisher's contract deadline. Then, perhaps, unfortunately there are very bad reviews and so on and so forth. Not surprisingly, toward the end of this process, historians tend to assume that the past will eventually be turned into the(ir) preferred history. Somewhat bizarrely, the time before now has to be run through the mill of the discovery of whatever engages them in the past. Historians almost invariably get out of the past what they want to discover. Obviously, this belief makes no sense unless you are a historian.

Despite their genuine belief that they can 'find' the most likely narrative that surely must have existed in the empirical past, it remains entirely unreasonable to insist they can 'expose and tell' the 'most likely history'. The process of engaging with 'the past' for what the historian wants to see or not in the past is, plainly, always an awkward undertaking. This is because history does not exist in the past and so—and ironically—history only exists in our perpetual present in many different forms *as* lectures, examination papers, journal articles, books, TV scripts, plays, and many other narrative forms. Hence: my aim in this book is to suggest our experience of the past can only be understood and fashioned by the multiple aesthetic history forms that, I believe, are the concepts I have suggested: the *Factional, Factitious, Fabricated, Factious, Factitive, Factive, Factualist, Fictitious, Fictive*, and *Figurative* aesthetic forms through which the past is turned into history whether most historians recognize it or not.

As I suggested at the start of this Introduction, then, each of these concepts are stand-alone. However, in terms of allowing us to understand the nature of 'history literary aesthetics' they will be novel to the substantial majority of academic historians. The reason for this situation is that historians deal with the nature of the past rather than engaging with the literary aesthetics of what they are doing, which is the process of turning the past into history/historying. I will not expend more effort in this Introduction on the nature of these key concepts, apart from again acknowledging that history should not to be confused with the past. However, if you want to involve yourself with the ontic nature of the past then you should engage with the realities of both the past and present.

1 Factional

More often than not, historians work in varying degrees of solitariness. However, at some point all historians invariably become *factional*. Being *factional* means that historians tend to choose to belong to a clique or coterie in terms of their historical interests and/or they cohere in terms of political ideology or some kind, as to their interest in a particular topic. The past, then, is always shaped, formed, and its meaning wrought by the reality of the past as perceived and there is always an unavoidable intervention of dissident and dissenter historians. Unfortunately, in the shadowy and obscure world of the nonexistent past, historians usually claim to have discovered 'the history'. Clearly, and as I have already noted from the start of this book, the past is not history and history is not the past. Thus, the past cannot be resurrected for what it was. All that historians (and everyone else) can do is resuscitate and/or review the past when it has been turned into a 'history'. So, it has to be clear to both the historian and their consumer that 'the historical past' has unavoidably been assigned 'meanings' and 'explanations' by historians (and everyone else), that there are numberless and preferred narratives of the past as authored into existence by historians and everybody else.

Unavoidably and nevertheless, engaging with the past can be delivered in a variety of forms to meet the needs of members of *factional* groups. These *factional* (factions?) include the 'written' and/or 'spoken' and/or 'danced' and/or 'built' and/or 'dug up' and many other forms that can legitimately claim to be a (re)presentation of 'the past'. Almost regardless of its 'presentational form' no one, and obviously including historians, can claim that the past can be resurrected or resuscitated or revived as it actually was. It does no harm to accept that the supreme irony in doing history, then, is that 'the history' can only be a substitute for a past. For every historian there is always a preferred history. History then is not the past. History is a substitute for the past that is authored in whatever 'form and content' the historian wants.

The historian's 'narrative creation of the past', even though it may be claimed to be 'the past as it actually was', that 'narrative creation of the past which we designate as 'the history', remains to be a form of imitation and/or simulation. Hence, no history can legitimately be regarded as a substitute for the past. Of course and on balance, historians insist that they know what 'really happened in the past' even though there may appear to be competing *factional* 'past realities'. Nevertheless, interpreting the available range of sensible possible meanings and explanations that historians contrive and create, still means that all histories almost invariably fail to produce 'the history of . . .'. For every history that every historian constitutes or creates or comprises there is always a *factional* differential.

So, historians always end up striving to 'recreate and reconstitute' the nature, meaning, and explanation of the contents of the past by organising, classifying, and systemising what happened in the past. Now, it is hardly news (I have noted it before) that historians 'process' the 'ontic' and the 'epistemic' nature of the past. Those two terms are not as awkward as they sound. The concept of 'the ontic' simply refers to 'the empirical stuff' defined by historians. Thus, historians collate as 'the facts' descriptions which they create/created about the past. The epistemic then refers to 'the theory' of how historians come to know what happened in respect of 'the knowledge of the past'. And there is plenty of 'the past' available that can be usefully turned into the historian's preferred 'history'.

Historians, like everyone else, deploy the simple mechanism of 'shaping the past' by turning it into 'a (hi)story'. The past, obviously, is just 'mush' until it is 'processed' into a history. However, turning the past into a description of what the historian believes to be previous reality—the past *as* it was—requires that the reality of the past can be adequately offered as a truthful description of the past. Obviously, the past is not history and history is not the past. You can have one or the other. So, historians along with everyone else have to define their preferred topics and events in the past with the aim of 'discovering' what they choose to believe is 'the history'. For every historian there is always a history to be discovered 'back there and then'. To discover the reality of the past, historians (like everyone else) are required to 'shape and form' past reality through 'the(ir) authorial mechanism'. This process involves deploying 'concepts', 'theories', 'themes', and 'leitmotivs'. Moreover, the past has to be fashioned and formed by concepts such as gender, culture, class, regions, war, peace, ideology, the rise and fall of industrial processes, art and aesthetics, cities, and so forth.

The past is particularly unhelpful for historians because 'the past' remains just 'stuff that happened' until the historian assumes they have 'discovered the explanation and meaning of the nature of the past'. But, obviously there is no end when engaging with the past. Doing history, then, is an exploration and investigation process. The myriad of subjects and objects in the past become what they are by the historian fashioning and designing (their preferred) categories of historical analysis. So, how many historical analyses can historians create and want? The answer is numberless of course. This (re)generation of the past is claimed to be a process of discovery, but historians devise and formulate the forms and means by which they bring the past (usually those parts they want) to their and our presence. Accordingly, how many ways can the past be constituted? Well, 'the history we think we need and want' is shaped through the forms and modes that the historian wants the shape of their history through which they can shape and construe the nature and meaning of the past.

This processing or turning of the past into a preferred history is almost impossible to exhaust. The past is both cramped and opened by gender, nationalism, periods of time, religious sectarianism, social class, the state of present and past science, politics, beliefs, ideology, sexuality, material objects, farming, technology, and so forth. Then there are also awkward problems such as the annoying aims of the publisher and most irksomely there are always the determined efforts of other historians to create, recreate, and sustain their point of view on the nature of the past. Plainly, there are so many pasts that historians will never run out of 'pastness'. And, of course, every historian is an expert on something that is so arcane that she or he may be one of half a dozen across the globe. Anyway, historians, unlike any other human being, invariably subject the(ir) past to a processing engagement that no longer exists. Obviously, every historian is unique in their engagement with the past and hence the *factional* nature of 'their turning of the past into a history'. Note: *the* history does not exist because *the* past always produces multitudes of meanings and explanations. Hence, the past is presumed never to change. But that makes no sense at all because our only access to it is through the historian's preferred history.

Unsurprisingly, then, historians exist in a perpetual *factional* condition. The nature of being a historian means having to cope with countless competing 'interests' and 'subjects' and their 'application of aesthetics' unavoidably shapes and creates meanings for numberless concepts that historians construe and deploy in order to shape and engage their interests in the past. The list I noted previously is actually numberless. Historians engage with gender, nationalism, economics, philosophy, religious sectarianism, periods of time, the aesthetics of narrative, the annoying demands of their publisher, and the determined efforts of the substantial numbers of historians who never give up their belief that they have discovered the truth of the past. Thus, 'doing history' is plainly a *factional* undertaking that sustains an academic, political, and ideological structure. This *factional* milieu sustains the historian's engagement with the past through the(ir) mordant and often desperate desire to support the perpetual disordered present through which the past is constantly disarranged. As a *factional* undertaking, then, the nature of history(ing) is sustained by the inclination of historians to both 'herd' and 'dissent' and 'rebel' and 'drove'.

The adjectival concept of the *factional* more often than not determines and/or qualifies and/or demonstrates the explication the function or meaning of the past. Now, common sense indicates that the nature of the past should remain constant. But clearly that makes no sense of any kind. The past is the past thanks to the efforts of historians (and everybody else). Now, historians can reconstitute or rethink or reconsider or reconstruct the past as they please. But the really awkward thing about 'doing history' is that it is also constantly deconstructed. Now, the past may never change but the ways we engage with it always do. So, the past is always and constantly changed *as* history. The worst confusion for historians and everyone else is that all we have in the absence of the past is a history that is constantly changing. If you want to cure a fault in your motorcar you get the tools and follow the handbook (or more sensibly put it in the hands of the expert car mechanics). Historians cannot do that with the past, although every historian will insist on repairing the past.

So, and unhappily, while there are many 'how to do history' texts that inform and explain the nature of the past, there is no handbook which can avoid the *factional* nature of turning the past into a history. Knowing what happened in the past and what it meant always requires the mediation of historians. So, how is it that the past can be turned into a convincing history given that every historian has his or her own 'take' on the past? Unsurprisingly, then, for every historian there is always his or her preferred authored history. Like shoals of the same fish at some 'coherence point' individual historians become a group. Hence, for every historian there is always a *factional* shoal. This is something of a clumsy description on my part. But, for every historian, there is always a different and differential past. Some versions of the past are very similar, most are somewhat differential, and in some instances the interpretational process of authoring a history produces an entirely different 'the-past-*as*-history'.

A list, then, of competing *factional* forms might include social movements, nationalism, gender, jingoism, regionalism, art, race, the eighteenth century, and all the other centuries on this planet. Then there are different forms and topics such as the Industrial Revolution in various countries, and then there are obviously topics themed as the political, social, economic, gender, philosophical, military, religious, regional, biographical, cultural, fashion, ideological and 'the history of history', and so on and so forth (this is a tiny list of course). Hence, there are many very specific histories from the past which can be done and forgotten and then resurrected and probably have been. The space for all this exists because historians are both individualists but also grazing herd animals. Moreover, historians are characterised by *factional* dissent. The process of *factional* historying is a problem that most historians are well aware of. Historians have the freedom to combine and emphasise, order and reorder, delete and insert, fill-in and fill-out, be accurate, and, at worst, mislead in their pursuit of 'the-past-*as*-history'. Now, and accordingly, historians will no doubt in the future continue to struggle with the obvious problem with truth. The reality of the past, then, is impatiently shaped and formed by historians in coteries, groups, and factions, also in terms of being gendered (obviously) and as far as I know there are histories of tall or short people, or whatever. Hence, there is no shortage of *factional* arguments among historians despite the ill-scarred nature of historical truth. So, what is historical truth?

Now, historical truth is a really difficult problem. The historian's propositions or beliefs concerning the nature of the reality of the past are unavoidably the result of many constraints such as language, gender, age, the unexpected sabbatical, or, if you prefer, the other way around, which means that historical truth largely exists propositionally. The disposition of historical truth assumes there must be a match (somewhere) between proposition and reality. Unfortunately, the historical explanation is beset by the tension between these two perceptions of truth. Today, most historians would probably accept that because the past is organised to make sense through the exercise of their historical imagination (more of this in what follows), this means they have to reject any absolutist notion of historical truth. But this is very awkward for historians because historical interpretations should be regarded as likely to be true through corresponding to the verified evidence and the coherence of the statement as judged by other historians.

So, the worry with the *factional* nature of doing history is that historians refuse to acknowledge the much larger problem of '*factional* history truth'. It is this '*factional*' truth that blights 'the history culture'. For historians, the trouble with truth is that it cannot be defined and/or tested by the agreement of the 'past world' and the 'historian's word'. The debate(s) between historians is rarely resolved and, of course, it is very useful for historians although the vast majority would probably deny it. Historians, in the vast majority, deny that there is any problem with tried and attested data. So, why is there so much debate among historians about past events and what they mean? Well, more often than not, there is less to the historian's debates than initially meets the eye.

The perennial and complicated nature of historical truth can be acknowledged very simply. The historian deals only with the past while, say, the psychoanalyst confuses/confused and blends the past with the present. For the historian the past is obviously distinct from the present even though there are causal links between the two. To have knowledge of the past is, well, to have knowledge of the past. The historian's 'facts of the past' are simply successions of events over time and which will unlikely ever be repeated. Thus, seen from a psychoanalytic standpoint, historical truth is not the factual truth that most historians are aware of. The truth of a history appears through an endorsed and validated event. Accordingly, the historian wants 'the truth' of a sequence and/or a single event. Accordingly, then, historical truth is a material truth. Truth in history is both a literal and literary truth that derives in respect of a 'direct present', which is also a referent in the past and hence also in the historian's present reality. As soon as a history is created it becomes its own history.

A major foundational problem with history, then, is that there is a persistent difficulty with *factional* historical truth. This claim is not quite as bad as it may seem—but there is still a problem. The notion of *factional* historical truth is always going to be awkward, this is because when disparate groups of historians make a claim as to the reality of the past by claiming its meaning and explanation, historians pursue the truth via 'the sources chase'. This enables historians to know what happened in the past (more or less), but ironically there is always a continuing and unavoidable issue with the nature and direction of truth. Just who is in the market for the knowledge of the past? To be clear then, *factional* historical truth will give the history the historian discovers and wants or hopes for or expects. The notion, then, of the 'discovery of history' is, literally, nonsense.

So, the-past-*as*-history is a *factional* enterprise amidst the many different 'competing historical truths' while every single historian claims to offer the (only) historical truth. Every historian has his or her own truth. Unhappily, however, many singular competing truths persistently rub shoulders with competing versions of the past through the (unnerving?) political and ideological frames of *factional* reference. Ironically, in the pursuit of the truth of the past, there are many *factional* competitors, which do, of course, create a milieu of *factional* irritation, exasperation, and touchiness. What this means is that far too many historians thrive on what I describe as *factional* historical truth. By this, then, I mean it is all too easy to take the past and revise, rethink, recodify, refashion, and readapt it not simply through the historian's preferred style of representation, but also cater to the uncountable bees in the bonnets of historian(s).

The substance/subject/styling of the past that historians create in our perpetual today exists in almost innumerable forms. History is offered in print, television, radio, lectures, acted, filmed, art objects, thought, written, and many other forms that carry their own style and hence the past is constituted as history with each form creating different(ial) meanings and explanations. Then and now, of course, the historical record is increasingly digitised. The immediate previous past generations of historians indulged/indulge their opportunities for their preferred historying. They do this through an increasing use of the computer in historical investigation and eventual construal. Today and fortuitously, the *factional* process of creating histories not only wallows in its various forms but also myriad disputes of meaning and explanation.

Now, while 'the history content' is always claimed to be at the heart of doing history, the nature of history still remains a *factional* undertaking. The irony in this should be obvious. But it is not. The status of *factional* historying is central to 'doing history' along with lots of other interventionist undertakings. This is because historians cannot offer an agreed definition of what is history and so also what is 'historical truth'. Today, and in the past and/or in the future as well, as far as I can tell, the trouble with historical truth is that it cannot be defined to the satisfaction of anyone let alone historians. So, what do I think is the truth about historical truth? Happily or not, depending on your preference, the notion of historical truth has no certainty of any kind. The constant trouble with historical truth is that it cannot be defined, let alone tested and attested because historians seek out the truth of the past in a very simplistic way. It is 'this happened' and 'not that' according to the 'present available' evidence. Moreover and very awkwardly on top of that, the truth of the past is entirely subject to the interpretation of the data.

This does not mean historians can go around imputing (attributing) and/or inventing (formulating) the past, as they may wish to. But, and it remains a very big but, history is an unavoidable act of aesthetic engagement which deploys several forms of 'truth'. The problem with truth for historians, then, is that there are several forms of 'truth' and none of them can be defined or tested in agreement with the non-scientific world. Not only do truths differ for different past worlds but also the same truths differ from each other. Historical truths are simply multiple versions of a preferred past reality. Hence there are as many past 'historical realities' as historians can offer. It is well known that all histories are short-lived contemplations of recently discovered (based on yet more) data. Thus, it is hardly news that historians can take the same sources and variously interprets what those same data means. This is called 'historical interpretation'. Historians, then, cannot possibly avoid this problem, and this is why historians differ in terms of 'the references', 'weightings', 'orientations', 'emphases', etc., etc.

So, the nature of 'historical truth' is—plainly—a weak and docile *factional* form of truth. This means that the truth, the whole truth, and nothing but the truth would be a wilful and paralysing strategy for any historian. The truth of the past is the version of the history that the historian believes they have and want. Histories, then, are simple versions of an inscrutable past reality. Obviously, knowing what actually happened in the past is embarrassingly simple to discover. So, the past is a precious commodity. Knowing 'what actually happened according to a historian' is largely worthless because the historian and all historians can only ever have *a* 'historical interpretation'. Hence, the notion of *the* 'historical interpretation' has very little to be commended to anyone, apart from other historians. In the absence of a form of truth that can guarantee the veracity of past reality, historians have to accept one or more of its four forms as I suggested in this chapter. Hence, *correspondence*, *correlation*, *coherence*, and/or *consensus* is the only definitions of truth that historians can deploy when they choose to shape the 'the-past-*as*-history'.

So, there is a real and continuing problem with each form of truth and consequently the *fabricated* and *factitious* understanding of 'the-past-*as*-history' as I have argued will always get in the way of the (un)reality of the past.

The major problem with *fabricated* and *factitious* historying (as I noted in this chapter and Chapter 2 and will again in the chapters that follow) is that the past cannot speak for itself and—somewhat awkwardly—neither can historians. This does not mean there is no truth in our knowledge of the past. As I have already noted, the truth of the past is essential but it is also an unavoidably awkward pursuit through *correspondence*, *correlation*, *coherence*, and/ or *consensus*. Because the past is insensible, it has to be 'made to speak' even though it may be often thought of as a discovery that can speak for itself. The past has no history until historians create one. Now, there are two main types of historical sources that historians can deploy and lean on. These are *primary* and *secondary sources*. A *primary* source is some 'thing' or 'artifact' or some other piece of detritus and/or debris that originated in the past. This 'stuff from the past' can be a chronicle or a journal, a piece of pottery and/or earthenware and/or a painting on a canvas and/or wall or even a piece of glacial ice that yields climate data about the levels of carbon in the atmosphere ten thousand years ago. But, for most historians the less exotic will do, such as ill-kept and scruffy archives, forgotten libraries, dubious records, half baked chronicles, tedious diaries, tiresome letters, tatty notes, and so forth. The role of sources in 'doing history' thus depends entirely on the individual historian's theory of knowledge. All historians adhere to a theory of knowledge (whether they know it or not) through which they pursue 'justified belief'.

Ironically (and not unlike medical professionals), historians dig up that which has expired. For the hardcore reconstructionist historian the past can be 'brought back to life (sort of)' and thus such historians can speak to the past. Unhappily, that silly notion doesn't work. The past never speaks for itself and so historians continue to believe in the serendipity of discovering 'the most likely' narrative back there and then, which can be a neatly tidy historical explanation. This, then, makes no sense. Happily, however, historians eventually always find themselves in the situation of being able to (re)construct the past as it was and thereby (re)produce 'the-past-*as*-history'. Happily, of course, all histories fail. The past is always subject to being renovated and renewed. Plainly then, knowing what happened in the past is hardly a struggle if there is sufficient data which can be deployed in order to 'discover the meaning' and eventually 'discover' the (or a) 'in-built' explanation of the historical sources. Unhappily that process is very unlikely to acquire *the* absolute truth of the past. But, the past is never secured. Shed loads (literally in some instances) can 'shed' fresh light on the past. But, eventually, both sheds and contents (di)scount for naught when new sheds and contents are regularly found.

As I have suggested, then, the problem with history is that it is not the past and the past is not history. Shaking the foundations of the past is a very good and regular undertaking especially as it often keeps historians in employment. Happily, then, this employment demands reconstructing, constructing, and deconstructing a useful 'past history' and thus historians have the histories they want. Or, to put it slightly differently, all histories are unavoidably *factional*. Every historian, then, engages with the past as much as they also 'disagree' with their equally engaged colleagues who have an entirely different past and thus a different history. Historians, then, are often herding creatures and this is a serious—almost debilitating—problem for historians. There is no mechanism that historians can deploy to test the nature of the past, apart from throwing more 'theories' at the sources. Scientists can 'do experiments' in a laboratory but there is no similar mechanism for social science historians as such and I have ended up throwing lots of statistical regressions at a shed load of data.

Now, it is true that very substantial numbers of historians endorse the mechanism of the 'social sciences'. Now, I have to admit I took an undergraduate social science degree and thanks to good fortune, I was engaged over several happy years as a Ph.D. postgraduate (thanks to my wonderful wife Jane who was the breadwinner) through which I created a stage model of urban immigrant political assimilation in the USA (between 1870 and 1920). I 'authored this model', which consisted of four stages which I invented. The first invented stage was Symbolic-Normative, the second was Operative-Positive, the third was the Transformation stage, and it ended with the final stage of Political Assimilation. I think four people actually read that Ph.D. Obviously I researched and wrote it, my wife Jane typed it, my supervisor supervised me and then, eventually, so did the External Examiner. Anyway, I came to believe (eventually) that more useful and sensible is the notion of not trying to reconstruct or construct the past, but deconstruct it. After this 'realisation' I was turned by the dark arts of 'postmodern history'.

After settling into my career as a historian, the period of 'deconstructing history' briefly flowered between 1990 and 2010 but those two insurrectional decades continued to leave an intellectual shadow over my thinking as a historian, even though the substantial majority of academic historians were never convinced and the next generation remains 'in the past' (ironically). At the height of 'postmodern historying' the truth, the whole truth, and nothing but the truth sat awkwardly and was (and it remains) a paralysing policy. Getting the (hi)story straight was and will always be unproblematic of course. This may seem a dangerous thought, but 'getting the data straight' is hardly difficult if one lives for enough months and years in a research library. Now, as the philosopher Nelson Goodman argued, our world—past and present and probably future also—is always human made. Hence historians, like every other human being, are unavoidably subject to the *factional*.

At this point historians, like everyone else, are very wary of the notion of the 'truth, the whole truth, and nothing but the truth'. Now, this applies in doing history, and as we all know, there are those very few historians who deny the attested reality of the past for their own devious purposes. So, we can find them out and duly dismiss them. Unfortunately, however, the whole truth of the past is beyond the grasp of human beings. To have the whole truth of the past is plainly impossible especially as historians are subject to their own legitimate constraints—lack of funding, getting a publisher, having a family, that long grapple with Income Tax Inspectors, and not least accessing the historical sources. The truth of the past, then, is simply too vast and measureless for all historians.

What this means is that historians unavoidably create 'the-past-*as*-history' and, who knows, quite often all of it might be true. Then, again, it might not. Now, it is always worth reminding historians (and everyone else) that knowing what happened in the past is not the same as history. Historians can offer insight. Historian can offer beliefs. Historians can offer principles. Historian can offer stylistic differences in profusion. But, ultimately, 'history' is 'not the past' and 'the past' is 'not history'. From what I just said, what then are the basics of 'doing history'? Happily, it is not too difficult to know and learn. There are five simple narrative principles to doing history. These are 'composition and decomposition', 'weighting', 'ordering', 'deletion and supplementation', and 'reformation'. These concepts should be known and understood by any 'historian-author' and their consumers.

Unfortunately from where I am sitting, it is very annoying that the substantial majority of academic historians are exclusively unaware that 'the-past-*as*-history' is almost entirely their authorial creation. This does not mean 'making up the past'. But, then historians are not in the serendipitous business of 'discovering the past'. Worryingly, historians tend to ignore the situation that 'the time before now' has to be 'authored' into 'a past existence' even if they may suggest 'the past' possesses its own 'history'. The notion of 'discovering the history of . . .' is not a process of inventing or creating or contriving or manufacturing the past. I do not expect professional historians to accept and endorse the notion of 'the-past-*as*-history' any time now. However, there remains the awkward problem of the *factional*. To be plain then: there is no history in the past until the historian 'authors' it into what they believe is its 'discoverable existence'. Unfortunately, before the historian's authorial tinkering in respect of 'weighting', 'ordering', 'deleting', 'supplementing', and 'rethinking' the forces that shape an 'authored narrative', there is no (hi) story to be 'discovered'. The *factional* nature of what historians do is embarrassingly simple. Historians insist that they 'discover' what the they think is the most accurate history according to the logic of their inferences, but then for every historian there is always a different inference.

As a source-based and interpretational undertaking, then, the past can only be 'authored into' what historians prefer past *as* the most likely history that they believe they have 'found'. Unhappily, there is much less to this process than historians and their consumers believe. What historians do in terms of their *factional* processing of the past is to *interpret* and *explain*. But, unfortunately, historians rarely agree with each other's understanding of the nature of the past and much less do they agree on what it means. This 'processing of the past' into 'a history' (or ideally '*the* history') is simple. Getting the history straight for most historians means modestly that 'the available new sources' are 'accurately interpreted' deploying a range of theories to explain *the* nature and meaning of *the* past. So, how does this actually work in practice given that there are lots of different histories/pasts? Well, and with no irony intended, most historians have a very tenuous grasp on how the past is turned into yet another history. This is hardly their fault of course because the past is never fixed 'for what it was'. This is because our access to the past can only be accessible through the process of *factional* analyses. It is hardly news that historians tend to herd. Historians gather, collect, assemble, and make huge efforts to turn the absent past into their real and present historying. But, for every historian there is always a different past.

History, then, is the individual historian's narrative of the past, but unfortunately, history it is not the past. At best 'the-past-*as*-history' can only be regarded as just another historical construction. Somewhat awkwardly, the process of knowing what happened in the past and what it meant is a very quirky undertaking. Think about it. All histories are compendiums of authorial styles and hence 'the-past-*as*-history' is an unavoidable 'aesthetic'. Now, of course, it is worth noting and quickly dismissing the notion of reconstructing the past as it actually was. This notion is a laudable undertaking and knowing what actually happened in the past is absolutely basic to our (and any other) culture. Nonetheless, it remains an impossibility to reconstruct the past as it actually was and hence the Battle of Waterloo is not a book, or a paragraph, or chat on a bus. No matter how much effort is taken to get the (hi)story straight on the Battle of Waterloo, that part of the past remains in the past and it cannot be resuscitated and resurrected and, of course, it cannot be refreshed and that is where the perpetual problem of the *factional* most clearly emerges.

The problem with the notion of reconstructing the past 'as it actually was' is that the past is the past and history is history. There is no (con)fusion of the two. The past is not a narrative. The past never changes for all we can tell. However, historians constantly change the nature of the past by re-constructing the possible realities of the histories the historians want. The immeasurable majority of historians are—obviously—determined to reconstruct again and again and again or construct again and again, and again, the nature of the past until they have tunnelled into its history. Unfortunately there is no history of anything until the historian has (hi)storied it into existence. The past, then, does not possess its own dedicated history awaiting its revelation. The foundational irony in engaging with the past is that 'there is no history' without various versions of the past which unavoidably generate *factional* disagreements. There is no possibility of 'diagnosing the condition of the past' in the absence of that 'past' the historian wants. Hence, when historians choose to reconstruct and/or construct the past they are unavoidably deconstructing the past through their preferred 'history'. Hence, the *factional* dimension of 'historying' remains and all historians eventually herd and/or flock and/or congregate and/or assemble. And then they rethink the nature of 'the history'.

The common sense understanding among historians is founded on the belief that for every historian there has to be 'a new and tweaked past'. This belief is, of course, ridiculous. Historians potter and fiddle in the past and most of us happily accept that certain events occurred and others did not. This situation, of course, produces the *factional* demand for a realist and common sense understanding of the referential, empiricist, and truth-conditional processing of the past. Happily for the *factional* reconstructionist historian, they assume the past speaks for itself though it be through the(ir) sources and which will, then, eventually speak as located and fostered by the historian. Thus far, too many historians only ever engage with and interpret the past when they believe they have built on preexisting historical facts. Now, and unhappily, historical facts are only descriptions of an event that historians agree upon or not as the case may be. Nonetheless and fortunately for historians, they have no objective and independent measure of the nature of the reality of the past apart from when they herd.

This herding process means that the reality of the past is rarely the same as the reality of history. Thus: we have to accept that the *factional* author and the *factional* reader must share the belief that not only is the events of the past are *as* described really happened, and/or, is a thing that is known or proved to be true. To sustain the credibility of historians they have to accept that what they say about the past corresponds to that which is described as 'a historical fact'. This means that what historians say about the past is a 'referential' truth-conditional statement about the 'actuality' of the 'past real world' and that it remains unaffected 'by the act of its description/interpretation'. What I think this means is that 'the past is not history' and 'history is not the past' and no one should (con)fuse the past with history and/or history with the past. Perhaps awkwardly, this does mean anyone can blithely ignore the realities of the past.

Now, there is both a presumption and also a very awkward problem with the past and how we engage with it. This is the problem of the 'common sense' belief that the past will never alter. However, the way we think about the past is in a constant state of flux. When I was a full-time university historian I engaged with the past most of my time. I was reading the constant flow of new 'histories', which invariably offered me new 'directions' and 'interpretations'. Clearly, historians cannot escape the(ir) self-imposed conflation of 'the past with its history' and 'history with its past' and, consequently, this is where historians 'herd'. All historians belong to a *factional* group even if it has only one or two members or a small clutch and regardless of their *factional* nature. This *factional* mindset is, of course, easy and simple to explain.

Now, 'the history' of 'the past' only exists in our perpetual present. Plainly, then, it is necessary to understand that 'doing history' is a presentist activity that constantly reinvents, reimagines and re-construes the past. Obviously, it happens quickly because the past comes before the(ir) history. Understandably, of course, the past must come before the history. There was no subject called 'the past' on the curriculum. But, because we are humans who have memories (some better or worse), 'the past' is always 'history' and 'history' is forever 'the past'. So which comes first, the past or the history? For me, the past always came before history. But very quickly, I soon had to acknowledge that all histories are '(wo)man-made'.

Every history, then, is subject to being recreated, reinvented, refabricated, remade, and so on and so forth. Happily, the foundational failing in the process of 'doing history' is that every history usually only has one generational life span. What happened to my 14 books? Such is life. So, the obvious fundamental problem with history is that it is unavoidably 'made' by many different clutches of historians who have their own agendas. Of course, the notion that historians can discover the actuality of the past is a classic instance of a form of 'artistic truth'. History was and still is 'made' and always will be. Historians (like everyone else) conjure up the appearance of past reality through all of those old photographs, wills, newspapers, records, and so forth. Plainly then, the past can only be accessed via myriad forms of media (written texts, lectures, theatre, TV). The reality of the past, then, is only accessible in the *factional* forms we create for it.

The aesthetic of historying is ultimately mystifying even as most historians will not accept this notion. Historians, by and large, will insist that any forms of mystification in engaging with the past are at best silly and at worst very dangerous. Unfortunately, the art of history eventually mystifies the past. The notion of rethinking the past usually ends up as yet just another processed act of historying. The composition of all histories—while they are claimed to explain the reality of the past—invariably end up as refreshed aesthetic observations or, as some disagreeable historians might say, a useless mystification of the straightforward. Like many artists, historians often end up as intellectual fugitives (whether they know it or not) and by that I mean they all too often do not see beyond the past into the(ir) history/historying space. Nonetheless, every historical text is a literary artifact as much as it is the creation of a *factional* undertaking.

It is well known that historians debate their sources with the aim of inferring their most likely meaning and obviously then reaching their conclusions. Then, other historians do the same, and by their preferred interpretation they have a different conclusion as to meaning and explanation. Without this process, there would be very few alternative debates about the nature of the past and there would be a substantial number of different ranges of disagreement. Historians, of course, deploy new research based on previous research. The aim and hope, then, is that new data redefines the issues and hope this 'opens up' the opportunity of reinterpreting the existing along with new data. The next stage is then to look to the context in which this new evidence is interpreted.

Beyond that simple process there is the role and functioning of politics, ideology, gender, geography, chronology, and so forth. This does not make the historian incapable of making independent judgments and it also does not require their interpretations to be subservient to political interests and, of course, there are also quarrels given the kinds of evidence the historian chooses to use. Many—probably most—historians have simply disregarded the 'historians debates'. However, having a 'new take on the past' can be worrisome. And, of course, there are historians, such as Keith Jenkins in his groundbreaking postmodernist *Rethinking History*, who offered a disturbing assault on 'classic historying'. And then there is your author who cofounded a history journal named after Jenkins' text. The brief postmodern assault on many historians cut to the very heart of what history was hitherto often regarded as being—and what historians can reasonably claim to do.

Now, for the majority of historians the reasons why they disagree on the nature of the past are usually very straightforward. It may be the competing choice of their methods of and in history, which might be philosophical, ideological, political, gendered, and myriad other predispositions and which for your author was initially their interest in visiting the Black Country Museum in Dudley, UK and their school history teacher. At university I chose history and specialised in American History and eventually I produced a Ph.D. on the political assimilation of immigrants in urban America between 1870 and 1920.

However, in due course I became increasingly engaged with the nature and functioning of historical knowledge and wrote my first book *Discourse and Culture: The Creation of America, 1870–1920*. Emanating largely from literary theorists such as Jacques Derrida and Hayden White I directly (en)countered the arguments of what was then known as (perhaps unhelpfully now) postmodernism and engaged with how historians can engage the past with history. Very quickly I began to engage with the nature of historical writing, especially *Rethinking History*

28 Factional

(Keith Jenkins). However, I soon became aware that the substantial majority of academic historians disagreed with my argument that the past is not history and history is not the past. So, I came to understand that for most historians' political ideologies or the philosophical and methodological disputes associated with postmodernism were not quite what they wanted that did not particularly worry me and the Histories of Herodotus was not what I was not interested in and certainly not the history of the Peloponnesian Wars.

So, it dawned on me that the very substantial number of historians had little in common with me (and vice versa). Happily, then, the *factional* nature of engaging with the past was (and remains) a splendid way for me to secure a niche in the nether regions of deconstruction. Now, 30 years ago continental philosophy made no inroads among most British historians so I ploughed my furrow, as did Keith Jenkins. Hence, the *factional* nature of history soon appeared. However, only a few other lusty pioneers of 'postmodern historying' appeared briefly and existed in some kind of purdah. Today, in the UK, there is less taste than there was a decade ago among historians in schools, and today historians largely fail to address the 'history aesthetic experience'.

In the UK, then, the national curriculum for history aims to ensure that all pupils know and 'understand the history of these islands' as a coherent, chronological narrative, from the earliest times to the present day. So, Britain has influenced and (much less) been influenced by the wider world, ancient civilisations and their expansions and dissolutions of empires, and so on. And, of course, there are always the achievements and follies of humanity. Histories then offer perspectives for historians by understanding the connections between local, regional, national, and international histories and also between varieties of history: cultural, economic, military, political, religious, and social history and between short and long term timescales, and so on and so forth. So, historians never discover the past until they have historied, as they desire.

Understandably, 'the history aesthetic experience' is required, historians and students are required to pursue 'historically valid enquiries' that they have framed for themselves so they can constitute, organize, and evidentially support the (hi)story narratives they prefer. So, the first profound irony in 'doing history' is that of recognising and accepting its *factional* nature. The notion of the past providing its own history is a useful but profoundly unhelpful and truly bizarre belief. The myriad claims of historians are always maintained 'in accord with the sources' but if that does not work, historians invariably fall back on what they will insist are contrasting arguments and interpretations. Hence, the history of the past has to be constructed and if that does not work it must be deconstructed. In planning to ensure all this, teachers (in the UK and probably everywhere else) are expected to combine and overview and offer in-depth studies to assist pupils, students, and everyone else to 'understand the nature of the latest *factional* relationships through which the past can be (hopefully) 'discovered', or far more likely 'devised'. So, why do historians always either bicker and/or herd? Well, I do not know. However, I suspect it is substantially about the(ir) deployment of differing sources as much as it is about their politics.

Either way, all bickering and herding historians are plainly *'factional* individuals'. Because the past cannot change, historians can only fall back on their preferred 'amenable colleagues to take over a class when the publisher finally demands to have the manuscript', and/or their own 'literary styles', and/or their deployment of 'dubious and different sources', and/or consequentially they produce 'differential interpretations'. An old adage comes to mind at this point in the context of medical doctors burying their failures. However, if historians are not exactly leeches, they are forced to come close to it. So, the old question still remains, what is the historian's task?

Well, for every historian there is a definition of what the historian should do and achieve. The American historian Carl Becker (1873–1945) wrote in his Presidential Address (1931) and which was published in the *American Historical Review* (vol. 37, January, 1932), 221–236. Now, dear reader, I strongly recommend you seek it out. However, if you do not, I will conclude this opening chapter with a very short summary of what I take to be his thoughts if not specifically the *factional* nature of turning the past into history. Becker noted the existence of 'Mr. Everyman' (and today that presumably includes women and the transgendered) in mind, he suggested that however accurately historians may determine the facts of history, the facts themselves and our interpretations of them, and our interpretation of our own interpretations, will be seen in a different perspective or a less vivid light as humankind moves into the unknown future.

I suggest, then, that most historians today are primarily authors who at once ignore and/or deny and a minority might agree with me, for the necessity to understand the nature of the *factional* turning of the past into a history. Now and plainly, all historians at some point are herd creatures. However, they are also individuals who are unavoidably contentious, partisan, dissident, sectarian, and, above all, disputatious. I structured this book then, as you will have understood from the 'title' and the nature of the 'contents' my judgment—among many other things—is that history is as much about history as it might be about the past.

2 Factitious

The past, then, is only accessible through the history we create for it. In practice, all historians, along with everyone else, are subject to the(ir) *factitious* expression of reality both past or present. Obviously, most people, and that includes historians, rarely invoke and/or deploy the concept. However, the concept is essential to the process of turning 'the past' into 'a history', which, of course, is synthetically and artificially created like every other narrative whether it is thought to be 'the reality' and/or 'the invention'. So, the belief that 'the history' preexists in the past makes no sense. While historians endeavour to discover the most likely nature of the past, it is they who as authors construe their preferred histories. The past then may be regarded as a discovery, but its meaning and explication is imprinted only through the historian's preferred aesthetic engagement with the events of the past. So, while historians may insist that they discover the history of the past, all histories are presented, of course, and aesthetically 'made by art'.

Like all human beings, then, historians express what is in their minds about the past through the *factitious* processing of the past into a history. While this is inevitable and whether they like it or not, academic historians can only 'express the past' through their paradigmatic thinking. Historians—fairly obviously—cannot escape 'human expression' which means all (hi)stories mediate and reflect the thinking of the historian rather than the empirical nature of the past. The past, thus, cannot escape the 'aesthetic', 'exaggerated', 'reproduction', 'presumed', 'spurious', 'contrived', 'replica', 'plastic', 'simulated', and 'unnatural' *factitious* nature of expressing 'the-past-*as*-history'.

History then, is the authored narrative of the historian and is not the product of the past and hence its nature is factitious. Hence, it is necessary to be very clear that the history is not the same as the past. To start with, conflating 'the past' with 'history' is an exercise in hope over experience simply because the past can never be rebuilt and/or restored. Obviously, then, the past is the past and history is history. Our multiple linguistic turns and twists as created by the author-historian mean that the past remains entirely inert until the historian looks ahead at the history to the past. History, then, is not a matter of inventing the past but of formulating processes, which will enable the creation of our preferred history(ing). Plainly, without 'description and style' there is no past. So, let me be plain. It is only the compulsion of the historian to engage with the(ir) past that permits and licenses the historian's engagement with the past.

Historians, like everyone else, have to accept that it is impossible to 'look through' language at past reality. The foundational irony in 'doing history' is that the historian's use of language always gets in the way of the past. Historians cannot look through their language at the reality of the past because their linguistic engagement with the past is constituted, composed, collected, gathered, assembled, and construed. The irony of the historical text is what it is. It may refer to the past but it never wipes, cleanses, washes, and/or dabs itself away. The glassy removal of past reality is impossible to expunge. Fortunately, though, the historical text never sponges itself away. So, the past is constantly 'back there' but it is inconstantly and changeable and reshaped as a series of 'historical maybes'.

History, then, is simply an expression (or series) of the individual historian's preferred engagement with the past. Somewhat awkwardly, there is no galvanic skin response that can 'tell the consumer' if the historian is telling lies. The vast majority of historians and consumers are expected to believe that they have discovered 'the history of the past'. However, this makes no sense of any sort. By confusing the past with history, historians invariably end up with 'the-past-*as*-history'. Somewhat awkwardly, then, the past is simply the narrative of some kind of history as preferred by a historian. Unhappily, then, history is plainly not the past and the past is not history.

Now, I make the assumption that most historians are content with the notion of their discovery of the (f)actual nature of the past, and that it is plainly that of a *factitious* activity. This significant notion is acknowledged by deploying the Latin verb facere, which means 'to do' and/or 'to make'. Consequently, then, history is 'authorially created' in the form of an aesthetic substitute for 'the past' in largely any way the historian prefers. Now, today, the process of '*factitious* historying' has come to mean the opposite of the realistic, which means 'being made' through 'artifice'. The notion of the *factitious* appeared (at some point) in the seventeenth century to define the human effort and/or skill instead of arising or emerging from 'nature'. Thus, the process of creating histories acknowledges the 'false' and/or 'artificial' and/or 'feigned' reconstruction of 'the past' as the individual historian believed it probably was according to the evidence they have chosen.

Still today, *factitious* historying defines both 'realistic' and 'common sense' and 'the history' is a synonym for 'the past'. Now, this is meaningless and a very odd notion, which is sustained by a concoction of 'self-styled common sense' and the application of 'minimal thought'. It has yet to become a common sense belief that, of course, 'the past' is 'history' and 'history' is 'the past'. Unfortunately, this notion is very silly. There is no connection between 'the past' and 'history'. This is simply because they have different phenomenal existences. Or, to be clearer: the past is the time before our perpetual present, and our perpetual present is, well, our perpetual present. So: in the unavoidable absence of 'the past' historians, along with everybody else, are required to create a 'history/historical narrative' to explain 'the nature and meaning of the past'.

Hence, then, all 'historical descriptions' are simply factitious narratives because all histories are synthetically produced which, understandably, confirms their nature not as 'discoveries' but some more or less complex 'authorial intervention' in the possibilities/probabilities of the past. This is why—and ironically—the past never stands still (obviously). Thus and then, all histories are constantly recreated, incessantly refashioned, unremittingly reformed, rebuilt, and unsurprisingly constantly aesthetically re-overhauled and redeveloped and constantly reinterpreted. The history of the past, then, is a process of perpetual overhauling, repairing, revamping, surpassing, renovating, and eventually rethinking the turning of the past into yet another preferred new version of the old past.

Now, dear reader, what do you think is *factitious* history? Well, is it the lies commonly agreed upon by historians? Or, who controls the past controls the future and whoever controls the present constantly controls the past? Or, is the study of history simply the people's memory, and/or is history a science, and/or is history no less than simply an argument without an end, and/or is historical knowledge that which precedes and eventually exhausts the field of useless knowing, and/or is history the conflation of the reckless assumptions of a loathsome generation, or can histories only cast a very dim and flickering light on the past? Given all this, is history simply a *factitious* failure? Well, no it is not.

History remains basic to our culture. For the ancient Greeks, history was a storeroom of illustrations and examples to guide future actions. The equivalent today is pretty much the same. Historians and everyone else are constantly being told to learn 'the lessons of history'. Fortunately and/or unfortunately depending on your judgment, 'the lessons of history' are obviously and understandably not 'the real thing'. Hence: the historical records have no utility of any kind until they can 'be deployed' and/or 'given to demonstrate' the individual historian's desire to 'trace history narratives back through time' for whatever purpose they want (usually political). Hence, there have been many if not myriad efforts over several hundreds of years to define 'what is history?' in terms of its *factitious* being and even if the term *factitious* has not often been deployed, the present-day *factitious* notion is simply the capacity to discover the nature of 'past reality', which is, of course, 'reality under a description'. Unhappily, this apparently useful endeavour demands a bizarre belief in the process of the (ironic) creation of imaginative constructions about the reality of the past.

Given its nature, as a *factitious* cultural undertaking, history is a classic example of 'irreal reality' in much the same way as is any other proposed 'constructed construal'. History, then, is simply that state of being insubstantial or imaginary. Of course, history can only exist as a secondary medium for our engagement with past reality. Nevertheless, history evokes powerful *factitious* imageries throughout the pursuit of (re)creating the past as it really was. Unfortunately, 'history' cannot escape its nature as a 'description-making' undertaking that can only have access to authorially simulated/stimulated 'past reality'. The central problem with 'the-past-*as*-history' as which most historians know and a substantial minority conveniently overlook, means they have to acknowledge that their recovery and repossession of the past is confined by the(ir) powers of imaginative (de)(re)construction. This process is, of course, based on the individual historian's grasp of their understanding of their evidential reality. Unfortunately, no historian's grasp of their evidential reality is going to be the same. Hence, the past never stands still. Accordingly, the upshot of this ontic imaginative 'history construction processing process' invariably offers a multi-meaning 'historical experience'. The short version of all this, then, is that you get the history you want to believe in.

Consequently, the *factitious* nature of history should force us to acknowledge (whether we like it or not) that the past is not an engagement with its history. History, then, is merely an authorial engagement with the time before our perpetual present. At this point in my narrative, I will insist that it would be erroneous to regard '*factitious* history' as a 'disorder'. At some time in their career, all historians will have been tutored to engage with the problem of 'reconstructing', 'constructing', or 'deconstructing' the nature of the past. Without going overboard in my analysis it seems to me that most historians demonstrate the symptoms of a historying *factitious* disorder. Now, and cumbersomely, all is not well in the sleepy hollow of *factitious* historying. This is because far too many historians unavoidably 'engage with' and 'graze in lush meadows' of overly strained inferential thinking. Their ability 'to draw inferences from the(ir) sources' (as most historians hope to do) will eventually shape, form, construct, reconstruct, and deconstruct the awkward spaces of the past. And, of course, the same applies for the consumer of the history. The universe of inferences, in which we all exist as consumers of history, call on an immense amount of background 'history noise' in which 'cause and effect' (relating events to each other) and 'facts' (events under a description) build up 'the stuff of the past'. Then, of course, there are always and also the historian's aesthetic representations of the past as (also) shaped by the processes of change over time. Whether it is acknowledged or not, of course, historians do not directly engage with the past. This is unfortunate, because historians can only engage with the past as a complex composite set of representations.

Thus: the pursuit of the past is a creative *factitious* turning of the past into what the historian believes is an appropriately suitable history for the themes they wish to engage in the past. Now, and of course, for many historians, doing history is little more than the application of their much-vaunted historical imagination and which fortunately is unpretentious. The historical imagination is no more nor less than that naïve creative and imaginative process, which is simply the positing of what might possibly/probably have/has happened in the past. This process is of course supported by the sources and data that the historian selects from the usually vast range of that which is readily available and which—eventually—is then deployed for yet more verification and confirmation. Thus: history is shaped by the author-historian as an aesthetic-imaginative (de)(re)construction of the past.

Plainly, then, all histories are *factitious* enterprises that are unavoidably subject to the historian's authorial shaping in the perpetual present. Ironically, the most outlandish belief of historians is that the past is still a reality. But, of course, the past reality is always retrofitted. In ontological terms, this is plainly nonsense because while 'the past once happened' does not mean it continues to exist. The past is never what it was because it is only ever 'history'. Even though it is sacrosanct in the hands and minds of far too many historians 'the present' is constantly absorbed by 'the past' in the shape of many (in)convenient histories which are created as *factitious* quasi-realist undertakings. Plainly, then, the past is the past and histories are, well, histories.

Given this situation, the foundational problem for all historians is that it is very difficult (probably impossible?) to distinguish the process of historying from some *factitious* form of 'correspondence truth'. This makes life very difficult for historians who want to seek out 'historical truth'. Even the most diligent historian cannot experience 'historical past reality as authored by the historian'. Reduced somewhat, then, history always fails as a truth-establishing process. The problem with truth does not mean the past is not to be what it was again. Historical interpretations are always both rejected and sustained in the light of the constant counter 'alternative data' that sustains or confounds the past.

Now, doubts will always exist about history because of the sources, the inadequacy of language, and the unfortunate situation that there are far more hopeless historians than we suspect, as there are bus drivers, brain surgeons, and civil engineers. Unhappily, then, there is—and very awkwardly—a problem with 'the-past-*as*-history' because there are unfortunately several kinds of truth. Yes, there really are several competing forms of truths for historians (and every other human being) to choose from. The four significant theories of truth (of which I am aware) shape the 'the-past-*as*-history' and these are correspondence, correlation, coherence, and/or consensus. Now, the most common of these 'truth-forms' deployed by historians (and probably everyone else) is correspondence. However, all of these forms have something aesthetically wrong with them (or not, depending on the individual historian).

The most straightforward form of truth is the correspondence theory. This theory of truth eventually and unavoidably leads to a desperately crude scepticism about our access to the external world, because the required correspondence between 'our thoughts' and 'reality' is never adequately ascertainable. Between 'past reality' and our present *factitious* understanding of 'the history' there is an insurmountable ontic and epistemic problem. It is that historians unavoidably get in the way between 'the past' and 'history' while maintaining that the past and history are synonymous. Unhappily, that belief makes no(n)sense.

Now, given this problem, and whether the substantial majority of historians realise it or not, they demonstrably prefer the correspondence form of truth because it appears to be the most conveniently straightforward. Hence, this is the classic form of 'what you see is what you get'. The convenience of correspondence theory and to a lesser extent correlation and/or coherence and/or consensus theories for historians lies in the simplicity of these forms of truth. Now, by and large historians very rarely (if at all) understand the form of truth they are deploying. Most of the time (like everybody else) historians are never quite sure which form of truth they are using. Now, to make it worse, very few historians either recognise or acknowledge the existence of 'the history aesthetic' through which historians tell the truth (or anyone else for that matter). The most significant history theorist in this issue of 'historical truth' was R.G. Collingwood who described 'historical knowledge' as a form of science that permitted the 're-enactment of the historian's past thoughts' as to the nature of the past but which unavoidably produced second-rate historying. But, here again, the past exists only as 'a history aesthetic'.

Arguably, the basic function of all historians is that they are expected to discover the 'truthful reality of the past'. Historians are in the business of impartiality and explanation but what, however, is historical truth? 'Writing the past as it actually was' is not difficult in one sense and extremely difficult in another. The past is not history and history is not the past. The past, then, is entirely in the hands and minds of historians who strive to reproduce 'the most likely' narrative which the historian presumes must have existed in those events which each historian construes as being 'the reality of the past'. For every historian there is a different past and hence all histories are unique in nature and meaning and explanation.

However, the theorist Collingwood seemed to have nailed the connection between the past and history, with his insistence that the 'author-historian' only needed to take into account the 'authenticity' of (the available) evidence and he also developed a methodology that 'in interpreting the past' he could and should deploy 'concepts of and in the present'. This chastening decision ended up creating the historical 'events', 'generalisations', and 'theories' and thereby Collingwood insisted on the fidelity to past ideas. For Collingwood, then, the past was/is always in some form or another an 'intellectualised history' in some form of 'social science'.

Somewhat, however, the overwhelming and overweening 'social science turn' of the past 50 or so years had to modes or forms—as an art or a social science. Thus, the American Social Science Association sustains the social science form of historying as also does the European Social Science History Conference, which is organised by the International Institute of Social History (IISH) and so forth. In our present *factitious* intellectual milieu, history has expanded as an intellectual and instrumentalist cognitive process—thinking your way through theories and discoveries. Unfortunately, the conflation of the concept of 'social science historying' with 'the past' remains an uneasy epistemic and ontic undertaking.

For the reconstructionist historian gathering sources and drawing inference as to explanations is straightforward. Alternatively, the 'social sciences' very rarely (if at all) wander into the fields of 'history aesthetic knowing and judgment'. However, for the social science historian 'aesthesis' is a weak 'kind' of 'comprehension' of the past, or present, or the future knowledge. The irony in this, nonetheless, is that most academic historians are simply not interested in 'form' over 'content'. For most academic historians, then, 'the-past-*as*-history' remains a mantra and the *factitious* aestheticisation of the past is quite simply beyond their understanding or interest even though they studiously deploy 'form' over 'content'. For the vast majority of historians, then, the foundation of 'the aesthetics of historying' is at very best a pointless undertaking, and at its worst it is simply a frail and dangerous undertaking. The problem of 'getting the data straight' and 'figuring out what the past may have been like' is not regarded 'as an aesthetic undertaking'. Now, for the vast majority of historians, their engagement with the past has no *factitious* contrived aesthetic role in 'in turning the past into history'.

The majority of historians, then, engage with the past by studying and engaging both their theory and practice and then they communicate their scholarship by knowing what happened in the past. Historians (by and large) like to believe they engage in social, economic, geographical, econometric, and political debates and also 'figure' and 'form' national identities. In recent years, new and novel ways of reconstructing, constructing, and deconstructing historical knowledge have emerged from 'local heritage' projects to 'websites' and eventually most historians rethink the ways they offer their work to the non-academic world. Historians also engage with a variety of debates on the nature of the past in the public world. Ironically, however, the majority of historians increasingly sustain their effort to communicate the presence of the past to the present. 'The-past-*as*-history' is what the past was even though this makes no sense. 'Doing history', then, is a *factitious* aesthetic undertaking and hence it is 'artificial' and 'contrived' and hence the past is not history and history is not the past.

Now, dear reader, if you were to be asked 'what is history?' what answer would you give? Obviously I do not know what you would say, however, it seems fairly clear to me (and for all I know maybe to you) that while a story in a novel is not obviously the same as a history, both are narratives. If I were to suggest that a vase in a museum has a history, does that mean it must have an emplotment and if so it must also therefore have a coherent poetic narrative? Or, equally, could all histories as vases, shoes, paintings, and historical plays have a meaning and an argument provided by the potter who made it, or the person who purchased it, or the unfortunate person who dropped it on the floor? So, historians, along with everyone else, have to be very clear that they can never directly engage with the past even though 'the history creator and/or consumer' may have chosen to believe that they have 'discovered' the(ir) most likely 'narrative' of 'the-past-*as*-history'.

Now, and perhaps unfortunately, 'the past' defined as 'the history' can only be regarded as some ersatz 'historical reality'. The past, then, is obviously not history and obviously no history can be regarded as the past. Fortunately, it is fairly obvious that the past is not history and history is not the past. This situation exists at both ontic and epistemic levels because all histories are *factitious* authorial creations. If this seems problematic to any historians reading this, I have to insist that every history is a simple authorial construal. No single history then can lay claim to being 'the history of the past of . . .'. Now, and perhaps unfortunately, the notion of 'the-past-*as*-history' is a far more complex undertaking than I have so far indicated. I have started with the concepts of the fabricated that is a verb that indicates how the past is (unavoidably) 'invented', 'devised', 'made', 'manufactured', and 'intellectually contrived'. Every history, then, is quite clearly both fabricated and also a *factitious* adjective construal and, eventually, all historians have to engage with the concepts of 'objectivity', 'explanation', and their preferred 'form of truth'.

Most historians, nonetheless, create rather then await the discovery of what is always their own aesthetic history of the past. The past then, which historians create as histories, entirely depends upon the preferred coherence they fashion and form in order to construe the nature of the past. Unhappily, the content of the past is blind, deaf, and dumb and so all historians (and everyone else) have to rely on the concepts of rationality and shrewdness. This demands a desperate hope among all historians (whether they know it or not) that the past is coherent because everything in the past can only be accessed as a figurative endeavour. This optimism 'over the historian's experience of the past' is what we commonly call 'history'.

All histories, then, are invariably very close to being 'the history the historian wants' because all historians insist that their histories are 'the histories'. This incredibly odd notion shapes the historian's conformity in what they say about the past defined as 'the reality of the past', demonstrates the very doubtful situation that all histories are the preferred and peculiar narratives that historians want. Hence for every historian there is always a history and almost always several versions of the past. Then and always, all histories are self-evidently falsifiable. New data, then, brings with it a new past. This is excellent news for all historians because that situation demands fresh meanings and renewed interpretations. The single most significant element in 'doing history', then, is that the meaning of the past is the usual maelstrom of interpretations. Happily, then the past is the past and history is not.

The other genuinely awkward problem that all historians have, and which by and large they sensibly ignore, is that if they did not they would be unemployable. The process of the turning of a past into the narrative about it makes no sense. Knowing what actually happened in the past is really very simple. Keep the records. Never destroy anything that can be turned into a legitimate and accurate history. However, the meaning of the past is entirely the province of 'the historian'. The past is the past and there are usually many plausible narratives that can be inaccurately or hopelessly plausible.

Of course, most histories can be very useful in cementing beliefs particularly in terms of class, nationalism, gender, and so forth. However, there are many histories that are weak, fragile, and, unfortunately, created to be constituted, reconstituted and constantly recreated in order to produce a preferred past reality. These usually vapid histories are, of course, unavoidably self-validated and most of them are directly associated with a variety of notions such as nationalism, gender, class, geography, imperialism, but perhaps most likely politicised self-construed history narratives which are regularly 'this new history' which is 'more accurate' than its hitherto 'explications' and 'explanations'. Now, the interpretation and meaning of the past emerges initially in the mind of the historian and which is sustained via a fresh evidential basis for 'the new historical explanation'.

All histories, then, are obviously artificially developed and created for specific functions. But, to start with, the notion of the historian as an explorer who discovers a new intellectual *terra cognita* in the past is, of course, downright silly. Many historians and hence their consumers may claim to be discoverers and/or explorers in the past but that is, well, a simple nonsense. Knowing what happened in the past does not dictate the meaning of the reality of the past. History does not have its own reality. Historians can know what happened in the past but that does not equate with 'knowing the history'. To begin with, the historian always wants to know what happened in the past. Of course, no one needs to be a fully paid historian to figure out that attested 'things' and 'stuff' happened in the past and what further 'things' and 'stuff' followed and on and on and on. There is no *factitious* end of history.

So, 'doing history' is a mélange (in no particular order) of conceptualisation, interpretation, derived meaning, moral imprint, and—obviously—all of these requirements serve the available evidence. So, what do most historians think about what they do? Well, most historians tend to think that what they do is twofold. First they gain a knowledge of what actually happened in the past, and then through their preferred sources they form and shape the(ir) history. Obviously, then, there is no history in the past awaiting to be discovered because in addition to the basic knowledge of what actually happened in the past—the evidence—there is conceptualisation, interpretation, and explicatory meaning.

Perhaps the most significant claim historians make is to insist that they produce bodies of knowledge about the time before our perpetual present. Now, I know many people who are not historians. However, they manage to operate perfectly well by knowing nothing about the past apart from that which they note as they go through their own life. However, many academics—invariably called historians—insist that knowledge of the past is essential to society. Lacking knowledge of the time before our constant present is claimed to be a dangerous ignorance claiming that we would have no identity as we floated in a boundless ocean of unguided time. Happily, my mother managed very well knowing nothing of history.

Now, most academic historians have other *factitious* problems, not least what they hope will turn out to be their discovery of the narrative truth of 'the-past-*as*-history'. So, what is *factitious* narrative truth? As I noted previously, what is essential to the process of turning 'the past' into 'a history' is to engage 'the reality' and/or 'the invention' of the past. This process demands a historical engagement that has been imaginatively invented and/or construed. A *factitious* history—unavoidably and unintentionally—is an authored intervention without the intention of deceiving other historians. Hence, a *factitious* disorder by proxy is a very common academic experience. This awkward and uncomfortable disorder is not hard to acknowledge among academic historians as when 'academic debates get out of hand'.

So, why do historians argue so much? Well, I suggest it is because 'doing history' is entirely a retro undertaking even if all histories are, of course, structured by our authorial aesthetic 'preferentialities'. Now, I suspect that most historians rarely admit to the peculiar situation that their historying is some kind of authorial creation. History, today, as it has generally been in the last couple of centuries (and probably earlier), the notion of 'the historical reality of the past' is an accepted 'actual reality'. Unhappily (or happily depending on the individual historian), all histories exist in some kind of hyperreality. Indeed, all histories are only given to us after some historian/historians has/have created 'a historical reality' as based on their choice of sources. Now, the French philosopher Jean Baudrillard offered the notion of the 'simulation' (simulacrum) and, as usually happens, academic historians entirely ignored it and most historians certainly do not engage with the concept of 'hyperreality'. So, the vast majorities of historians have little or no engagement with the idea and so, for most historians, while the past is plainly still not 'here' it certainly was and had an objective existence.

Historians, then, have very little time for the awkward notion of either 'simulation' or 'hyperreality' in their pursuit of the resuscitation of the past. However, in the absence of the past all that historians can do is—as I have noted already—either endeavour to 'reconstruct' the past, which is plainly a silly notion, or they can make the effort to 'construct' the past again. This is only slightly better, or they can deconstruct the past, which is the most problematic. To be blunt then, historians just have to fall back on authoring 'a past' they cannot engage with. So, as the French intellectual Gilles Deleuze argued, history is a simulacrum, which has an image without a resemblance. This is not at all bad news for historians because it permits them to engage with 'past reality' with 'their representation' of it and call it a new and enlightened history. Fortunately for historians, it is harder to think in the present than historically.

The really awkward problem that historians constantly have (and which they cannot overcome) is 'hyperreality' which means they simply ignore it. Now, historians have not ventured seriously to engage with the problem of the past. Whether historians realise it or not, our contemporary culture is in the midst of a crisis of representation. This is really bad news for historians and also everyone else. These days there is a crisis of representation in 'doing history'. Just where does the past exist? This may seem a bizarre notion? Surely it exists in history? Now, and possibly unhappily, the past exists wherever the historian wants it to be and what it means in different places and cultural situations. And that is why there is a serious problem 'with doing history'. To be blunt then: the signified and signifier of the past implodes not just 'in history' but also in every representation.

Ironically, then, the past may be fixed but we all have our 'preferred histories' and if you do not want one past just read another historian. Obviously, then, and you may have already come to this conclusion, past signifiers collapse in upon each other, annihilating meaning in the past, causing all signs to be unbalanced and 'the meaning of history' to become a crude mechanism for inventing perpetual past realities. The irony in all this is very obvious because the past is the past while history is a *factitious* engagement with that which no longer exists. No doubt many historians (and others as well) will be unnerved when it becomes even clearer to accept and acknowledge that the past is not history and history is not the past.

So, where can we go to for the original past(s)? Well, the obvious place is the past, which is a bogus unreality. The past was what happened in the past but its history comes out of our presence. Famously, then, Jean Baudrillard's allegory of Disneyland and fantasy leads us back to the legendary hyperreality. So, how can we engage with the past? Well, all we can do is constitute 'reality images' or 'simulations' that purport 'to depict' a 'real existence' but which nonetheless come to constitute 'reality past, present, and future'. Now, most historians who have got this far (and their students as well) will insist that history is a reconstruction (ideally) and not a construction (next best thing) but it is certainly a deconstruction of the past as the historians want. Of course, while trying to get 'the (hi)story straight' historians, by and large, insist that the history narrative is a detective process. Unfortunately, that makes no sense for the very simple reason that history never existed in the past. History, of course, is unavoidably layered by prejudices, intolerances, chauvinisms, jingoisms, nationalisms, patriotisms, and so forth.

What does this mean? As I have suggested, our access to the past is only through the histories we construe in the forms of a 'reconstruction' or a 'construction' and/or a 'deconstruction' of the past. The past then is what went before (obviously) but that remains a problem for the very simple reason that 'that which went before' is entirely the construal of the historian or anyone else who wants to engage with the time before our constant present/presence. Now, the 'infamous' postmodern semiotic concept of 'hyperreality', which was deployed by the French sociologist Jean Baudrillard in his (in)famous text *Simulacra and Simulation*, was and still is often dismissed as of no utility to and for the vast majority of historians. This remains awkward for historians. This was and still is simply very awkward. This is because the majority of historians just ignored his ideas for whatever good, bad, or indifferent reasons but primarily because his philosophy offered 'models of reality' without an origin or given reality apart from the historian.

So, why am I resurrecting the notion of hyperreality? Well, it is because most historians wilfully ignore it. Obviously, it does not worry me too much because historians simply and contently ignore the nature of their ontic and epistemic failures. Obviously, most historians rarely worry too much about history even though it is a series of representations they have constituted. So, they do not worry about the concept of the hyperreal simply because in the absence of the past (and dear reader you may have recognised this situation) all histories are, well 'historical representations'. Now, hyperrealism is just another sign of the past or anything else you want to describe in the past and the future the historian wants to insist was once an original referent. These original referents are the stuff of the past as 'sorted out' by the individual historian.

History, then, is an embarrassingly simple notion. This is not to annoy the utility of history of course. However, our perpetual present plainly is not the past and that is because without the past we create *factitious* histories. So, our histories are those notions that replace the past as a simulated past. Historians, then, are 'history cartographers' in order to create 'history maps' or, as Marshall McLuhan insisted, the 'medium is the message' and information devours its own content. Hence, historians invariably and constantly 'update the past' in their history texts. The irony in this is that the world of 'the history' is constantly 'updated' because history is a moveable feast in the murky universe of that discipline of historying. This is not really a problem because for every new edition/version of the past there is always going to be, well, for every new edition/version of the past there is always going to be and so forth until the historian dies.

So, in the universe of history the past is constantly remade. So, the cartography of the past is constantly rethought although 'history-hyperreality' is just another simulation of what might have already been a reality—or not. Hence, the point of this text is (in part) to point out that while historians desire to engage with the past all they can have is the *factitious* 'past by proxy'. History, then, is the classic mechanism to recoup that which cannot be recouped. As the proxy for the past, history remains as the means by which in our culture we can constantly rethink past reality and make it seem new. Now, the central failure with history is that it demands rethinking not just history but the past itself. It seems odd that the past can be rethought, reimagined, reconstructed, refuted, refused, rebuffed, reassembled, reconstituted, and so forth. But, then, can we imagine there was only one past? But that is what we have of course. All histories, then, are proxy pasts. However, histories constantly shift and move and simulate real reality.

Obviously, there are constant hazards for historians and their consumers because histories are invariably confused with 'the past' and like everyone else historians can only 'imagine/image the past'. Obviously, of course, historians do not discover the past because—understandably—they constitute it as authorial interventionists. Hence, historians all too often construe successful celebrity or failed celebrity or hero-worship or whatever description they want to hang around the person or create. Historians are in the business of blending reality and representation. The foundational problem with 'doing history' is that it is 'doing history'. Thus, all histories are simulations, which are simple examples of hyper-reality. By that claim I suggest that historians rethink the past in order to constitute a simulated past, which they believe is still reality.

Now, that is obviously nonsense because history is a simulation that is no longer a 'real territory' or a 'referential being' or a 'substance'. History, then, is that imitation that no longer takes place in a physical dominion because it takes place in an 'intellectual space' not categorised by physical limits, i.e., within our selves and increasingly also within 'a history' which is an image without resemblance. Arguably, the foundational problem with history—and which cannot be erased'—is that it is never found for what it was. History, then, is nothing more than a retro-reality, which might be 'useful' or 'misleading' or 'convenient' or 'expedient' and so forth. History defined as what it is—a simulacrum—which is a copy without being a resemblance. History is the classic illustration of a reflection of past reality, or which may turn out to be a perversion of reality or a pretense. History is possibly the classic characterisation of that which bears no relation to any present reality whatsoever. Thus, history is an authentic fake without being a reality but which is not quite a Disneyland.

Thus, 'history' unavoidably traffics in a reality that offers an illusion and which makes it more desirable for people to buy the reality of the past and it is very well known that very few historians are dangerous interventionists in creating a false reality of the past. Of course, histories are not endless copies of the past. Histories are versions of the past but they are not hyperrealist. Nevertheless, history is an original created by the individual historian. So, nothing is original, but all histories are endless copies of the historian's reality. Accordingly, since we do not imagine the reality of simulations, both the imagined and real are equally hyperreal; for example, the numerous simulated rides, including Disneyland, and/or Brighton Pier, and/or Fantasy Island, Skegness, and so forth.

In his book *Simulacra and Simulation* (1981) Jean Baudrillard (1929–2007) argues the 'imaginary world' of Disneyland creates a 'real' concealment that is neither true and/or false that refreshes the *factitious* real. Now, as the theorist Jean Baudrillard put it, 'history is our lost referential. History then becomes a "historical reality" '. Hence, today then, the past is a constant reality, which is both at once an ontic and epistemic construal. Now, no single history can lay claim to being 'the history of the past of . . .'. Now, and perhaps unfortunately, the notion of 'the-past-*as*-history' is a far more complex undertaking than I have so far indicated.

Now, most academic historians—should they have come across it—will have very little time for the concept of the *factitious* nature of what they do. I think I should be clear that in my view, historians today, in the wake of the death of 'the postmodern', have happily returned to the naïve notion that the past is the past and history is the description of what it was. Now, very few Anglophone historians ever engaged with the philosopher Jean Baudrillard. As I write this, I am well aware that the vast majority of Anglophone academic historians continue to accept that the past is 'what happened in the past' and 'what it probably meant' and that then the job is done.

Nevertheless, Baudrillard's postmodern views had some impact, if brief, on numbers of theorists. However, and moreover, the philosopher Frederic Jameson argued that our culture had lost contact with 'the real' in many ways and Baudrillard also argued that what you 'see' and 'feel' is not the 'actual' and/or the 'authentic'. So, Baudrillard offered an ersatz 'reality' that historians could not accept. Baudrillard's world—a dystopian simulated reality—was about as far from conventional historying that anything can be because the past is what the past was, and history is that which 'controls' past reality. Nevertheless, most historians happily ignored and still ignore that roughed up cultural invention insisting that the past is the past and happily the past will still be the past. Now, that makes no 'sense'. Now, knowing what happened in the past is not history. That President John F. Kennedy was shot in Dealey Plaza, Dallas, Texas on November 22nd, 1963 at 12:30 pm is an event that, like all past events, can be attested. But, as I have suggested, the past is not history and history is not the past.

Now, the substantial majority of historians will reject the notion that history is a retro referential undertaking. However, history is thus—quite plainly—a simulation. Hence, historians (and everyone else) have to accept that history is an imitation of the past. Histories can only exist as 'documentaries', 'TV programmes', 'lectures', 'seminars', and so forth. Ironically, today, all histories are about forgetting and rethinking historical histories. Historians constantly revise and reconsider and rethink the past. However, and somewhat awkwardly, the past is a presentist retrocultural engagement. All histories can only exist through their form. For every history form there is a different history. So, instead of discovering the past historians can only mediate it. Today, all history is simply an aesthetic act of hyperreality. No longer television, film, and the internet separate us from 'the real' even as they seek to reproduce it more fully or faithfully: So, all engagements with the past as history is an act of hyperreality of communication and of meaning. Hence, all engagements with the past are, of course, created not by the past but by the historian.

In the perpetual absence of the past, all historical engagements are merely acts of artifice. In the absence of the past all historians can do is create, proliferate, and design ready-made histories. As Jean Baudrillard said and/or claimed (or if he did not he should have) that all historians like everyone else are unable to compare and contrast reality with a simulation. What you are reading now is an example. Histories are classic instances of a replication/simulation of past reality. Histories, then, are useful until they are discarded and disregarded. History then is a classic example of consumption and trashing. Historians, obviously, consume the past disguised as 'past reality'. 'Doing history', however, is a classic demonstration of our culture of consumption and disregard. While most academic historians might deny it, 'getting the data straight' does not mean they are producing the and/or the most likely history. Historians today work within a consumer society that is crudely filtered by ideology, philosophy, political dogma, doctrine, canon and constant rethinking and while they offer the 'cool smile'.

So, most historians will continue to exist in a universe of simulation and simulacra while thus failing to figure out the distressing nature of their universe of concepts, impressions, perceptions, theories, acuities, debates, and so forth. Obviously, the past cannot speak for itself and—understandably—historians only speak for themselves. Obviously, then, all histories are simulations as created by historians. When I was a student I came across the thought that history was the same as the past. Indeed, I was told it had to be the same. But the universe of simulacra and simulation quickly wiped the smile off my face. I also soon discovered 'rhetoric', 'stylistics', 'textualism', 'genre', and why a novel was different to a history, and so on and so forth. I also came across poststructuralist thinking at a time when historians not only continued to engage with the past but also notions such as stylistics and some 'thing' called 'modern and for a few postmodern criticism'.

Now, that was an awkward situation as I had enough with my hands full with the past and so I had very little time for 'simulacra', 'signs', and 'signifiers' but it would be a sacrifice for me and historians and for anyone else for that matter to lose the dimension of the past through a crisis of *factitious* representation. While the postmodernist moment was at its height between the 1970s through to the 2010s most historians (almost all of them) managed to ignore it all. Obviously then, the central postmodernist problem was 'alterity' aka the state of being other or different. The irony in this was that the vast majority of historians did—and still do—insist that the past is history and history is the past. Unfortunately, however, the past is the past and history is history and they do not exist in the same ontic and/or epistemic intellectual universe.

There is an obvious irony in this that goes to the heart of 'the-past-*as*-history'. Historians regularly confront each other with their preferred 'differential versions' of their 'histories' and subsequently they constantly doubt the utility or bizarre nature of histories based on weak interpretations and/or insubstantial data and sources. So, the foundational problem that all historians have is directing the 'transfiguration process' by turning the past into history and/or history into the past. Now, all historical narratives by their nature always run far too easily to be able to claim to offer the 'realistic representations' of the events they describe. So, all historical narratives run far too smoothly to be able to seriously claim that they are 'the past of . . .'. Indeed, our knowledge of history is always fragmentary, is always incomplete, is always partial, and is always limited. All histories then are enquiries into that which no longer exists even though most historians would not believe that was bad news. The past, then, is useless until it is (hi)storied.

Now, what historians tend to do with the usually abject and wretched detritus of the past is to recycle preferred historical explanations through (possibly) 'meanings', 'denotations', 'significations', 'dialectical engagements', and even 'useful suppositions'. But, and it is obvious, there are no in-built explanations in the past until the historian implants them. All events in the past then are implanted and embedded historical events. Historians, along with everyone else then, have to accept that 'past events' are 'destiny' or just 'good or bad luck' or somewhere in between. With this going on, then, it is hardly surprising that 'historical events' allow the historian plenty of scope for 'rethinking and redefining the past'.

3 Fabricated

Our experience of the past is that which we usually refer to as 'the history'. Ironically and unfortunately, there is a problem with this notion that cannot be resolved. The perpetual problem with 'doing history' is the unavoidable distinction between the historian's 'representation' and/or 'description' of the reality of the past. Now, and obviously, there is no prepackaged history in the past which can be discovered and/or recovered by historians (along with everyone else). The time before the perpetual present can only constitute 'the past' through that ersatz substitute of 'the history'. The central and substantial problem that most historians have, then, is that they perpetually fail to distinguish their present representation from past reality. To be clear then, and like every other human being, historians can only engage with the past as a history even though its representational accuracy may be dubious.

This means that every history narrative is a fabricated construal (as a verb) about the possible nature of the past. To be clear, then, every history is unavoidably a textual/visual/voiced and physical assembly as to the likely nature of the past. Now, all historians like every other human being have a serious problem. All histories are, well, histories. They are not the past because all histories are 'made'. However, histories are 'prepared', 'contrived', or 'manufactured' in the sense that they are authorial inventions of historians. Of course, all responsible historians are very clear, in their belief that to engage with the past they are obliged to reconstitute and/or reconstruct what they believe was the past in accord with the presently available data and/or the state of the archive. The central and unavoidable situation that all historians and everyone else have is the foundational problem that history is not the past and the past is not history. So, via our unavoidably crude language use, historians and everyone else have to do their best in turning the past into a presentist and rapidly revisioned (hi)story.

So, the simple situation we all have is to circumvent the central and unavoidable problem with history, which is that it is not the past. Thus, while historians have to compare and contrast their histories, they cannot compare and contrast 'the pasts' that are available to them. Hence, historians have to accept (or they should?) that the past is not history and history can never be the past. Somewhat awkwardly then, this means that in the absence of the past (and, dear reader, you maybe have noticed that the past is always absent?) all we have is an enduring and constantly aesthetic engagement with the past but which is simply an authorial processed narrative. Hence, all we can do as historians is to engage honestly with both the empirical content of the past and the aesthetic nature of the histories they create. The central problem still remains of course. Historians, then, can only engage with the past by substituting their presumed authored narratives of and for the past. As, dear reader, I assume you may have fully understood by now, in the absence of the past we have to offer a substitution. Obviously, that substitution is the historian's 'discovery and array' of 'the facts'.

Unhappily, like everyone else, historians will always experience the same perennial problem with 'the facts'. This is that facts are 'events under descriptions' and obviously all facts are fabrications. This does not mean our descriptions of what we believe to be reality must always be 'made up false realities' which would be irresponsible, reckless, and negligent. At this point far too many historians and most other folks as well eventually fail to acknowledge that 'the worlds of the past' as well as 'the present' are always engineered by historians. The fabrication and/or the assembly of facts create the worlds of the past and the present. What you are reading now is a version of the past, which is made by me from a massive range of symbols, which originate in 'my intellectual world(s)'.

Now, I learned many decades ago that you should never rely on historians. This is not because they are inveterate liars but because they are authors who are unavoidable 'compositors' and 'deconstructionists'. Hence, the pleasure when engaging with the past is to deconstruct the 'existing worlds and sub-worlds' of other historians. Historians do not invent the realities of the past (although a tiny minority might invent the history they wish existed in the past). But all historians unavoidably exist in their subworlds, which they create by their fabrication of 'the facts', as I noted just now 'events under descriptions'.

Plainly, there are many worlds that historians, politicians, steel workers, airline pilots, and window cleaners occupy. So, all we can catch are their preferred 'descriptions', 'views', or 'ways how the world is'. World 'versions' are 'symbolic systems' that come in several forms. They can be described and expressed in words, music, pictures, dancing, and any kind of symbols they want. The descriptions we deploy are usually literal/numeric, but in the arts they can be free-formed. None of the worlds that human beings and that obviously includes historians, is more real than others. Historians always select a 'past world', which they and their consumers call 'the past actual'. Of course, the genuine world of the past differs when the historian changes their point of view.

The nature of engaging with the past means deploying 'weighting', creating 'sub -worlds', and fresh 'connections' which enable the historian to both 'create and combine the parts again' in a new way. Obviously, differential 'histories' come with differential authorial emphases, which are deployed by 'ordering' and 'contextualising', and there is the notion of 'deletion' and 'supplementation'. And then of course, historians 'describe', 'correct', or 'corrupt' the nature of the past. Then, how can historians truthfully evaluate the nature of past worlds? Historians have a real problem with the nature of truth. To begin with, 'historical truth' concerns propositions, which can be both verbal and written, and there are always contradictory truths.

But how can historians test 'the truth of the historical past'? Well, they cannot. It is impossible for historians to compare the present presentation of the past in their perpetual existence. All too often 'the truth' in the sense of 'correspondence' depends on 'consensus'. Unfortunately, historians are almost entirely constrained by their own measure as to how useful the(ir) past was. Historians are usually presumed to discover 'the facts of the past' but, of course, 'the facts' do not slouch about waiting to be usefully deployed. Historians have plenty of problems in turning the past into a history or, if they prefer, discovering 'the past narrative' that must surely be back there and then? Historians have several measures, which make their history useful. How plausible is 'their argument'? How coherent is their 'history narrative'? How valid is their deductive inference through their theorems and premises.

So, the logic and content of the 'aestheticised historied past' is plainly not necessarily 'the reality of the past' because it is authored in the present. The common sense logic of 'the-past-*as*-history' is a mix of actuality and artifice. History cannot be anything other than a convenient 'narrative substance' and which, dear reader, such as you are presently reading. So, every 'history' is no more than a 'history' and, while there are (usually) very good reasons for preferring one historical interpretation to another, the empirical foundation of 'a history' by the historian remains something of a mundane undertaking. The most useful element in a history, then, is the historian's figuring out the nature of the narrative substance that constitutes 'the-past-*as*-history'? Now, and of course, very few historians would go much further than engaging with that process of 'what probably happened' and 'why'? This simple process then constitutes the most likely narrative of the history. Unfortunately, the absence of the past means the past can only be construed and interpreted as a history and the nature and meaning of past events are never more than 'authorial', 'contingent', and 'circumstantial'. The past then is never more than the 'past-*as*-history'. This situation, of course, is unavoidable given that all histories are fabricated authorial creations.

All histories then are authored and aestheticised 'story creations'. This means that while they purport to be referential in their nature, they are unavoidably a fabricated aesthetic experience of the past, in the sense that they are subject to the historian's 'understanding' and 'interpretation' of the 'sources' as adjudged by each individual historian. It is not at all surprising, then, that historians tend to 'herd' and/or 'school' and/or 'group' such as Marxists, postmodernists, Tories, unsuspecting students, and so forth. Consequently: while the 'evidence' supposedly determines the true or most likely probable nature of the past, histories always reshape, redevelop and revision the past as their authored (and obviously) preferred history. Thus: 'the-past-*as*-history' constantly and unavoidably changes. Histories change because of the predilections, partialities, and likings as shaped by the historian who, in addition, will be likely to have an ideology or a religious belief or no religious belief and they are likely to have a preferred philosophy, viewpoint, perspective, assessment, evaluation, and so forth.

Now and then, of course, there is the worry of the research grant running out, the publishing editor playing up, their impending divorce and the(ir) debts that for all I know may lead them to excessive drinking alcohol, and so on and so forth. Thus: all histories are created and developed at the impulse and caprice of the author-historian although she or he may insist they are (and will continue) in the business of 'discovering the history of . . .'. Unhappily, there is no history in the past. There is no history 'in built' in the past 'to be discovered' and if there were they would quickly be re-visioned and re-versioned. To be clear then: historians do not discover the past. Historians discover only those parts of the past, which they believe ought to be in any useful history. Indeed, 'history' is an entirely sweet confection and/or an endeavour that can be liked or disliked.

Plainly, then, the past is all too often (re)created as an aesthetic on steroids. This description may seem like I am going overboard, but the past must be constantly reconstituted, reorganised, restructured regularly in terms of being modified, adjusted, fine-tuned, honed, and so forth. Imagine a past that cannot be revisioned? There would be no need for history? There would be no need for a past? There would only be the perpetual present as shaped, schooled, and controlled by a number of intellectual and academic assumptions and constraints. The most basic of these limitations is the bothersome process of hermeneutics. This is the notion of 'textual exegesis', and still today historians are taught to follow the post-Reformation practice of 'textual explanation'.

This activity is rarely dangerous if it is recognised as what it is, i.e., the simple written inference of the meaning of the past by the historian. To be clear on this then: while historians invariably insist that their judgments, meanings, and understandings are wrapped up and carefully deployed, there remains the very odd notion of discovering the nature of the past and what it probably meant. Now, this activity is invariably a harmless undertaking, something akin to trainspotting. If you miss one historical interpretation another will soon arrive at the station. This means that our understanding of history as an authorial, i.e., fabricated undertaking, is an unavoidable proxy problem. By this I mean is that the nature of history is almost entirely founded on the notion of interpretation (aka hermeneutics). This means that in the absence of the past all we have is the perpetual deconstruction of our own process of historying, which—hopefully—eventually leads to a historical explanation.

But, there is a very awkward problem that historians cannot resolve and so consequently most ignore. This problem is the massive effort to feed and sustain both the historical consciousness and the historical explanation. The historical consciousness is the historian's orientation toward preexisting (and aestheticised) historical narratives. Obviously, the past is by definition inaccessible, which means historians have to generate and constitute their own historical consciousness, which, of course, is sustained by its empirical, analytical, and representationalist structure. This, of course, feeds that vast range of preexisting historical narratives that historians sustain by rethinking, reconstituting, reconstructing, recreating, refashioning, and so forth.

Given the nature of our perpetual present and which presumably in all likelihood into the future, the process of the interpretation of texts - hermeneutics - enables us to produce the nature of the past as a historical explanation. Unavoidably, then, the past is and will remain a fabricated undertaking. This is because the past is built and constantly built again until the historian (and everyone else) is satisfied with their preferred version of the past. Plainly, then, the past is the most egregious problem for historians (and everyone else?), given the common sense and naïve desire to recover from the relativism that has underpinned the immanent author-reader relationship. The notion of objectivity, presumably in the pursuit of the history of the past, makes no sense. In the face of the irretrievable past, all historians can do is accept the highly dubious concept of the historical explanation.

Not surprisingly, then, when historians 'author' aka 'stitch together their preferred histories' they soon have to accept and/or at worst acknowledge that there is no utility in the notion of the historical explanation and so another historical explanation has to be created/constituted. Through this unavoidable mechanism historians, like everyone else, must categorize the past for what they think it was and thereby invoke one or more of the classic four emplotments of tragedy, comedy, romance, and/or satire. Hence, there is no meaning in 'the-past-*as*-history' until the historian emplots it. This rather crude 'processing' of the past into a history is, of course, invariably described as the 'historical explanation'. Unfortunately, this makes no sense of any sort if the historian wants to dig out and/or discover the aestheticised narrative reality of the past.

Now, this makes no sense. It makes no sense because explaining the nature and meaning of the time before now can only be offered and/or presented as the individual historian's constituted, reconstituted, and, as I prefer to describe it, a fabricated history. This does not mean all histories are fabricated in the sense of they are a likely historical explanation that is not necessarily untrue. Acquiring, gaining, procuring, and securing historical explanations are a very basic and simple common sense activity, which then seems to deliver its own inherent narrative emplotment. This is egregious nonsense of course. Only historians insist that it is they who can produce and deliver why, how, and what happened in the past. The notion of discovering 'the-past-*as*-history' is almost entirely dependent upon the historian's preferred and contrived historical explanations(s). It may be tasteless and tactless to admit to it, but the historian's history is a straightforward invention through the concept of discovery which is generally preferred that hopefully will fill the void of the past.

Among historians then, there are three worrying questions that historians invariably cannot avoid. They are that there is no historical explanation in-built in the events of the past. Unfortunately again, there is rarely 'the cause' of anything in the past that all historians can agree upon. And, then, historians still tend to herd shifting and changing as they re-author or deny the readings of their histories by their colleagues. Obviously, then, there are myriad preexisting historical narratives available to explain the past. Unhappily, most historians, like every other human being, aim to offer an 'historical explanation' which might (they hope) pass muster as the most likely (hi-)story. So, what this adds up to is that every historian's engagement with the past has to be 'described' and 'explicable'.

Now: it is well known that historians deploy explanatory methodologies in order to understand and elucidate the nature of the past and its possible\probable meaning(s). Unhappily, there is no science which can explain why 'what happened in the past happened'. To be blunt: historians can and do offer their assumptions and explanations about what happened in the past, but—because they are human beings—they cannot prove in a scientific fashion why and what occurred. The past is 'the past' but history remains a narrative about the past, which is plainly outside the past. At best most historians agree a history is a 'reconstruction' or a 'clever construction' of the past. Very few historians try to deconstruct the past by rethinking the hitherto agreed upon reality. This is problematic of course given that the past is the past and history is, well, not the past. History, after all, is the preferred authorial narrative of the individual historian (although many do still herd of course).

So: in respect of engaging with the past the best historians can hope for ('in doing history') is producing a history ('as a discovery') that is authorial(ly) self-conscious in respect of the poetics, aesthetics, and philosophy of the history narrative in the past. Unhappily, most academic historians ignore this simple logic. They take the road, which is 'telling it like it was'. Unfortunately, the majority of historians (and I suspect non-historians also) constitute their engagement with the past in accord with their ideological, political, class, nationalist, gendered, and myriad other preferences. Hence: the notion of 'historical objectivity' is a convenient notion to beat past reality into submission.

Thus: history is neither more nor less than an authored 'narrative explanation' about the past and so there is no '(hi)story explanation' until the historian fabricated it. Now, this claim of 'the fabricated history' is possibly more than a little awkward for the historian who is desperately determined to sustain the presumed smooth processing of the past into history. 'Doing history' is obdurate and always awkward because every history is, well, fabricated. This sounds somewhat awkward at best and at its worst it is an act of an intellectual rough and tumble assemblage that is hardly scholarly. But, dear reader, if you elect to take the time to think about it, all histories cannot be more than an authorial creation. This is because there is no given history in the past to be discovered despite all the historian's investigations. Now then, all histories are 'brilliant', and/or 'good', and/or 'bad', and/or 'awful' authorial construals. Obviously, getting 'the data straight' is embarrassingly simple even if it takes months/years to obtain and sift and then (often unhappily) process as a good, bad, or indifferent 'interpretation' and/or as a 'clarification', and/or as an 'understanding', and/or as an 'analysis'. So, what do all forms of history have in common? So, put straightforwardly then, all histories are the inescapable fabricated intervention of the historian.

Now, happily, the nature of processing the past into a history is not particularly complex. Historians do it in many different forms such as lectures, seminars, tutorials, books, articles, TV presentations, radio programmes, and so forth. Fortunately, and whether all historians do or do not acknowledge this situation, the form of 'the historian's history' is always and unavoidably as significant as the content of the form. Unfortunately, there remain far too many historians for whom form and content in their engagement with the past is not significant. Now, I may be harsh in my judgment in this, but the breadth, depth, and persistent belief of the vast majority of historians continue to insist that they have done their job when they get the data 'straight'.

Now, the substantial majority of historians believe they have done the(ir) job when they have delivered what they believe 'the most likely nature and meaning of the past' as they recognize the aesthetic dimensions of history. Somewhat awkwardly, however, the historian cannot avoid 'making', 'fashioning', 'forming', 'shaping', and 'construing' the past for what they believe it was, but the past is permanently out of the historian's control of the past. What follows then is that all histories are '(re)construed aesthetic fabrications'. So, the process of 'doing history' is understandably never a discovery because every history is the historian's preferred narrative. To be brief and blunt: the vast majority of historians constitute past events through their preferred description of the past.

Obviously, then, while all histories are subject to their 'historical content, i.e., what happened' they remain authorial creations. Evidently, then, there is a substantial range of (pre-)fabricated forms available for the historians creating 'the-past-*as*-history'. Happily, of course, the metaphysics and ontology of 'doing history' is embarrassingly if not disconcertingly simple. Like every other human being, historians always have and express their 'preferred philosophies' whether they know it or not. They also choose their preferred and 'selected concepts' and they all have their 'favourite theories', and some of them have 'intellectual yearnings' and 'personal desires' about the past and, not surprisingly, the individual historian also 'shapes', 'forms', 'arranges', and 'assembles' the past for their use.

The expression of that artifact we call 'history' and/or 'historying', then, is simply just another synthesised version of the past. To be blunt, history has only one reason for its existence. It is a signpost to the past at best and at worst it is a self-regarding and self-expression of what historians want to believe in accord with their inferences, interpretations, and clarifications. In one very important sense, then, history has very little to do with the past because its nature is that of a manufacturing process about a product historians cannot control, i.e., the past. Of course that does not mean the past can be denied, disallowed, and rejected and it may turn out to be an exercise in simple (or complex) lies. Happily, the vast majority of histories are demonstrably clear and factual expressions of beliefs are sustained and anchored in evidentially past reality.

So, and obviously, all histories are differentially authored narrative forms. The-past-*as*-history, then, comes in lectures, books, films, seminars, roundtables, radio, TV programmes and documentaries (of various kinds), chats on the bus, and so on and so forth. But, again and obviously, every form of 'history' is construed and constructed, which is always intended to reconstruct and/or construct and/or deconstruct 'the past as it actually was'. Unhappily, though, every history is a demonstration of hope over the now unreality of the past as we live our lives in our perpetual present. Unhappily, then, the best that historians can do with the past is to demonstrate that it is an aestheticised fabricated narrative that is made for the past. Hence, 'the-past-*as*-history' can only be utilised when it is put into 'the lecture' or 'the seminar' or 'the book' or the 'radio talk' and/or 'the article' of the historian. Engaging with the past, then, is simply a range of offers of 'meanings and explanations' that are retrofitted to the past by the historian.

Now, as the historian-philosopher R.G. Collingwood argued, historians usually evade the past by 'rethinking' what was the nature of the past. Thus: the empirical past is what it was 'as far as we can tell' but it cannot be engaged directly. It is well known that historians lean heavily on the notion of 'the fact' and most historians would agree that a 'fact' is a belief that can be corroborated and verified and which, hopefully, can be proved and ultimately demonstrated to be true. Unfortunately, the concept of 'the historical fact' is never really going to work for historians (or anyone else) because statements of facts about the past are just simply events under a description. Hence, the notion of 'a history laboratory' would be and it is plain nonsense. To make matters worse, while there may be a consensus that certain events occurred and there can be traces of consequences of such events there is rarely a consensus as to what it all 'meant' or 'means'. This is why historians insist that 'their' fabricated interpretations are histories. To be clear then: the past is the past (for what that is worth) and history is history (and again for what that is worth); however, it is impossible to conflate them, i.e., the past and history, because, in ontic terms, the past is not history and history is not the past. The upshot of that unfortunate situation is that historians, like everyone else, have to live with the oxymoron (contradiction) of 'the truthful interpretation of the past'. For all historians, then, their histories are never duplicates although many may seem similar.

Given this unavoidable situation the embarrassing logic that blights the historian is that the history of the past is contrivance as much as it is 'engineered', which is unavoidably a 'fabricated correspondence' between 'the historian's description and that which is being described'. Hence, all historians have to live with and/or simply ignore the situation that a fact is nothing more than their description. A historical fact, then, is a reference to an aspect of the past that is sustained by the historian's preferred selection of data. Thus, given the nature of the 'fabrication' of 'the historical fact', every historian has to accept that the past 'for it to come alive' is a 'construal', 'understanding', 'elucidation', 'explication', and/or a 'clarification' and so on and so forth. This is where the crucial notion of 'justified belief' is foundational to historical thinking and doing.

Accordingly, history is that creative process (fabricated) that styles and fashions the past in a variety of intellectual and authorial forms. All histories, then, are 'built', 'lectured', 'written as texts', 'radio programme scripts', 'Sunday newspaper magazines', 'idle chit chat on the bus' but are rarely intentionally 'made up'. Thus, 'historying' is variously a process of 'discovery', and/or 'detection', and/or 'uncovering', or 'simply a diversion' that remains as a cultural, political, economic 'construction' and/or 'deconstruction'. It is to state the obvious then, that a history is a copy without the original. This leads to a very awkward problem especially for academic historians. Now, most people have little engagement with the past apart from a rough and ready notion of it. For most people this is not particularly problematic. Most human beings manage to go through life knowing nothing about history and, should they come across 'a history', it is usually just a vague diversion.

The irony in this is demonstrated in today's deployment of 'a history' which has become a substantial cultural 'stayer' and it has become an aesthetic 'built process of cultural diversion' that shapes, forms, and processes our society. So, and not least for all historians whether they acknowledge it or not, the nature of the past 'as it actually was' cannot be recouped. Of course, this flies in the face of the unavoidable situation that there is always a constant proliferation of contemporary pasts and their meanings that historians (all too often) constitute and create. Nevertheless, and more than somewhat awkwardly, the past has to be habitually reconstituted through the process of 'historying'. Eventually, the 'history processing course' ends up as some form of deconstruction. Now, there is a depthless irony in all of this because the historian never controls the past even though they are self-styled as the custodians, guardians, and protectors of the past. The irony in this is that historians constantly and happily (re)create and (re)vision and (re)think the 'past'.

Consequently, and ironically, the 'definitive history of the past' is always available because historians cannot ever 'occupy the past' and neither can they 'acquire what the past actually was and/or meant' by acknowledging the aesthetic dimensions of 'the-past-*as*-history'. The best situation that historians can wish for when engaging with the past is to create a new and/or fresh 'trawling the archive' and/or 'smarter inferences'. Happily, as long as there is a past, there will always be historians seeking out 'the new aestheticised interpretation' thanks to 'the latest evidence' and/or smarter 'inferences'. Hence, there is no end to history and consequently and with an impressive irony, 'doing history' seems to be the only human pursuit that will never end and never reach a definitive conclusion. The perpetual, continuous, unremitting, and assiduous creation of 'the-past-*as*-history' is thus the foundational undertaking of the historian. Happily, for historians (and possibly everyone else) there is yet more to 'doing history'.

Every history, then, is an authorial (re-)creation and/or a (re-)fashioning as a fabricated undertaking. To be clear, then, the past is obviously 'the past' and 'history' is the historian's present 'narrative' they have created about it. Ideally, of course, and as I have already noted, historians are supposed and/or presumed to be objective and hence their claim to 'the histories' can be sustained. Unhappily, that situation always fails and historians cannot reconstruct 'the past' as it actually was. The past, then, is what the past was as certified by the available evidence; however, because all histories are unavoidably aesthetic undertakings the reality of the past can only be fabricated in form and content. The concept of the fabricated refers to the situation (which is yet again unavoidable) that history is an authorial creation. The empirical (observable) nature of the past can be discovered but not its histories. The obvious reason is because the past exists 'in waiting' for 'what it was' for the historian to author it into an existence.

Now, this situation is entirely due to the nature of the range of 'sources' that the historian choses and which then 'sifts to discover' the most likely existence and meaning of the past. Annoyingly, only the briefest engagement with history reveals that the past always has a surfeit of explanations and meanings, which are formed by the authorial decisions of the historian. Now, whether they realize it or not, historians unavoidably reduce the past into their history. A history is entirely pointless until it is 'formed into' some kind of engagement with the past. This engagement is systemised and controlled through the historian's reduction and/or construction of the past that is defined and construed as some kind of history. But every history is also a deconstruction of both the past and its history.

All histories, then, are a work of art but plainly it is the historian who is the origin of their preferred history. Now, the source of all histories is plainly the past as understood by the historian. But there remains the nature of truth in history. So, where does the truth of the past actually come from? There are two foundational concepts that constitute and drive the nature of our knowledge of the history of the past. These are phenomenology and hermeneutics. Phenomenology is the science of consciousness as experienced from the first-person point of view, while hermeneutics is that branch of knowledge that deals with interpretation. Most historians are to some degree well aware of these two concepts, which shape and form the nature of any history. Some of the most significant connections between phenomenology and hermeneutics, then, both shape and form the nature of history. It is obviously important that historians and everyone else generally tend not to engage in such esoteric notions.

Nevertheless, 'what you see is what you get' when engaging with 'the-past-*as*-history'. However, history, then, is never discovered because (and obviously?) history is that practice of the processing of the past into history. Hence, the past can only be captured through the process of establishing the correspondence of the history with the facts. Now, all histories are connected events 'under a description'. So, the concept of correspondence is basic to 'historical truth'. Hence, the notion of history not as a discovery but is some kind of 'truth' as some kind of disclosure. In the 'universe of the past' all that historians can offer is a range of 'artwork descriptions' as to the possible/likely character of the past as shaped by us.

As I have already noted, the most meaningful connection between phenomenology and hermeneutics is the historian's effort to form and shape the nature of history as the historian reads it. All that histories can offer us is 'the past in our perpetual present'. This means all we can hope for as historians and history consumers is to engage 'the past' through image and resemblance. But the world of the past is only what it seems to be through the engagement of the historian. And, of course, for every historian there is 'the past world' they believe they have found and can represent. But and so for every historian, there is always an unavoidable meaning and explanation available, and, to be even more accurate, meanings and explanations constantly multiply. And many of those denotations and accounts are yet to be determined. But, as all historians understand, their historical imagination is always modified and neutralised. To be very clear on this, the reality of the past always appears in chapters, in parentheses, or in quotations marks. The reality of the past that the historian 'imagines' and/or 'images' only works because the words, paragraphs, and chapters deny the unreality of the past with every new page of their history.

All pasts, then, are fabricated because that is what historians provide to their consumers. But the irony about the past is that history is always a reality game. Even if the reality of the past is offered as an image, shadow, shape, and/or form the historian creates it. So, all histories are ersatz. Getting the data straight is a tiny element in authoring the past. Historians offer their version of past reality, which they prefer. By their mixes of colour, form, place, intellectual torsion, and evidential remains, all historians remain strangers in a strange land. Historians will often say that the 'thing' speaks 'for itself' and if it does not then the historian can come to the saving of the past in some way or another.

However, the reality of the past is entirely image and similitude. As I have already noted, the phenomenology of consciousness cannot be other than experienced from the historian as a first-person point of view. Now, the phenomenology of histories is such as they are the historical pasts. So, for all as we can tell, there are multiple pasts and historians just have to work with them. This means that there is nothing more enigmatic and mysterious than a history. Hence, there is no transparency despite the historian's efforts at accessing past reality. The past only exists between the historian's inverted commas. Thus, all histories are 'the independent realities' of historians (and everyone else) but they remain misrepresentations.

Ironically then, in their effort to bring the past (back) to our present, historians can only engage with what is a perpetual 'disincarnated past' and that in the 'disincarnating of past reality' is precisely what historians do. So, all historians can do is work with their resemblance and a sort of image of the past. The phenomenology of the historian's images and many other representations are entirely dependent upon the historian's representation. Ironically, every 'historical' representation of the past is created in the present. Now, the notion of the 'historical imagination' plainly makes no sense of any kind even if it seems so basic to what historians do. The reality of the past exists, at best, in 'prefaces', 'chapters', 'quotation marks', and/or 'parentheses'. The unreality of 'the-past-as-history' is obviously as all historians know given that they constantly update both the irreality and unreality of all history(ies).

Now, as I have already noted in this book, history is that intellectual process that turns the historian's preferred narrative of the past into a history. But as an art, all histories are representations. As I have already made clear, in my judgment all histories are representations of the past. If you want a history that you like and which you believe informs us as to what happened in the past, all you can do is create that representation of the past we call a history. So, it is essential for historians and history consumers to understand how historians deploy the notion of representation. Now, I have 'sought of' meandered and circumnavigated the notion of representation but there is more to discuss.

I have already referred to the theorist Hayden White and his 'rhetorical models' for historical representation and primarily the common sense explanations of the four basic emplotments of tragedy, comedy, satire, and romance. So, as I have already noted then, these apply as much to histories as any other authorial literary endeavour. Thus, the individual historian-author's narrative is obviously composed of 'events that happened' and why. But, as is well known, historians can engage with the same selected 'chunks of the past' and end up with an entirely different history.

Now, the notion of the past remaining as it was as a history is obviously nonsense. Knowing what actually happened in the past obviously makes sense. Denying the attested actual nature of the past is plainly meretricious and deceiving. However, and obviously, turning the past into a history remains and fulfills the historian's job description. Reduced to the basics of what historians (and everyone else) do in terms of their engagement with 'the-past-*as*-history' can only make sense through a process of representation. So, the problem all historians always have comes down to the fabrication of a 'historical representation'. The primary reasons for this are the result of the usual deployment of authorial processing, prefiguring, emplotting, offering arguments and/or their ideological positions.

Now, that artwork we call history plainly has a cognitive value. The historian's history, then, must obviously be a rational understanding of the past inasmuch as it makes sense in 'the terms of the historian's preferred history'. So, then, the notion of discovering 'the history of the past' is all that historians and everyone else can hope for, that their fabricated authorial representations make some sort of sense. However, the concept of history as a fabricated undertaking is a poor description of how we unfortunately can only engage with the past so shabbily, because that concept seems to be associated with dubious descriptors such as invention, falsehood, misrepresentation, caricature, and no doubt cartooning. However, the central historical forms I have engaged in this text remain representations of the past.

As I have suggested, when the historian engages with the past the aesthetics of 'doing history' rapidly becomes the primary element. It is hardly unsurprising given the various natures of the other foundational constructs I have offered in this text, that the irony of 'doing history' is not the discovery of the past for what it was but is the historian's authorial process of taking the past and engaging with the historian's preferred fabricated 'past-*as*-history'. So, all history narratives are examples of fabricated truths and/or inventions whether the historian knows it or not.

Now, and as I have suggested, all histories have cognitive value as well as being an artwork. Getting the data straight is obviously foundational to authoring 'the-past-*as*-history' as I have noted, but after the engagement with the sources, the past is entirely the historian's responsibility because it is they who have chosen to turn the past into the(ir) history. So, the epistemology preferred by the historian (their favoured theory of knowledge) has to take the past again (and again and again) and thus consequently presenting it for what they think it was. Unfortunately, the past is what it was and hence all the author-historian can offer is their (re) presentation of the(ir) past. So, what can historians do—as I have already noted—with the concept of representation?

Like all authors, regardless of their specific engagement with the past, and as I have already noted briefly, representing the past is an unresolvable problem. In the absence of the past invariably all we have are the histories we fabricate given the nature of both the ontology and the epistemology of history. The form for this engagement is, obviously, representation. The reality of the past, of course, can be represented in many different 'ways and forms' although many historians regard their undertaking as some kind of 'social science'. Regardless of the problems of hardcore laboratory interventions, social science historians tend to offer their 'findings' in varieties of forms. Nonetheless, at the start of this chapter I suggested that there are many ways of representing the nature of the past, however, the vast majority of historians are obliged to accept that they fabricate the facts of the past.

So, then it is time that I come clean because much of my argument in this chapter I owe to the philosopher Nelson Goodman's analysis of 'the fabrication of facts' as found in his text *Ways of Worldmaking* (1978). Particularly in his chapter on the fabrication of facts he offers what is arguably the most significant contribution to 'doing history' in the past half century. His analysis of the relationship between 'actuality' and 'artifice' offers historians a dramatic insight into how they are forced to engage with the unavoidable fabrication of facts. To be blunt, he insists and thus annoys those fundamentalist historians, i.e., most of them, who still insist that 'facts' are not authored into existence.

The fabrication of facts is the foundational dimension of 'doing history' and that means all histories are not—and this is obvious of course—not discovered but fabricated. The vast majority of historians then have to face up to the foundational failing of 'their doing history'. This is the fabricated nature of facts. This does not mean inventing, designing, and conceiving those 'bits of the past' that the historian finds convenient. Whether most historians like it or not, facts are 'historian made'. This does not mean the historian's facts are inventions but all facts are *fabricated* which means that we must be clear that actuality and artifice work

Fabricated 61

together. What 'once was' always has to be described in some kind of 'historying' process.

My logic is fairly obvious (I hope). I do not advocate a radical relativism when engaging with the past. The past cannot simply be 'taken' and 'rebuilt' as the historian wants. Denying past reality is stupid and mindless. However, and obviously, 'turning out' the past into its history is the perpetual problem. The only definition of truth that is worth anything is—ultimately—correspondence truth. Unfortunately, however, I assume (especially) historians, have the ultimate responsibility of distinguishing between the versions of past reality that they are persuaded is probably more likely. To be as blunt as I can be, specifics about the past are invariably all too often turned into little concepts, which with enough effort can be turned into 'the' past. Where one history is foreclosed, another is born.

Historians have a very easy intellectual life. All historying, then, is unavoidably a process of reduction, construction, and deconstruction. The devastating problem with history, then, is that it is never reliable. The central problem that too many historians have is that the past is always available to be reduced and reconstructed and/or constructed and/or deconstructed. Historians and their consumers, then, should always be wary of believing that the historian's effort at 'past world making' is always subject to its rethinking. Thus, two histories of the American Civil War (or any topic in the past) are unavoidably authorially biased. And, moreover, historians are also trained not to confuse fact with fiction but worse, distinguishing metaphorical truth and metaphorical lies.

Historians, by and large, are not trained to distinguish, depict, describe in their visions, words, lectures, seminars, and so forth. These forms just come naturally. But it is far from being natural to deploy all the many differential mechanisms through which the past can be delivered. For every form for engaging with the past there is an entirely different meaning and explanation. The bane of historians (in my judgment) is 'reference'. Reference is usually simple. But there are symbols in the processing of the past that cannot be denied. All histories exemplify (whatever the author wants) via a range of symbols from the book cover to the numbers of chapters, the nature of the bibliography, and the index.

Now, when engaging with the processing of the past into a history, the historian, the publisher, and the consumer are very likely to have a rendition in their mind as to the nature of 'the history'. All histories, however, are not 'made' by the author alone. The reader, reviewer, publisher, and so forth will create their own meanings and sustain their intellectual 'rightness' as to the 'translation' from the 'proffered past' as to their 'preferred past', aka 'the history'. Now, the *fabricated* nature of history rarely crosses the mind of most historians who—as I have noted—will deliberately not philosophise the nature of 'the(ir)-past-*as*-history'. But, to make things worse, historians (by and large) tend not to philosophise the nature of their discrete philosophising when endeavouring to engage with the nature of the past. Now, the very substantial numbers of historians 'transfigure the past' into their preferred history. The irony that unavoidably exists in the historian's universe, then, is their situation of illusion and art in the pursuit of past reality. So, as an aesthetic, which history is, the past can only be engaged as some kind of transfiguration of time and place. So, how is a history of the past possible?

Well, it should be obvious to all historians (and hopefully eventually everyone else) that the past can only be useful when it is transfigured into forms and ranges of histories. So, how can the historical representation of the past be possible? Well, fortunately, it is simple. Because history is a representationalist art that means history can offer almost innumerable pasts. And it does. Historians, then, and like everyone else, have an impossible task if their aim is to explain the nature of the past. Knowing what actually happened in the past is not difficult to figure out. However, the obvious situation quickly develops. How can historians actually conflate the past with its history? Well, making and matching the past with its history is the aim, but the past constantly changes by the delivery of new sources and fresh interpretations. The past never stands still.

Indeed, the past both contains and constrains through the historian's preformed notion of the past. Historians never discover the past because they deliver their preferred 'history' like an unknown parcel on a front door step, which then offers several surprises. The past is never what you hope it to be. By forming the nature of the past as a history the historian endeavors to 'close up the past'. Every history is an aesthetic even if all too often it simply turns out to be a weathered engagement with the past. With a delightful irony, history is never more nor less than a contemporary literature which is always on the verge of plunging off the cliff of time. The only saving grace for historians and their consumers is to accept that the past is never 'the past' for too long. Historians, of course, work very hard to sustain the novelty of the past and when it runs out there is always another past to discover and sustain. Fortunately, the numbers of historians only limit the numbers of 'historical pasts' that historians can create. Now, far too many historians (the vast majority) happily and readily accept the notion of 'the-history-in-the-past'. It would be more sensible to throw this notion out of the nearest historian's window.

The past is—obviously—not a history. At best the past is an obsolete past which historians grab and grasp at. Most histories are weathered, wrinkled, and scoured by time. Hence historians have to constantly prefabricate, shape, and form the(ir) fabricated past. The ultimate irony for historians is the situation that there is an unavoidable aesthetic symbiosis in engaging with the past, when all they can engage with is the(ir) preferred history. Now, all historians can do is sightsee the past, at least those parts they have engaged before the scholarship forecloses and the sabbatical ends.

All historians—unfortunately—suffer from the same problem. This is that the history is never the original and hence all histories are of necessity fabricated. But this is hardly a severe problem because it is how our universe works. History, to be as clear as I can, is a very 'weak forming process' when it comes to examining the past and that is why the past has to be acknowledged to be a fabricated undertaking (among all the other problems in this book). When the history consumer along with historians demand 'the reality of the past', all they can have is the(ir) fabricated history/histories. This situation is not to deny the utility and culturally significant importance of engaging with the past. As the philosopher Frank Ankersmit argued, history is a sublime experience and it will remain as such. In the next chapter, then, I will address another associated notion, that is, the unavoidably *factious* nature of history.

4   Factious

All 'acts of historying' are an exploration in the shadowy world of the nonexistent past. Obviously, then, the past is not revivified, resuscitated, or renewed through any history. No historical past that has ever been written (or spoken and/or danced and/or built) can claim to be the past and certainly no history—regardless of its form—can claim to be the past resurrected as it actually was. The supreme irony in doing history, then, is that the past can only be a substitute (in whatever form the historian wants) because it is the historian's narrative creation even if it is claimed to be the past as it actually was. Hence, no history that anyone can create will be an accurate substitute for the past. Obviously, of course, we can know what happened in the past, more or less, and that is what historians do.

Now, historians very rarely contrive to create the contents of the past. What would be the point? It would take a poor historian to out invent past reality. Historians may and do organize, classify, systemize, and/or give varieties of forms to the past in order to organize, well, the ontic and epistemic nature of the past. Historians, then, deploy the simple mechanism of shaping history through their preferred subjects, themes, and topics such as gender, culture, class, regional studies, war, ideology, and so forth. Historians thus explore the myriad of subjects and objects in the past by creating categories of historical analysis such as aesthetics, gender, periods of time, nationalism, religious sectarianism, the annoying aims of the publisher, and the determined efforts of other historians to create and sustain their point of view on the past. Hence, historians are invariably subject to their engagement with the *factious* nature of their turning of the past into a history. Note: never *the* history.

Unsurprisingly, then, historians exist in a perpetual *factious* condition which generates countless competing interests that range across the range of approaches and subjects via the application of aesthetics which shape and create meanings for gender, nationalism, religious sectarianism, periods of time, the annoying demands of their publisher, and the determined efforts of the substantial numbers of historians who never give up sustaining the usual personal attacks. Thus doing history is quite plainly a *factious* undertaking that sustains an academic, political, and ideological structure. This milieu sustains the historian's engagement with the past through the(ir) mordant and desperate desire to support the perpetual disordered present through which the past is constantly disarranged. As a *factious* undertaking, then, the nature of history(ing) is sustained by the hard-wearing inclination of historians to herd and dissent and rebel and drove. Historians, then, lean on and sustain the usual topics that feed their 'historical content'. These topics/themes are myriad. The next paragraph may upset some readers who have not quite grasped that historians really do not have far too much time for anything in the past apart from their tiny and thus insignificant small subject matter.

A list, then, might include social movements, nationalism, gender, jingoism, regionalism, race, the eighteenth century, and all the other centuries on this planet. Then there are different forms and topics of historying such as the Industrial Revolution in various countries and then there are obviously topics themed as the political, social, regional, cultural, ideological, religious and 'the history of history', and so on and so forth (this is a tiny list of course). Hence, there are many histories from back there and then which can be resurrected and probably have been. The space for all this is vacant historical space because historians are both individualists but also grazing herd animals, and, hence historians are characterised by *factious* dissent. The process of *factious* historying is a problem that most historians are well aware of. Historians have the freedom to combine and emphasize, order and reorder, delete and insert, fill-in and fill-out, be accurate, and at worst mislead in their pursuit of 'the-past-*as*-history'. Now, and accordingly, historians will no doubt in the future continue to struggle with the obvious problem with truth. The reality of the past, then, is impatiently shaped and formed by historians in schools, coteries, groups, factions, and so forth. Hence, there is no shortage of *factious* arguments among historians despite the ill-scarred nature of historical truth.

Now, historical truth is a really difficult problem. The historian's propositions or beliefs concerning nature of the reality of the past are unavoidably the result of many constraints such as language, gender, age, the unexpected sabbatical, or, if you prefer, the other way around, which means that historical truth largely exists propositionally. The disposition of historical truth assumes there must be a match (somewhere) between proposition and reality. Unfortunately, the historical explanation is beset by the tension between these two perceptions of truth. Today, most historians would probably accept that because the past is organised to make sense through the exercise of their historical imagination (more of this in what follows), this means they have to reject any absolutist notion of historical truth. But this is very awkward for historians because historical interpretations should be regarded as likely to be true through corresponding to the verified evidence and the coherence of the statement as judged by other historians. So, the worry with the *factious* nature of doing history is that historians refuse to acknowledge the much larger problem of *factious* history truth. It is this truth that blights the history culture. For historians, the trouble with truth is that it cannot be defined and/or tested by the agreement of the past world and the historian's word. The debate(s) between historians is rarely resolved and this, of course, is very useful for historians although the vast majority would probably deny it. Historians, in the vast majority, deny that there is any problem with tried and attested data. So, why is there so much debate among historians about past events and what they mean? Well, more often than not, there is less to the historian's debates than initially meets the eye.

The foundational problem with historical truth is that there is a persistent difficulty with *factious* historical truth. This claim is not quite as bad as it may seem—but there is still a problem. The notion of *factious* historical truth is always going to be awkward because of when disparate groups of historians make a claim as to the reality of the past by claiming its meaning and explanation. Historians are infamous for herding together in the pursuit of the truth. Of course, 'the sources chase' enables historians to know what happened in the past more or less but, ironically, there is always a continuing and unavoidable issue with the nature and direction of the truth. Who is in the market for the knowledge of the past? To be clear, then, *factious* historical truth will give the history the historian wants. The notion, then, of the 'discovery of history' is, literally, nonsense.

So, the-past-*as*-history is a *factious* enterprise amidst the many different competing truths while every single historian claims to offer the (only) historical truth. Unhappily, then, many singular competing truths persistently rub shoulders with competing versions of the past through the unnerving political and ideological frames of *factious* reference. Ironically, in the pursuit of the truth of the past there are many *factious* competitors, which of course create a milieu of *factious* irritation. What this means is that far too many historians thrive on what I would describe as *factious* historical truth. By this I mean it is all too easy to take the past and revise, rethink, modify, refashion, and adapt it not only through the historian's preferred style of representation but also cater to the uncountable bees in the bonnets of historian(s).

The substance/subject/styling of the past that historians create in our perpetual today exists in almost innumerable forms. History is offered in print, television, radio, lectures, acted, filmed, art objects, thought, written, and many other forms that carry their own style and hence the past is constituted as history with each form creating different(ial) meanings and explanations. Then and now, of course, the historical record is increasingly digitised. The past immediate previous past generations of historians indulged their opportunities for their historying through an increasing use of the computer in historical investigation and construal. Today, and fortuitously, the *factious* process of creating histories not only wallows in its various forms but also myriad disputes of meaning and explanation. Historians just live a row.

Now, while 'the history content' is always claimed to be at the heart of doing history, the nature of history still remains a *factious* undertaking. The irony in this should be obvious. The status of *factious* historying is obviously central to 'doing history'. This is because historians cannot offer an agreed upon definition of historical truth. Today (and in the past or in the future as well) the trouble with historical truth is that it cannot be defined to the satisfaction of anyone, let alone historians. So, what is the truth about historical truth? Unhappily or not depending on your preference, the notion of historical truth has no certainty of any kind. The constant trouble with historical truth then is that it cannot be defined, let alone tested and attested, because historians seek out the truth of the past in a very simplistic way. It is 'this happened' and 'not that' according to the 'present available' evidence. And, on top of that, the truth of the past is entirely subject to the interpretation of the data.

This does not mean historians can go around imputing and/or inventing the past, as they may want to. But, and this remains a very big but, history is an unavoidable act of aesthetic engagement which deploys several forms of 'truth'. The problem with truth, then, is that there are several forms and none of them can be defined or tested in agreement with the non-scientific world. Not only do truths differ for different past (or present for that matter) worlds but truths differ from each other because the past is notoriously nebulous, tenuous, and always has to be formulated in some form or another. Historical truths, then, are simply multiple versions of a preferred past reality. It is well known that all histories are (a) short-lived contemplations of (b) recently discovered (based on yet more) data. Thus, it is hardly news that historians can take the same sources and then variously interpret what those same data mean. Historians, then, cannot avoid this problem, and this is why historians differ in terms of references, weightings, orientations, emphases, and so forth.

So, the nature of 'historical truth' is—quite plainly—a weak and docile *factious* form of truth. What is worse, the truth, the whole truth, and nothing but the truth would be a wilful and paralysing strategy for any historian. Histories, then, are simple versions of an inscrutable past reality. So, the past is worthless without it being turned into a 'historical interpretation'. Hence, 'the historical interpretation' has very little to be commended to anyone, apart from other historians. In the absence of a form of truth that can guarantee the veracity of past reality, historians have to accept one or more of its four forms, which as I suggested in Chapter 1, are *correspondence, correlation, coherence* and/ or *consensus*. These four theories of truth constrain and shape the 'the-past-*as*-history'. So, there are serious problems with each form of truth and consequently the understanding of 'the-past-*as*-history' (see Chapter 1) will always get in the way of the (un)reality of the past.

The major problem with *factitious* historying is that the past cannot speak for itself. The past has to be made to speak even though it may be often thought of as a discovery that can speak for itself. There are two main types of historical sources that historians can deploy and lean on. These are *primary* and *secondary sources*. A *primary* source is some 'thing' or 'artifact' or some other detritus and/or debris that originates in the past. This 'stuff from the past' can be a chronicle or a journal, a piece of pottery and/or earthenware and/or a painting on a canvas and/or wall or even a piece of glacial ice that yields climate data about the levels of carbon in the atmosphere ten thousand years ago. But for most historians the less exotic will do and these are archives, libraries, records, chronicles, diaries, letters, notes, and so forth. The role of sources in 'doing history' thus depends entirely on the individual historian's theory of knowledge. All historians adhere to a theory of knowledge, expressly in regard to the methods, cogency, and scope through which they pursue 'justified belief'.

Ironically (and not unlike medical professionals), historians dig up that which has expired. For the hardcore reconstructionist historian the past can be 'brought back to life (sort of)' and thus such historians can speak to and through the past. The past never speaks for itself and so historians continue to believe in the serendipity of discovering the historical explanation. This, of course, makes no sense. Historians always find themselves in a rather awkward situation. The bizarre notion of (re)constructing the past as it was and thus and thereby 'the-past-*as*-history'. Unhappily, of course, all histories fail. The past is always renovated and renewed. Plainly then, knowing what happened in the past is hardly a struggle if there is sufficient data which can be deployed in order to discover the meaning and eventually the (or a) explanation of the historical sources. Unhappily that process is very unlikely to acquire *the* absolute truth of the past. But then the past is never secured.

As I have suggested, the problem with history is that it is not the past and the past is not history. Shaking the foundations of the past is a very good and regular undertaking. Denying the past, of course, is senseless and futile. This is why the past is never discovered and hence the past is always reconstructed, constructed, and deconstructed into a history and so historians can choose the historical description they like. In the absence of the past, then, what historians have are the histories the historians want. Or, to put it slightly differently, all histories are unavoidably *factional*. Every historian, then, engages with the past as much as they also 'disagree' with their (equally engaged) colleagues. Historians are herding creatures. Now, this is a serious—almost debilitating—problem for historians. There is no mechanism that historians can deploy to test the nature of the past. Scientists can 'do experiments' in a laboratory but there is no similar mechanism for historians. Hence, the notion of social science is unlikely to speak for itself.

It is true that a very substantial number of historians (*factionally*) endorse the mechanism of the 'social sciences'. I was once a very hard-core social science historian. My Ph.D. was an incremental 'stage model of urban immigrant political assimilation in the USA between 1870–1920'. I 'authored this model', which consisted of four stages. The first stage was Symbolic-Normative, the second was Operative-Positive, and then the third Transformation stage, and it ended up with the final stage of Political Assimilation. I think four people actually read that Ph.D.—me the author—then my wife Jane who typed it, my supervisor, and the External Examiner. Anyway, I came to believe (eventually) that more useful and sensible is the notion of not trying to reconstruct or construct the past, but deconstruct it. After this process I was soon turned by the dark arts of 'postmodernist historying'.

The heyday of 'deconstructing history' (roughly 1990–2010) is now over (I assume) but those insurrectional decades continued to leave an intellectual shadow even though the substantial majority of academic historians were never convinced and the next generation remains 'in the past' (ironically). At the height of 'postmodern historying', the truth, the whole truth and nothing but the truth, sat awkwardly and was (and remains) a paralysing policy. This may seem a dangerous thought, but ironically getting the data straight is hardly difficult if one lives for enough months in a research library. As the philosopher Nelson Goodman argued, our world—past and present and probably future also—is always human made. Hence historians, like every other human being, are unavoidably subject to the *factional*.

At this point historians, like everyone else, ought to be very wary of the notion of the 'truth, the whole truth and nothing but the truth'. For the historian, seeking out the whole truth and nothing but the truth would be perverse and paralysing given that the past is not history and history is not the past. Fortunately, the whole truth is beyond the grasp of *factious* historians. To have the whole truth of the past would be paralysing for any historian. The truth of the past is simply too vast and measureless. 'The-past-*as*-history' is 'made up' by historians and, who knows, quite often all of it might be true. Then, again, it might not. This is unavoidable. Knowing what happened in the past is not the same as history. Historians can offer insight. Historians can offer beliefs. Historians can offer principles. Historians can offer stylistic differences in profusion. But, ultimately, 'history' is 'not the past' and 'the past' is 'not the history'. From what I just said, what then are the basics of 'doing history'? Happily, it is not too difficult. There are five simple narrative principles to doing history. These are 'composition and decomposition', 'weighting', 'ordering', 'deletion and supplementation', and 'reformation'. These concepts should be known and understood by any 'historian-author' and their consumers.

Unfortunately and very annoyingly, the substantial majority of academic historians are not happily aware that 'the-past-*as*-history' is almost entirely their authorial creation. Historians are not in the serendipitous business of 'discovering the past' and somewhat more worryingly, historians also tend to ignore the situation that the past has to be 'authored into past existence'. This is not a process of inventing or creating or contriving or manufacturing the past. I do not expect professional historians to accept and endorse the notion of 'the-past-*as*-history' in the next few weeks given the ontic and epistemic universe in which they (and everyone else) exist. Thus: the substantial majority of historians do and will continue to believe that the past can be discovered and revealed for what it was (turned out as its history) given 'the sources they have deployed'. This, of course leads to the awkward problem of the *factious*. To be plain then: there is no history in the past until the historian 'authors it into what they believe is its discoverable existence'. Unfortunately, before the historian's authorial 'weighting', 'ordering', 'deleting', 'supplementing', and 'rethinking' of the forces that shape an 'authored narrative', there is no (hi)story to be 'discovered' because of the *factious* nature of historians 'discovering what they think is the most accurate history'.

As a source-based and interpretational undertaking, the past can only be 'authored into' the historian's preferred 'past-*as*-history'. So, what do historians do in terms of their *factious* processing of the past? According to conventional thinking, historians examine 'methodologically' and 'in detail' in order to *interpret* and *explain* the nature of the past. But, unfortunately, historians rarely agree with each other's nature of the past and much less do they agree on what it means. This 'processing of the past' into 'a history' (or ideally '*the* history') is embarrassingly simple. Getting the history straight for most historians means simply that 'the available (and hopefully new) sources' are 'interpreted' and 'nudged' and all too often 'pushed around' along with a range of dubious theories to explain the nature and meaning of the past. So, how does this actually work in practice? Well, and with a very serious irony, most historians have a very tenuous grasp on how the past is turned into a history. This is hardly their fault of course. 'The-past-*as*-history' is never fixed 'for what it was' because our access to the past is only accessible through the process of *factious* analysis. It is hardly news that historians tend to herd. Historians gather, collect, assemble, and make huge efforts to turn the absent past into their real and present historying.

History, then, is the historian's narrative of the past. Unfortunately, history is not the past. At best 'the-past-*as*-history' can only be regarded as an 'informed' construction. The process of knowing what happened in the past and what it meant is a very quirky undertaking. All histories are compendiums of authorial styles and hence 'the-past-*as*-history' is an unavoidable 'aesthetic'. Now, it is worth noting and quickly dismissing the notion of reconstructing the past as it actually was. This notion is a laudable undertaking and knowing what actually happened in the past is absolutely basic to our (and any other) culture. Nonetheless, it remains an impossibility to reconstruct the past as it actually was and hence the Battle of Waterloo is not a book. No matter how much effort is taken to get the (hi)story straight the past remains the past and it cannot be resuscitated and resurrected and, of course, it cannot be revivified and refreshed and that is where the perpetual problem of the *factious* emerges.

The problem with the notion of reconstructing the past as it actually was is that the past is the past and history is history. The vast majority of historians are—obviously—determined to reconstruct again or construct the past through what they choose to believe its history. Unfortunately there is no history of anything until the historian has (hi)storied it. The past, then, does not have its own dedicated history. The past only 'has a history' when historians constitute it through the process of *factious* disagreement. There is no possibility of 'diagnosing the condition of the past' in the absence of that 'past'. Hence, when historians choose to reconstruct and/or construct the past they are unavoidably deconstructing the past through their preferred 'history'. Hence, the *factious* dimension of 'historying' unavoidably remains. Hence, historians herd and/or flock and/or congregate.

The common sense understanding among historians is founded on the belief that for every historian there has to be 'a new and tweaked past'. This belief is, of course, ridiculous. Historians potter and fiddle in the past and most of us happily accept that certain events occurred and others did not. This situation, of course, produces the *factious* demand for a realist and common sense understanding of the referential, empiricist, and truth-conditional processing of the past. Happily for the *factious* reconstructionist historian, they assume the past speaks for itself though it be through the(ir) sources and which will eventually speak as located and fostered by that historian. Thus, such historians only ever engage with and interpret the past when they believe they have built on preexisting historical facts. Now, and unhappily, historical facts are only descriptions of an event that historians agree upon or not as the case may be. Nonetheless and fortunately for historians, they have no objective and independent measure of the nature of the reality of the past apart from when they herd.

This herding process means that the reality of the past is rarely the same as the reality of history. Thus: we have to accept that the *factious* author and the *factious* reader must share the belief that not only is the events of the past are *as* described really happened, and/or, is a thing that is known or proved to be true. To sustain the credibility of historians they have to accept that what they say about the past corresponds to that which is described as 'a historical fact'. This means that what historians say about the past is a 'referential' truth-conditional statement about the 'actuality' of the 'past real world' and that it remains unaffected 'by the act of its description/interpretation'. What I think this means is that 'the past is not history' and 'history is not the past' and no one should (con)fuse the past with history and/or history with the past. This does mean anyone can blithely ignore the realities of the past.

Now, historians cannot escape the(ir) conflation of 'the past with its history' and 'history with its past' and, consequently, this is where historians herd. All historians, yes every single one of them, belongs to a *factious* group or clutch and hence their *factional* nature. Historians herd. This *factious* mind-set is, of course, easy and simple to explain. The history of the past thus only exists in our perpetual present and so it is necessary to remember that 'doing historying' is 'a presentist activity' which is continuously 'reinvented' and 'reimagined'. History then is not the past and the past is not history. Thus, it is essential to acknowledge that the other dimension to their *factional* thinking is that history is unavoidably a *factious* activity.

Historians, then, while they are inclined to being *factious* they are also and always also inclined to *factious* dissent. Unlike many other 'employments' such as surgery, airline piloting, engineering, gardening, and many other pursuits, historians constantly debate the nature and meaning of what they do, that is, construe the reality of the past. Now this is really bad news in many ways because the past is obviously not history and history is certainly not the past. Beyond the simple (and they are simple) basic rules for doing history it is always impossible for historians to reach the same conclusion in terms of their 'historical explanation'. The reason for this is simply that historians cannot agree about their history of almost anything. Architects build and move on. Ship captains deliver the boat to its destination. Politicians get into a mess and then move on denying all responsibility, but the irony in the historian's *factious* dissension about the past ('what it was' and 'what it meant') is that historians tend to 'herd' and 'deny'. The irony in being a historian, then, is that 'the past' is only ever 'the-past-*as*-history' and hence for every 'historical explanation' there is always invariably *factious* debate, discord, and disputation.

Every historian has—more or less—a convincing alternative historical explanation to fill in the history blank, or gap, or opening, or alternative, or whatever the historian desires from the(ir) preferred past. So, just what is the nature of the relationship between the past and history and the role of historians? For sure the past is not history and history is not the past and to claim otherwise is at best silly and at worst dangerous. What then, dear reader, do you think about the past or do you think about history? Is the past the same as history and history the same as the past? Well, obviously that notion fails without a second's thought or it should. The past is not history and history is not the past. As I have already suggested, 'the connection' between the past and history is a process of deconstruction and/or construction and/or reconstruction. Choose the answer you want. When you have made up your mind you will have engaged with the persistent *factious* debate on the nature of historying. This is not the same, of course, as debating what happened or did not happen in the past.

What should not be surprising is that at the centre of the debate on the *factious* nature of historying, there is a very big problem. It is 'the historical imagination'. It is well known among historians that the nature and meaning of the past is the(ir) historical interpretation. Plainly, the first lesson when pursuing the past is not to confuse it with the historical imagination. This is because the historical imagination is a constant and perpetual 'reimaging' of history, not the past. When I first came across 'the historical imagination' (as an undergraduate student) I was flummoxed. Surely learning about the past was, well, learning about what happened in the past? Wrong, very, very, very wrong. Of course it is essential to know what actually happened in the past and hence getting the data straight and inferring what it probably meant is only a tiny part of doing history. But this notion is also wrong. It is wrong because 'the historical imagination' has very little to do with either the *factional* and *factious* nature of history.

It is hardly news to acknowledge that every historian imagines, envisages, and/or sees the past as they believe it was in accord with the data and sources they have selected (aka designated, labelled, characterised, identified). Now, because the past is no longer with us, 'the historical imagination' (obviously) substitutes for the past. Lest we forget, then, the past is the time before now and history is a contemporary narrative we decide to author about the past. For every historian there is always another history of the(ir) perceived past. Unhappily, however, the problem with engaging with the past is that every historian has and is subject to their own 'historical imagination' and hence every historian deploys the(ir) own 'historical imagination' in order to engage with the nature of the past which they think they have 'discovered'.

Thus: historians exercise their historical imagination by deploying the basic processes of cause and effect in the(ir) effort to discover 'the-past-*as*-history'. Unhappily, the historical imagination is often harmless but most of the time it is pointless. Given the absence of the ability to rerun the past in a 'history laboratory' all that historians can have is a very shaky purchase on past reality, and so they invoke the dubious concept of 'the most likely possibility of the nature of the past was . . .'? However, and obviously of course, the past is irrecoverable for precisely what it was and what it meant. Accordingly, in the absence of the 'real' reality of the past we reach for our 'historying'. The further irony in all this then is that historians are always reduced to debating that which is unknowable.

So, and as I have suggested, 'history' would wither, weaken, and sooner or later fail entirely without the sustenance of the historical imagination. To be clear then, in the absence of the past historians have to fall back on their 'imagining of the past'. Now, this metonymic figure of speech is demonstrated by the historian's processing of the 'historical imagination'. All historians without a second thought deploy this. Thus the late nineteenth century American historian Frederick Jackson Turner in 1893 famously said, 'The existence of an area of free and, its continuous recession and the advance of American settlement westward explain American development'. Without his famous history speech at the American Historical Association in 1890, this *factious* figure of speech was 'in fact' substituting the name of 'an attribute' for that now of 'the thing meant'. Turner thus fashioned what he assumed was the generic characteristic of American democracy—freedom—as supplied through the 'free land' in the West.

Now, it is plain that all historians at some point are subject to being *factious* because they are inclined to dissension and therefore to some level of to being quarrelsome, argumentative, disputatious, discordant, troublesome, and so forth. Moreover, historians are also intemperate by sustaining various kinds of self-interested baleful designs and interests. This is most obvious, of course, when ideology shapes the nature, meaning, and explanation of the past. So, why would we be surprised that historians are unavoidably *factious* given that all histories are only 'authorial preferred' descriptions of the past? Ironically, then, the reality of 'the past' is 'revealed' as a 'reported' text and that which is attested by the sources the historians prefer. So, for the very substantial majority of historians 'common sense' demands that 'the narrative history of the past' be apparently removed from the realm of literary artifice.

This is because neither history nor history(ing) are found nor discovered. The-past-*as*-history is unavoidably made, formed, wrought, influenced, and predisposed entirely by the historian's historical imagination. Thus: the imagined/imaginary that we commonly associate with fiction (*fabricated, factitious, factional*, and now *factious*) is no different in form from history. Like any coherent narrative, every history is invariably 'formed' (contrived and compiled) as a description of 'what happened' and which then (hopefully) also explains 'why' historians think the past was like it was. History, then, is what we have in the absence of the past. Promptly and nevertheless, while historians understand that they are authoring the most likely past in accord with their choice of sources and their ideological preferences, historians always infer their preferred historical narrative of the past.

Plainly, then, history is not the past. This is because histories, whether they are literary or some other sort of text (a stage drama, a radio play, a ballet, are subject to human interventions) all historians have inclinations, imaginings, pictures, evocations, and then educing, inferring, gathering, surmising, and so on and so forth the past they hope for. What I have just said (which I trust is common sense) is a process that is dependent on two foundational philosophical concepts. They are those of epistemology and ontology. Epistemology concerns the process of knowledge acquisition. In the case of knowledge of the past, it is usually assumed to be that process of discovery of the evidence of the past (the sources) and they are assumed to both refer to and validate the ontological reality of the content and nature of past events.

This is the nature of being, form, procedures, and methods that yield and/or generate the nature of history. Thus: the historian's reference (aka allusion) to past reality is entirely fashioned by the historian and is an act of authorship through which historians represent (re-present) their knowledge of the past. Plainly, then, a basic foundational principle, and perhaps the most significant principle among conventional historians, is that the past and history should be identical as far as possible. However, there is a well-known problem with 'the-past-*as*-history'. It is that—obviously—the past is not history and history is not the past. That problem is of course irresolvable because it is the historian who authors historical narratives into existence. History is not a discovery engine. To be clear: historians do not discover the (hi)story, they author it into what they believe was and/or is the past.

There is a very important and somewhat awkward implication to this sloppy and disordered common sense. It is that the past can only be engaged in terms of the historian first 'imagining' the most likely meaning/explanation for a set of events given the historian's (re)sources as they have selected (or the grant has run out). The situation all historians end up with is that their *factious* historying they believe is the most likely meaning of the (hi)story invariably is always 'revisioned'. This is a 'win' situation in one sense because they assume 'the past' is 'history' and 'history' is 'the past'. Now, this logic makes no sense because the past only exists in that set of events in the historian's imagination and so the past can only turn out to be a *factious* construal. So, while history is (commonly) assumed to be a 'meaningful message from the past' it is only the historian's competing and contending and challenging and thought-provoking narrative account. So, 'the history' is never more and never less than an act of the 'historical imagination'. There is a lot more (perhaps unfortunately) to be said about of this later in this book when I get to the concept of the '*fictive*' in Chapter 9.

For the moment, then, the historian's understanding of the (most likely) meaning of 'the evidence of the past' remains a fairly unproblematic act of 'finding out data' and turning it into narrative descriptions as approved by the historian, i.e., it is 'historied' and this turns out to be the simple process of 'historying the past'. Fortunately, turning the past into history is very simple (embarrassingly simple). First, the historian locates the evidence, which *they* chose to deploy, then they infer the most likely meaning of that evidence in *their* judgment, and sooner or later 'the history' comes into existence *as* a seminar, lecture, journal article, book chapter, and so forth. In terms of straightforward 'history practice', then, the historian's narrative of the past is what results from her or his authorial imagining and testing of connections between the multiple and selected events of the past. Here again the historian is pivotal because the past remains the past while history is the historian's preferred *factious* history.

The unavoidable problem with this situation, though, is that all histories are authored by the historian who can only presume that the(ir) most likely (hi)story 'back there and then' becomes 'history'. Happily and joyfully for historians, getting the data straight is extraordinarily and astonishingly straightforward. The only tricky problem for historians turns out to be embarrassingly simple. This is figuring out what the past meant as demonstrated in the form of the historian's (hi)story. The key problem in doing history, then, is literally figuring out the nature of historical meanings and explanations. In the process of historying then, it is expected that the historian will infer the most likely meaning of the documented 'past events' of 'what actually did occur'.

This processing of the historian's *factious* acts of 'what if' obviously require that the historian will infer the most likely 'historical' meaning. Hence, 'reference to the sources' is assumed to be the foundation of history and only by comparing and contrasting sources can historians become increasingly confident in their aligning of the past with the historian's most likely (hi)story. However, this process raises the unavoidable problems of 'the practical and realist notion (aka common sense)' that 'the past' and 'history' can be conflated. Plainly this is impossible. For most practitioner historians, their job is done once the(ir) description is aligned with the past as they believe it to be. Fortunately, then, 'the history' is regularly 'refreshed' when the next historical meaning turns up.

An obvious example of how the past can be 'revived *as* history' is when existing historical narratives are 'reimagined' and/or 'reconstructed' and/or 'constructed' and/or 'deconstructed'. So, historians might do well to go back to the philosopher of history Arthur Danto. His rendition of the simple form of the 'explanation of history' is simply deploying the history narrative form of beginning, middle, and end (Danto 1982, 17–32). This mechanism also confronts the vexed issue of the 'discovery' of functioning of 'covering laws'. These laws are deductive/nomothetic (law making) in form, and which are adopted and adapted to explain cause and effect in the past. But, of course, even those historians who believe in such 'covering laws' still have to fashion and design 'their' history narrative even if they think that their historical creation is 'the' (most likely) history narrative.

Generally speaking, then, historians both explain and illuminate the nature of 'change over time' by employing the(ir) authorial narrative mechanism of 'timing'. The past does not have an in-built narrative structure. Historians have to supply that. Thus: the (hi)story is authored into existence through the simple (but unavoidable) classic and unavoidable literary authorial mechanisms of 'order', 'duration', and 'frequency'. Thus, one of the most odd beliefs held among historians (and also along with everyone else) is that there is 'always a history narrative to be found and described for what it was'. Unfortunately that is serious nonsense. There is no (hi)story in the past to be discovered. Historians readily and more often than not will be blunt in 'their discovery of *the* history of *the* past' even though it makes no sense of any kind. Obviously, the past is the past and history is history but the-past-*as*-history is never discovered. It is not discovered because all histories are authored, fashioned, formed, and directed just like any other narrative, even though 'the change over time' refers to 'real events' in a 'cause and effect' milieu.

Paradoxically, then, cause and effect is certainly not the foundational trope for historians. Rather, the basic tropic feature of doing history is the authorial process that turns the past into a history. The foundational element in doing history then is the authorial timing of the history text. Now: this is not much of an insight because common sense recommends all forms of discourse (including opera, ballet, theatre, masque, written fiction, cinema, re-enacting, or just sitting in the pub having a chat with your friends). Plainly, then, 'telling the past' deploys all narrative forms. There is nothing special about narrating a history. Now, the three most common textual mechanisms for the 'narrative management of historical time', whether the reference is real or imagined, are initially '*when*' the events occurred, their '*duration*'(how long the events happened), and '*how often*' the events reoccurred. So, 'telling change over time' which is the central feature of doing history is not simply a chronological 'this happened, then that happened' exercise. Producing a history, then, is an authorial narrative timing exercise. Hence, then 'the-past-*as*-history' is almost certainly accurate but is not to be confused with 'truth', which (as I have already noted) is far more complex than the notion of 'the-history-*of*-the-past'.

So, why are historians in the pursuit of 'past reality' so happy to engage with both their *factional, factitious, fabricated*, and *factious* 'processing of the past'? Well, it is not hard to figure out. Historians always 'tend to herd' in terms of 'ideology', and/or 'vague politics', and/or 'philosophy', and/or 'opinion', and/or 'viewpoint', and so on and so forth. Apart from this annoying list, historians also ask different questions of the past and hence there is always a different past for every historian. For every historian there is new history. This situation is unavoidable because the past is an intensely political, social, and intellectual subject. It is not surprising, then, that historians ask so many different questions of the past in the hope—presumably—they will get the answer they desperately want. Obviously then, historians select and deselect data. This process means that historians can choose as many different methodologies to engage with the past that they want. Historians, then, have their preferred engagement with the past in terms of disciplines—politics, economics, psychology, sociology, aesthetics, and stylistics—and their preferred publishers (if they have a choice) and so on.

Now, the greatest joy and luxury the historian relishes is—obviously—hindsight. However, while this retrospection is a freedom it is also a desperately strong straightjacket. The historian enjoys the freedom of constituting the(ir) preferred historical past in respect of meanings and explanations, but this freedom is always soaked in a substantial amount of *factious* hindsight. At the mundane level of primary evidential sources historians usually manage to find various ranges of evidence on the same topic and theme. The historian's Holy Grail then is to discover new information by scouring the archive and that generates new conclusions, deductions, and interventions that are almost immediately contested (not necessarily a bad thing). In my career as an American historian I have produced a number of interpretations, which turned out to be clarifications, explanations, justifications, amplifications, elaborations, and rethinkings. Plainly then, the past is always and invariably constituted *as* a history but which is never fixed and never will be (I suspect). Indeed, and happily, the process of 'un-fixing the past' and then 're-fixing it again' is what sustains historians in employment.

Unhappily, the vast majority of academic historians does not address or engage with the aesthetic dimensions of turning the past into history. I started out as a social science historian and ended up preferring to engage with that aesthetic process that I call 'the-past-*as*-history' and this meant having to 'figure out' how 'artworks' and their aesthetic consequence (if there was any) influenced the nature of history narratives. Now, and with heavy irony, academic historians very rarely engage with the notion of the 'aesthetic nature' of the concept of the historical past they have offered. So, social science historying was good enough for me (to get my Ph.D.) until I recognised (several years later) that 'doing history' was much broader than I imagined it to be thanks to the failure in the authorial historical past.

Historians know that they engage with 'the-past-*as*-history' as an empirical undertaking and so that history is a science. Unfortunately, all histories are also shaped by ideology such as Marxism, Liberalism, Conservatism, Positivism, and Postmodernism, and all of which are shaded and influenced by more or less individual idiosyncratic 'bees in the bonnet' of individual historians subject to varieties of nationalism and idealism. History is also subject to history's entitlements to be a science and—clearly—Marxism as one obvious tradition that has melded ideology with science. In Anglo-American historiography (primarily in the 1970s and 2000s) the postmodern challenge of Hayden White and many others also rejected the positivist tradition. The historical topics of race, class, gender, science, technology, the body, nationalism, and so forth stimulated debates on what kinds of 'history' could and should be pursued through subjective authorial intermediations.

The notion of 'getting the history straight' is plainly a form of controlling the past and most obviously with Hayden White's infamous text

Metahistory (1973). His intervention famously widened the space for new sensibilities in creating new forms of 'histories', which increased the self-consciousness of historying in terms of 'history aesthetics'. Unhappily, this shift did not make much of a dent in the everyday work of those historians (the substantial majority) who continue to ignore the aesthetic character of turning the past into history. The function of historying is to recognise the nature of the past, which, of course, is constituted *as* a history.

All histories are the articulation of the past *as* an art. Hence, all histories shape our emotions and thoughts about the past. Historians thus create meanings for the past. The aesthetic historical models that historians create for the past, are shaped by many diverse forces and constraints such as ideology, philosophy, viewpoint, opinion, overview, understanding, plausibility, gender, epistemology, social context, the grant running out, and being run over by a Giraffe (if it has not happened yet it probably will). For many historians the past is shaped by their simple unawareness as to what happened in the past, and/or the book contract running out, or their employment ending. Then again the historian may select a methodology that ends up being useless. After all, how many methodologies can historians deploy in connecting between the past and the(ir) preferred history?

The past is also engaged via 'history workshops', the aim being to (re-)create the past, but the meeting only ends up with an argument over key concepts, terminologies, lexica and formulations. Historying, then, is an intellectual process that is often entirely subject to its context unlike science of course (well maybe), and so 'the-past-*as*-history' is regularly shaken and stirred in various measures precisely because it is not a science. Actually, I should admit I started out as a social science historian but that is a different narrative. So, there are political, economic, cultural, and intellectual self-inflicted demands by historians which shape and form the(ir) histories.

Then there are other constant issues such as the nature of the history text itself. Obviously, then, 'historical meanings', 'explanations', and what was and/or is a 'historical fact' (an event under a description) still remain unsure. Thus, all histories turn out 'the history' that is always caught in the web of 'ideological interpretations' and/or and hence the *factional* and *factious* product of the ideological leanings of varieties of groups (herdings and herrings) of historians. Now, the substantial majority of historians (academic or amateur) rarely connect their knowledge of the past with the(ir) historical narrative. This is usually unrecognised despite the processed connection construed between narrativity and historical knowledge.

Without a considerable understanding of the connection between 'events in the past' and 'history for the past' all narratives are all too often subject to the (infamous) fallacy of *post hoc ergo propter hoc*—the cow awakes before sunrise, therefore the cow waking causes the rise of the sun. 'Doing history' is always and seriously subject to this unfortunate gobbledygook. However, there is much worse. Thus, the past has no inherent history until the historical narrative is injected by the discovered aka authored into existence, which, then, and obviously, is the discovered past. It is hardly news to acknowledge that all narratives, which include history narratives, are a fundamental process, which turns the past narrative readily into a historical narrative that is—obviously—a *factional, factitious, fabricated,* and *factious* process. The next step in this examination of the historian's turning of the past into history is how it is shaped and formed through the concept of the *factitive*.

5 Factitive

By now dear reader, I hope you are starting to understand that I define history as a form of literature as much as some kind of 'historical' engagement with the past. What makes history different to all other narrative forms, however, is that a history is a narrative about the probable/possible actuality and reality of the past. It is important to acknowledge, then, that all histories are 'contrived explanatory narratives' about a preferred 'past reality'. So, it is important to understand that for the historian and/or anyone else for that matter, history and the process of historying are to 'bring about' and 'invoke' the past. Thus, for example, a historian may refer to John F. Kennedy as the direct object of their history of Kennedy. However, Kennedy's presidential function would be the *factitive* complement just like I am the author who is guiding you.

So, narrating an attested past reality, aka a history, is an exercise in authoring a narrative of the past as understood and envisioned by the author who may wish to engage with the presumed reality of the past through their construed historical narrative. Now, I have reached the halfway point in my engagement with 'the-past-*as*-history' and, as with all the other chapters in this book, I offer two further concepts that I suggest work together in the aestheticising process of turning the past into a history. Note, yet again, I mean that all we have are innumerable historical realities and, of course, there is no single history of 'the past of . . .'. As with the previous concepts (in the prior chapters in this book), there is another further concept—the *factitive*—that is 'made' and 'constituted' by the historian's authorial engagement with the past and I hope my argument is by now plain. Thus, 'the-past-*as*-history' is entirely determined by the individual historian's preferred authorial engagement with the past. To be as clear then as I can be, it is essential to understand that the past has no in-built history awaiting its discovery. It is the historian who constitutes 'the-past-*as*-history' because the past has no history of its own. The past is what the past was, but that does not mean it was the history.

Obviously then, a history of the past cannot exist until the historian 'authors it into existence'. In this chapter, then, I will examine the concept of the *factitive*, which I suggest (insist?) would be useful for historians to acknowledge. The concept of the *factitive* is deployed by historians whether they know it or not, to further sustain the basic process of making and/or calling into existence a history of or for the past. To be very blunt, there are as many ways to constitute the past, as there are historians readily available to take up the strain of their acts of 'authorialism'. The past, then, has very little to do with the historian's preferred process of 'doing history'. This might seem bizarre, however, the *factitive* processing of the past is simply just another 'meaning for a history' for the historian's preferred past.

As you may have gathered by now, my foundational assumption that all histories are a 'narrative making' undertaking is predicated on my ontological assumption that history has the status of a narrative and/or a narratological act. It is my judgment—skeptical though I am—that the past can only be constituted and understood through the historian's act of their 'authorial fashioning' of their preferred narrative past. This, of course, does not in any way imply or suggest a denial of the status of single statements of justified belief and appropriately drawn inferences. Again to be blunt, historians create and/or if they prefer, 'establish their historical narratives' through which they insist will enable them to 'discover the past' which, happily and supposedly, speaks for itself. Somewhat awkwardly, this makes no sense of any kind. Unfortunately, then, there is very little to discovering 'the history of whatever'. Yes, historians can studiously seek out what they believe about the past according to their data. However, unfortunately, no one—and obviously that includes historians—can discover the traces of the past, but they can never discover its history.

To be as clear as I can then, historians 'turn' the past into 'a preferred history narrative', which has the benefit of implanting itself (*post hoc*) as 'the most probable past'. This implantation is what the historian does. All histories, then, are intended to be interpretive factual narratives; however, the foundational problem with this notion is that all factual narratives remain what they are—authorial devices. In describing the reality of the past every historian has to 'authorialise' her or his 'objectively construed' histories. But there is a further problem with 'doing history'. The *factitive* processing of the past into the historian's preferred history could not make any sense of any kind, if the historian did not already know what they think the nature and meaning of the previous past already existed. All historians invariably know what they think about the past long before they create, produce, fashion, and construe their histories. All historians, then, are very well aware that the ontology of what they produce is the *factitive* oil that smooths over the intellectual wheels of 'the-past-*as*-history'.

So, all this leads historians to acknowledge that the distinction between the past and history is foundational to 'doing history'. Unsurprisingly, then, historians happily accept that they can legitimately 'author' and/or 'discover' those historical narratives and they choose to believe that they can acquire the knowledge of the past and what it most probably meant. Unhappily, I have to suggest that such source-based knowledge is entirely interpretational and which may then be permitted to constitute 'the-past-*as*-history'. Now, basic to this process of turning past reality into a history are a number of foundational concepts of which far too many historians are unaware. These authorial concepts are 'the story', 'discourse', 'narration', 'story space', 'voice', 'focalisation', 'timing', 'agent intentionality', 'characterisation', and 'action', all of which 'shape' and 'form' the past as 'history'.

Hence, while the attested past cannot be denied, history remains what history says. The past is nothing more than a series of narrative creations contrived by the historian (along with everyone else). As I have already suggested, autobiography, histories, news reports, and so forth are not generally regarded as inventions in respect of what they are because of what they are 'made' to mean. No histories exist in the past, then, awaiting discovery. As I have already noted, history is 'built' because all histories are reconstructions, constructions, and/or deconstructions. Hence, all hi(stories) are authorial creations. The single and undeniable important point when engaging with the past and the only vehicle we have is the narrative the historian believes they have discovered. But, as I have already suggested, the concept of narration can be regarded as a *factitive* processing mechanism.

Obviously, history narratives are specific to what they do if only in the mind of the historian. However, all history narratives are dependent upon a myriad of circumstances, which can (and should) be considered as a *factitive* undertaking along with the other constraints I have examined and the others in the rest of this book. The history text, then, like any other text, is simply a process of 'telling'. Unhappily, most historians are rarely taught that the past is not some kind of revelation or disclosure. This is because of the rather simple-minded notion that the past is some sort of sublime historical experience. Unfortunately for historians and other human beings, the past is a vast sea of 'telling' and 'retelling'.

Now, the (hi)story text is simply a succession of events. Of course, it is the function of historians to stitch, fashion, and construe 'what happened' in the past. All histories are usually unpretentious concoctions of varieties of narratives that include histories and other narrative forms, without which there would be no meaning, no explanation, and, most worryingly, no past reality to recall. Now then, the problem with this is that the past is not history and history is not the past even though the vast majorities of historians sustain and maintain a very strange notion. That notion is that 'the history of the past' is a discovery. Now, with very little serious thinking, this is quite clearly nonsense. Allow me to be very clear now. History does not exist snugly and comfortably in the past awaiting its discovery. The past is not history and history is not the past.

Unfortunately, then, because history is not the past the historian's authored narrative of the past is all we have. To be clear then, and as I have already suggested, there is no single history in the past to be discovered. The past then, is not just a depository of data (which it is of course), but in the absence of the 'history of the past' sooner or later some historian will author it into their what will be their preferred existence. Obviously then, the past cannot speak for itself and so it has to be constituted not simply by being based on the data of 'what happened' and/or as selected and/or discovered and/or revealed by the historian, the vast majority of academic historians choose to believe that the past and history are consonant. Unhappily, the past is not history and history is not the past. The reason is because they exist in different ontic and epistemic universes.

Of course, this notion makes no sense to historians who insist that history is a discovery rather than the narrative invention of individual historians. Knowing what actually happened in the past must be understood as best as we can in accord with the presently available evidence. So, 'telling lies about the past' is quite obviously stupid, senseless, and ultimately pointless. However, it is essential to acknowledge that in engaging with the past the key to 'doing history' is to acknowledge that all histories are 'built narratives'. The logic in all this is that in acknowledging that histories are authored narratives as based on the 'balance of evidence', historians can only engage with the past through their authorial mechanism of the *factitive*.

Given that 'the past' can only be engaged through an 'engineered intervention' on the part of historians, all histories (yes, all every one of them) are *factitive* acts of historical engineering. Many historians, I suspect, will respond to my radical sceptical argument in a twofold way. They can insist that being too engaged with narrative self-reflexivity just gets in the way of doing history 'properly' and/or might just produce a threatening authorial narcissism that obscures the knowable reality of the past. And, of course, this also imperils the verities of truth and objectivity that keep all historians honest. Unhappily and plainly, then, all historians are in a bind as deep as the Marianas Trench. Historians can dive into 'their preferred histories' and take other historians with them but schools of historians constantly float about wondering where the tides will take them. So, it is impossible to guarantee that any historian's narrative is the 'right narrative'. The past then, and as I have suggested, can only be known and be knowable when the historian composes, constitutes, and institutes their history of and for the past.

As I have already noted, the past does not become the history until it is 'historied' by the historian. Now, of course, in addition to getting straight what happened in the past there is also the historian's ideology, the contract deadline, and the bad reader reports. Historians, however, also create 'the(ir)-past-*as*-history' which is unavoidably infused with what they believe is the history of the past and also what other historians sincerely believe is their undoubtedly correct analysis. Plainly, then, the historian's skill is not that of 'discovering the history of the past' but rather lies in authoring a meaning for the past through their authorial making, shaping, forming, fashioning, and framing and hence what they believe to be the most likely true nature of the past. Consequently, historians provide the(ir) versions of the past and then further offer what each version might have meant and/or the historian can reasonably have been right given the sources and the(ir) interpretational probabilities. Obviously and consequentially, the process deployed by historians—even if the vast majority does not think in these terms—is that of the *factitive* structuring of the past.

Now, the *factitive* is significant like all of the other key concepts that I refer to, because it is closely associated with, but is not to be confused with, any other narrative verb processing. In this chapter, I am suggesting it is necessary to examine the manner and the way that historians variably deploy the innumerable *factitive* verbs and whether or not they know it, when they engage with the past and the present like everyone else. Historians thus variously create, assign, assess, suggest, deem, name, judge, make, and designate in their extraordinary effort to engage with that which no longer exists—the past. Here, then, are some very simple sentence examples of the disposition of the possible *factitive* engagements historians can deploy. Examples are 'The people elected Donald Trump, President of the United States' and/or 'Margaret Thatcher was a British Prime Minister' and/or 'Rosa Parks was an American Civil Rights activist' and so on and so forth. Such simple *factitive* sentences, however, are plainly not the same as the past. They are descriptive statements about Trump, Thatcher, and Parks.

Obviously, that hugely over worked concept of 'the history of the past' is always unavoidably blind, deaf, and dumb until the historian constitutes and/or reconstitutes a narrative explanation for it, whatever 'it' was, in the past. At this point, most historians (in my experience) will say they have discovered the most likely nature of the past, given the probabilities in terms of the available sources, but what historians also 'author into' existence is a *factitive* history. To be as blunt as I can without annoying too many historians who desperately insist on conflating the past with history, I suggest that all history narratives simply represent the author-historian's intellectually construed paradigms, patterns, premises, principles, and the all too often hypotheses for and/or of the past as they see fit. Unhappily, or happily depending on how you read it, there is no inherent meaning in the past. And so all historians can do is float about without an anchor.

The historian-author can swim in a gooey slush of the poetics, aesthetics, and (more than likely) paradigmatic hopes about what the past was and meant, but happily all histories can be turned into what the historian thinks and trusts is authorially useful for them (and their editor?) to desire to believe. Now, beyond those worrisome suggestions (which cannot be avoided), the *factitive* has a very serious significant role in creating 'the-past-*as*-history' (along with all the other italicised concepts). Thus, *factitive* verbs describe a situation where there is a result consequent to the action, as in the historian's claim that 'they made her (or him) Prime Minister in the absence of anyone better' or those historians who claim to interpret, well, whatever they want to interpret.

Unfortunately, the substantial majority of historians very rarely understand the nature of how their unfortunate presentist authorial undertakings—aka the(ir) histories—become the past. The notion of the past as being history is, of course, an example of the worst form of hope over experience. The past is what it was because it is in the past, but it is not the same as its history in our perpetual present. The nature of the past is obviously only accessible through its transfiguration by the historian who turns the past into their preferred, desired, stipulated, and postulated history. This means that the art (or science if you prefer) of historying is plainly not a form of imitation, it is at the very best some kind of simulation and/or it might be a re-creation, or it may have been a restitution and the rest. Hence: there is no history lurking in the past awaiting to be unearthed or pushed out of the thickets of hope over experience. History, then, is an ersatz and/or sham replica and/or just another febrile imitation of the past. Now, this is never nor necessarily a bad thing. A surfeit of historians is essential. Without that overabundance we would end up with a politicised but most worryingly, lots of poor, insignificant, petty, and trifling histories. So, eventually and happily we accept that in the absence of the past all we can—hopefully—create are various good, bad, or hopeless histories.

Now, and fortunately, getting 'the past straight' was and remains a very small element in the processing of the past into a history. History, then, is neither a mime nor a caricature nor is it any kind of substitute for the past—and hence—the past cannot be re-realised as anything else other than the historian's preferred history. Ironically, the only way the historian (or anyone else) can access the past is to acknowledge that doing history is a frail, insubstantial, and unstable imitation of the past. As Aristotle famously said, it is not the role of a poet to relate what happened in the past. Unfortunately for academic historians and their consumers, they exist in a no-win situation and (oddly?) very few of them seem aware of that predicament. Getting at the truth of the past, i.e., knowing what actually happened in the past is a very small part of what historians actually do. The perpetual problem that all historians and their consumers have, and which none can escape, is that history is an imitation of what is plainly an ersatz past reality. Historians cannot exist in the past and happily surely very few folk really take historians seriously?

So, how can historians be taken seriously? Well, now and obviously, every history is unavoidably threaded through with the usual narrative history emplotments. These, of course, are tragedy, comedy, irony, and romance and/or more often all of them. Now, as Aristotle argued (sort of), this authorial construal is often so aligned that reconstituting and/or reconstructing the past in terms of its likely meaning actually ends up as some kind of *factitive* deconstruction of the past. This unfortunate situation then is always impossible to unscramble. Hence, historians always and consistently end up by somehow clumsily constructing and/or deconstructing the(ir) preferred past rather than reconstructing its reality. This is not necessarily a problem of course. The factitive expression of the historian's interpretation of the past always depends entirely on some 'thing', or 'event', or 'incidence', or 'occurrence', and so forth, which the historian will always insist, is the single event that constitutes and happily shapes and construes the nature of the past. So, how far can historians really go with the subterfuge of claiming that their narrative is the (most likely) past?

All histories, therefore and fortunately, have no shared inherent characteristics that shape all their meanings/explanations and their unavoidable implications. The past, then, cannot be devoid of its *factitive* nature and the reason being is that the past has no 'inherent history' available to be discovered. But, historians have a problem (among many others). In creating (authoring) a history, historians conveniently and erroneously conflate 'the past' with the(ir) preferred 'history' and vice versa. So, it is not at all that startling that the history of (whatever) must have a conclusion. Thus, regardless of its form the author-historian brings together the components of the(ir) preferred emplotment. This means that all histories not only offer what happened in the past but also explain what it all meant. However, there is—obviously—no given and/or in-built emplotment in any series of past events, which means that historians cannot discover the past apart from a perceived in-built history.

The *factitive* verb, then, is significant in creating historical meaning(s) given the unavoidable nature of the intellectual crudities of historical interpretation. The deployment of *factitive* verbs obviously operates at the heart of 'the process of doing history'. Hence, the deployment of simple descriptions thus permits historians like everybody else to choose what parts of the past they want to arrange as they further choose to select and/or privilege some data over other data when they judge a historical agent's action, and/or the historian names a process, or the historian further privileges one historical act over another. Historians thus have a heavy responsibility to acknowledge their intellectual and ideological input into 'the-past-*as*-history'. So, the past is what the historian's choice of language is, which constitutes the nature of the past.

Now, there is a serious problem with 'doing history'. To be brief, and as most literate people know, histories are claimed not to be narrative fictions. Unfortunately, the notions of 'story', 'text', and 'narration' are completely useless in 'learning' and 'knowing' what actually happened in the past. By that claim I do not mean knowing what actually happened in the past, however, what did happen in the past is not really that difficult to figure out. But in that process of figuring out what happened in the past it is unavoidably subject to the mechanisms of 'story', 'narration' and 'text'. Knowing what actually happened in the past is unavoidably embedded in the historian's communication about the past and so a history book or a journal article or a seminar or a lecture is plainly not bits of the past. However, because they are expressive narratives created by the author who is presently engaged with the past then it is likely the history consumer will accept what the historian claims.

Now, one of the most awkward problems in (doing) history is how the historian constitutes, manages, and deploys the aesthetic and moral value of history. Most historians (I suspect) will recognise that they 'layer the past' with ideology and moral certitude and also insist that they can be objective. This, of course, is an odd stance because very few historians are impartial, and/or unprejudiced, and/or objective, and/or dispassionate and very rarely do they try to keep the more obvious moral elements out of doing history. Furthermore, historians do not address the moralities of historical agents if it does not fit into their prejudices or vice versa. No historians are objective (like every other human) but in engaging 'their preferred history of the past' historians constantly regenerate history and offer almost numberless reinterpretations. Historians, then, are obviously 'makers' rather than 'discoverers'. The idea of discovering the past for what it really was is some sort of Holy Grail. In addition, think of that entire rethinking historians that have to go through when exploring the nature of their *factitive* historying.

It seems reasonable for most historians to believe that they can discover the reality of the past. Unfortunately, apart from their rock solid beliefs in 'what happened in the past' historians have to imagine what the most probable past was like. The brief and now passed recent postmodern years, the empty shoreline of deconstructing the knowledge of the nature of the past is no longer. And so, the substantial majority of historians again believe in the simple possibility of truthfully knowing the nature of the past. Now, most historians, despite the brief postmodern blot on the intellectual landscape, remained dedicated to the crude empirical-analytical view of the 'given' connection between the past and its history. Despite the continued broad belief today, that the past is history and history is the past (which is a seriously silly belief), the only connection between the past and history is a professionalised faith in the knowledge of what happened in the past, and which usefully reveals the most likely explanation of the nature of the past.

Unfortunately, that notion remains rooted in the minds of the substantial majority of historians who agree that their findings as to what happened in the past and what it meant will be rendered truthfully to them. But, of course, the academic forms of history remain what they are, just more restructuring of the past, which (fortunately) constantly piles up. To circumnavigate this problem means that fair, balanced, and secure accounts of key causes of past events must be provided so history can be regarded as 'the' past. For the vast majority of academic historians conflating the past with history and history with the past requires little to question. Unhappily, however, historical knowledge is not the same as historical truth. Hence, it is more essential these days than ever before, to assess the sceptical contention that every history text by its nature unavoidably destabilises any claims to truth whether its forms are coherence, correspondence, consensus, and/or the contextual. All histories are comprised of form, substance, and content. But, that mix is never enough. The past does not speak for itself nor does it see for itself, and its physicality is always plastic in terms of its imposed meaningfulness.

Unfortunately (perhaps?), this means that there is never a final historical truth. This is useful for the employment of historians. Of course, knowing what actually happened in any set of past circumstances is invariably worthwhile. However, without entirely rethinking the nature of the past as it was (or might have been), then what the past meant remains entirely subject to interpretation. This is an excellent and happy *factitive* situation for historians. Unfortunately this situation makes no sense of any kind. Now, the substantial majority of historians insist (whether they know it or not) that they can discover the nature and meaning of the past. But this is both illogical and therefore pointless. The subject of the past that the individual historian wishes to engage with can be presented in varieties of forms. If they were willing and able, historians could offer their preferred history as a narrative in the form of a ballet, a novel, a short story, a movie, a chat in the common room, and so forth. But, if historians want the truth of the past (and they do by and large) they have to be well aware that their preferred form for the past is not to be confused with the substance of the past.

Now, historians are very keen (correctly in my view) to get the data straight and what it most likely meant. Unhappily and all too often awkwardly, far too many historians actually know very little about the presentation of their 'captured past'. Thus, historians do not prefer to engage with the past in other forms than books, lectures, seminars, and the odd oral and visual media and, who knows, possibly a ballet while flying on the wing of a biplane? Of course, the job of all historians is to make choices concerning the kind of truth they want and can live with. Truth in history is authorially constituted in such a way that fresh discoveries in the archive are available for yet another history narrative, which can be constantly both provisioned, previsioned, revisioned, and rethought. Like any other narratives, histories are always and invariably 'political engagements' simply and obviously because the author-historian selects what they hope their reader should believe about the past. The process of truth in creating history, then, is never more than a shaky 'historical truth' and which is (obviously?) just another truthful history narrative. The nature of historical truth, of course, means acknowledging the varieties of truth forms that the invention of history demands.

Conventional (and invariably simple notions of) truth requires deploying the argument of most historians but not all that somehow they can escape into history. This notion is seriously misleading of course, but what perhaps is even worse is that historians invariably fall into the trap of empathising with people in the past. The reason for this annoying and pointless situation occurs simply because the substantial majority of historians (being trained by other historians) inevitably chooses to deny the most fundamental principle of their engagement with the past. This notion leaves no room for all the 'pasts' that can be accessed through the historian's authorial intervention. To be blunt, then, the only thing(s) we can share with people in the past is the historian's insistence that their 'discovered narrative' is at best a heartfelt reconstruction of the past.

Now, if the historian waits long enough, the historian's preferred history turns out to be either a construction or a deconstruction. Plainly, there is no possibility that the historian can reconstruct the past as it actually was. I mean that the past is the past and history is a narrative about it. So, unfortunately and definitely, historians cannot reconstruct the past. In spite of the archival sources and the deployment of the empirical-analytical and/or narrative bridge between the past and history, the past continues not to be a history and a history is certainly not the past.

Now, this claim does not mean to deny the past as it is engaged with. The best that historians can do is to choose the empirical-analytical route into the past (which historians do of course), and always demand the inter-(in)vention of histories which are, simply and plainly, examples of the author-historian's narrative preferred dipping into historicity (authentic history). So, what the historian writes about the past is, well, what the historian wants to write about the *factitive* past. Our only engagement with the past, then, is that the history is neither more nor less than our authorial preferred history narratives. Historians, then, are not explorers and/or discoverers much less investigators because the intellectual milieu of the *factitive* is yet another intellectual context for the historian's engagement with 'the-past-*as*-history'. This means historians can only create history in a very uncooperative intellectual condition. Historians not only have to seek out the intentionality of agents in the past (why did they do what they did?), but historians also have to figure out their own intentions toward the past through their historying. Obviously, historians are very (very!) far from being explorers and/or discoverers. The notion of meddlers comes to mind?

Anyway, if this description may seem a clumsy way of my denying that historians exist in the world of 'serendipity history narrative making', so

Factitive 91

be it. However, and fortunately, historians usually manage at some point to figure out why and what happened in the past at least as they measure it. However, and unhappily, there is another very awkward problem. This is that 'past historical agents'—aka people in the past—only existed in the past through the histories we provide for them. Accordingly, it is the historian's responsibility to turn the reality of 'the past' into their 'history narrative'. So historians tend to only engage with the 'agents' they prefer to engage with and talk about.

Now, as I have already noted, there is another fundamental problem with history. This is the unavoidable deployment of the causative verb. If, dear reader, you want a succinct definition of the central problem of history it is that historians seek out 'historical agents' that fit into the historian's plans for, well, those historical agents. To be clear, then, the *factitive* element in writing history is almost entirely organised and prearranged through the deployment of preferred causative verbs. Happily, historians cannot avoid verbs such as 'let', 'allow', 'have', 'make', 'must', and so forth. Historical interpretations, then, are simply convenient descriptions of that which the individual likes. Conservative historians write conservative history. Marxist historians tend to write Marxist history.

Moreover, reconstructing the past as it actually was is plainly impossible, and so all that historians 'can do with the past' is to reconstruct, construct, and/or deconstruct it in accord with the historian's preferences. Obviously, historians cannot reconstruct the past as it actually was because history is not the past and the past is not history, and the most likely meaning of the past, then, can only be construed and/or interpreted through the individual historian's preferred history narrative. Obviously, of course, that does not mean historians can legitimately offer 'their preferred past reality willy-nilly'. Unfortunately, however, and of course, that is exactly what they do. So, what this means is that there is no given history in the past awaiting discovery (which is obvious) and hence all historians are destined (which again is obvious) always to create their own 'past-*as*-history'. Obviously, then, getting the data straight is the number one function of all historians. However, all historians have their own preferred individual history narratives which, given their (selected) sources, means all historians have are their preferred 'pasts-*as*-histories'.

If they are so inclined, then, historians tend to create the(ir) narrative which they choose to believe exists back there in the(ir) preferred 'historical past'. So, Horatio Nelson died in 1805 and/or Abraham Lincoln was assassinated in 1865 and Neil Armstrong was the first man on the Moon in 1969. But, among all its other constraints, the process of 'historying the past' is unavoidably subject to its 'being created as . . .'. Hence, all histories are *factitive* narratives. Hence, 'the-past-*as*-history' is simply (or complexly depending as you read it) a description of what the historian believed happened in the past and what they decide it probably meant, i.e., this is their historical interpretation. Hence, we have so many pasts because we have so many interpretations and probably far too many historians?

Now, all historical interpretations offer descriptions both specific and general as to the nature of the past but, and obviously, history never comes pre-wrapped. The worryingly large number of disagreeing historians demonstrates that. The past then, is what it is for every historian—different. The foundational element in doing and delivering history is the interpretation of the most likely cause of whatever the historian wants to seek out. Happily, historical interpretations are very simple because they are the historian's generalisations. Histories then, look, smell, mean, and feel like what the past was like as observed by every historian but differentially. Now, this is a very simple illustration of the *post hoc ergo propter* hoc fallacy which states that since A is followed by B it must have been caused by A. Anyway, nothing in the past is useful 'as history' until a historian conjures it into existence 'as the history'.

Now, there remains the most significant and inevitable problem when it comes to the concept of the *factitive*. This is the situation that 'the past cannot be history' and 'history cannot be the past'. How can historians sort out this problem? Well, they cannot. Given that the past is the past and history is history, consequentially and unfortunately, constantly rethinking and/or refashioning 'the-past-*as*-history' there is yet another problem. Ironically, most historians are aware of a situation that they cannot resolve and hence they conveniently ignore. This situation is the historian's awkward and problematic authorial *factitive* past.

Now, if there is a central problem with connecting the past and history, it is ironically the creation of multiple histories of the same past, which means that there are almost innumerable versions of the same past. At the simplest level historians believe there is a narrative 'back there and then' that can be (re)discovered and eventually it will be (de)constructed (again and again and again . . .). Thus, the central problem that all historians have is that 'the meaning of the past' does not exist until it is articulated as 'the meaning of the past'. This is the foundational intellectual problem all historians have and so does everyone else. To be clear: the past must be provided with meaning and explanation. The constant problem with history is that 'historical meaning' never exists before it is communicated as history. So, when engaging with the past, historians (and their consumers) cannot escape 'the-past-*as*-history'.

So, historians will always place what they think occurred in the past was/is bound to be a discovery and so not an authorial creation. But that—unfortunately—is nonsense. Think about it. The meaning of the past does not exist before it is articulated and understood and perceived by the historian who intends their engagement with their preferred narrative. Then, somewhat amusingly, perhaps, historians more often than not prefer narrative history structures that they have themselves authored into existence.

Now, this boils down to a very simple situation. All histories of say the rise and fall of a generally regarded buffoon American President are likely to be plainly narrative structures that present recurrent and regularities in his actions. So, what we have of the past is neither more nor less than a constructed/contrived narrative that can be probably loosely suggested as a 'historical analysis'. However, all histories have deep narrative *factitive* structures through which they can deploy meanings and explanations. This is commonly defined as discovering the emplotment, which eventually is authorially connected to a range of events, decisions, outcomes, and so forth.

So, a (hi)story is a story which can be either present or absent at the will and pleasure of the historian-author. Or to be obvious, some narratives are discovered by historians and others are a shaky construal. This is where history usually comes seriously undone. Histories are not novels and novels are not histories. However, and perhaps unfortunately, common sense is either far too common or must be uncommon depending on the author's desired consequences. Now, I argue that the past has no structure to it until the historian construes it *as* a history. The flexibility of this is at best an awkward situation. The past, then, is constantly revised and amended and re-re-trodden if the author's publishers allow it.

Now, there is another problem. Historians are not born as authors. However, most of them tend to assume that they are discovering the past's history. Now, most common sense historians assume that several events in the past constitute the past. Now, these common sense historians (and most of them assume that is what they are) tend to accept that events in the past constitute a (hi)story and so they can gauge what that narrative was most likely to be emplotted in the usual ways, as either/or comedic, tragic, satire, and/or romance. Obviously, it is assumed that for every set of events in the past there must be a history back there in the past. The key to engaging with 'the-past-*as*-history', however, is that the historian has to decide which came first—the past or the history or the history before the past? For the past, then, there are countless histories. So, it is literally a pick and mix arrangement.

Now, it has to be accepted that history is a constant and contemporary and perpetually changing literature. Now, it has to be admitted that the past is ultra-flexible in terms of what it was and what it meant. Knowing what happened in the past is what makes the past, well, the past. Unsurprisingly, this means that history is always secondary to the past given that we do not experience the past at some point of reverie. However, the notion of engaging with the past is obviously silly and at its worst stupefying. Because history is a narrative form—even if it is claimed to be the resurrection of the past (the idea of which is obviously very silly)—all 'historical agents' (in the past) have to be categorised, classified, labeled, and pigeonholed. The shortcut at this juncture then is to engage the admittedly somewhat simple theorising of the Soviet scholar

Vladimir Propp who argued that there are eight character types: 'hero', 'dispatcher', 'villain', 'helper', 'donor', 'princess', her 'father', and the 'false hero'. Now, I have to admit most historians are probably not *au fait* with Propp's list of 'stock characters' and would also deny that they approach the past with such a mechanism. However, even if they do not engage with such a list self-consciously, as authors, all historians lean on stock agent/actors.

Now, I doubt that most jobbing historians would or will knowingly or unknowingly lean on Propp's categorisations. But, like it or not, historians are authors engaged to discover the nature of the time before now. The essence of knowing the nature of the past, then, demands an understanding by the historian's preferred *emplotment*(s) and/or *argument*(s) and their *ideological inclination* which they believe—based on their data and preferred interpretation—will disclose what they insist is the true nature of the past. This notion is hardly news. However, of course, in the absence of the past all we have that we can substitute for that absent past is history. The deep irony that exists in all history/histories is that the key characters and events are stable/unstable and/or they succeed/fail. I also presume that all human beings, and that includes historians of course, have to accomplish their preferred goals (as historians), and they believe they have comprehensive mechanisms for succeeding in explaining the nature of the past. Happily, this is usually simple because the historian deploys those elements that enable the historian's 'analysis' to, well, make some sort of passable sense.

So, all historians have methodological, procedural, and operational mechanisms, which they deploy and which enables them to explain the nature of the past. Now, all consumers of history/histories obviously create and constitute their preferred *factitive* 'historical explanation' (even if they do not recognize the concept of the *factitive*). Now, we all know that historians seek out the data and the sources that will clarify the nature, meaning, and explanation of the past and obviously, then, for every historian there is almost certain to be a different past. This means that the (hi)story as preferred by individual historians obviously permits multiple accesses to the numerous versions of the same set of past events.

Now, simple logic suggests that for every different history narrative there has to be a differential past. But this seems to be daft, dippy, dozy, or all three. So, to be blunt, every set of past events is characterised in the way the historian wants or believes it should be. So, because every history is an authorial construal, or if you like a construction or a deconstruction and somewhat much more unlikely 'the true narrative back there then', that becomes 'the-past-*as*-history'. Anyway and nevertheless, and whether the majority of historians like it or not, the past (*as* history) becomes immanent, and the past becomes what the historians want 'to narrate for the past' and so the past immediately becomes history, and then again another history, and another and so forth. The past, then, is what the historian wants in their history but it never lasts.

What happens then is the unavoidable situation of what might be called the historian's translation into the narrative of the past. As I have noted already, the (or a preferred) meaning of the past can only exist when it is 'historied' into history. Now, if successful, the trail of the past shifts as the individual historian desires and prefers. Now, all this leads to the *factitive* subterranean narrative structure of all histories and every other narrative creation. To be clear then, all histories are 'deep' descriptive narrative structures, which are accounts and portrayals of that which no longer exists. So, whether historians realise it or not, they create a history for a 'construed engagement with the past' which they wish—as I have already noted—to reconstruct, construct, or deconstruct the 'past-*as*-a-history.'

What this means is that all historians along with every other human being have to face the *factitive* problem of labelling the process of 'causing a result' within the text, which might or might not enhance the process of understanding 'a causality' which engineers 'the existence of the history'. This is possibly the central problem all historians have to resolve even if they do not recognise it. Causality, then, is probably the most significant feature of 'doing history'. Chronology and succession are foundational to 'doing history'. Every history narrative is shaped by events that are authorially arranged, organised, and ordered in a sequence through time. Obviously, this does not mean the historian invents this process but—and understandably—will if they wish, and they usually do, juggle temporality.

So, there are obvious historical situations that arise which are not created by historians but which as I have just noted, they authorially juggle in order to squeeze out some hitherto situation not acknowledged by other historians. A recognizable 'story situation' of this is when Fred died and then his wife died. This is obviously a narrative. However, if Fred died and then his wife died of grief, then that is now an emplotment. The reality of the past then demands reasons and causes and so no histories can exist and have any significance without an authored causality. Now, historians have a real problem with this situation. Which conclusion to adopt? But, then, does that matter given that every historian is in a *factitive* win-win situation? It is called 'choosing the most likely interpretation given the sources selected' by the individual historian. But, not to worry, the constant cycle of 'the new most likely interpretation' will always come to the saving of the historian.

Happily then, histories offered in books, lectures, journal articles, seminars, chats over cups of tea, and throwaway lines in a pantomime continue to hover between deconstructing, reconstructing, and constructing the past. The unfortunate problem that both historians and consumers of history have is their collective failure to recognise and appreciate that their '*factitive* telling' is just another eventual collapse in the effort to constantly engage with the past. Reaching back to the past for a support for the perpetual present is never going to work. Before we can engage with the past we have to distinguish the range of concepts that historians could and should deploy in engaging with an absent past.

Ironically, in the empirical world of the past (which is irretrievably gone) all the historian can engage with is their intervention. The historian is, at best, some kind of *factitive* agent who will try to recapture, recall, and evoke 'a narration' of the past. So, what can historians do in the face of the implacable past? Well, very little in the face of the forms through which the historian (and anyone else) deploys. In this book, for example, I am offering a variety of concepts through which we can engage conveniently and usefully with the past. When historians (and anyone else) want to engage with 'the time past' using verbs, which are intended to prod the past into being a useful history, we must select, elect, name, appoint, deem, judge, designate, and assign meanings which hopefully will prod historians into rethinking 'the-past-*as*-history'.

6 Factive

So, authoring a history is all about acquiring and (re)presenting the actuality of the 'historical past' as best historians can. Unfortunately, as I have already noted and suggested, the 'historical past' must not be confused with the actual past (and certainly not to be confused). Hence, historians invariably have to deploy the *factive* verb (whether they know it or not) in the presumption that all (or most) historical claims they make are true or very probably true. However, the reality of the past is simply a history masque through which histories can be engaged with via manuscripts, records, books, journal articles, lectures, tutorial plans, and so forth. Historians, then, and fairly obviously, have two severe problems that they cannot resolve. These are 'facts' and 'intentionality'. However, in the historian's universe of '*factive* historying' there is a problem.

Historians are sustained by 'facts', which, of course, are defined as events under a description and which are primarily constrained by 'agent intentionality'. Unhappily, 'the historical fact' (hence the notion of the *factitive*) is both complex and contentious. For a start what are historical facts? Well, most historians would agree that they are 'past events under a description'. This means facts are agreed as *factive* statements of belief. Thus, historical facts when added up are taken to produce a collective consensus concerning the genuine nature of the past. So, the Battle of Waterloo took place on June 18th, 1815, and another fact is that Wilbur and Orville Wright made four brief flights at Kitty Hawk on December 17th, 1903 and the first landing on the Moon was on July 20th, 1969, and so on and so forth. Consequently, there is no limit to historical facts and historians (or anyone else for that matter) constantly and relentlessly create all of them.

So, the *factive* dimension to doing history demands the creation and tracking of a consensus among historians not about the nature of the past, but their ability to historicise it. Thus, a particular statement as to what is truthful in what we say historically about the past immediately becomes itself an item of historical reality. To ascertain the truth of a description requires a belief in the alignment between the past and the beliefs of the historian about the past. Hence historians have an insuperable problem.

The problem is that they know that connecting 'the past' and 'its history' is, well, impossible. At best, the past event is, well, a past event *as* a description. Is there a way out? No. It is impossible to discover the history of the past.

This may seem awkward and it is. In order to be connected to the past as it actually was, historians have to create historical facts. However, that cannot work in practice because the past is the time now gone while history is a perpetual presentation of that which no longer exists. So, to be clear on this *factive* problem (again?), that which is historical is not the past and that which is the past is not necessarily historical. Most historians find this a vexing situation but they, rather than having to cope with it, generally ignore it entirely. This is why for every historian there is always a differential past. In part, this may be because of the use of different sources by dissimilar historians, which require diverse interpretations of the past and hence miscellaneous histories.

Yet another problem with history is not so much getting the data straight, as I have already noted, but describing it. Hence, the nature of history has a *factive* nature. Arguably, a central problem that historians find particularly annoying with doing history is not getting the nature of the past but, as I have already noted, how the historical facts are construed, constructed, and eventually deconstructed. As I have already noted, 'the-past-*as*-history' is a series of connected causal events, which are, of course, simply descriptions. The central problem for historians in doing history is that they fail to acknowledge that language is a form of representation. Hence: the meaning and explanation of 'the historical past' can be acknowledged and accessed not only through our language but also in all our representational forms—films, journal articles, academic books, chats in the local café, school classes, theatre plays, playing in the playground, TV programmes, speeches, and so on and so forth.

Unhappily, however, the historical imagination still cannot access the past. Indeed, the historical imagination cannot either *reconstruct* or *construct* the past again for what it was. And, whether they like it or not, no historian can *deconstruct* the past via their historical imagination. Obviously, the human mind can 'suppose the past as . . .' which can then be tested in the empirical data. But this means the historical imagination is simply the application of the capacity of the historian's mind to compare through connection, likening, analogies, comparisons, and so forth. The problem that faces all historians along with every other human being is crossing the line between imagination (fancy, creativity, and innovation) and inference (interpretation, construal, and understanding). All historians, then, have to create and/or picture the past through inference. Thus, there is the unavoidable *factive* processing of the past and which we usually describe as 'doing history'.

Historians are divided in many ways. They have different interpretations because of their sources. Some have more travel grants to seek out hitherto untouched sources. Others insinuate their political leanings into their histories. And, of course, there are publishers who insist on book contracts that must be written and sent in by a deadline. And then, of course, as the theorist Frank R. Ankersmit suggested in his classic text *History and Tropology* (1994), there was always 'the reality effect' in the writing of history. Knowing what actually happened in the past obviously surfaces in histories; however, histories are always differentially construed and that is why we have so many different histories and interpretations. And, of course, there are other differentials—age, gender, the sabbatical acquired or denied, the Head of Department who never liked you, the latest fad in terms of 'the historiography', so on and so forth.

In addition, and whether the individual historians acknowledges and recognises her/his shifting *factive* states of mind, i.e., being sentient and sensitive that permits the historian to access states of 'knowing', which hopefully link to the truth of the past. Plainly, of course, there are by contrast, non-*factive* states whereby historians believe or think that what appear to be truths to them about the past but which eventually can only be demonstrated as untruths because they misconstrued the sources or just got the wrong end of the straw. In this *factive* state of mind, historians can be 'reality-congruent' or probably more annoyingly exist in irreality-congruent states of false belief (the wrong end of the straw). This situation is hardly problematic in the sense that historians tend to believe what they want to believe about the nature of the past. Reduced to its basics, then, historians can believe what they want (and usually do) and regardless pursue their own intentions (again as they usually do) in respect of the historical agents that they refer to.

So, the difficulty with *factive* thinking, which we all experience and usually unwittingly undertake when authoring a history and which we also engage when we also go shopping or going on holiday, 'knowing', 'being aware' and 'insightful', can only link 'an agent or thing in the past' to 'the present author's perceived truth'. The contrast to non-*factive* mental states can very easily (which is fortunately) link an agent, which includes author-historians, to either truths *or* falsehoods. Historians usually draw a sharp line between the capacity to accurately attribute states of 'the mind of past agents' which appear such as 'them knowing', 'their being aware', and 'his or her insightful thinking' that can only link 'an agent in the past' to 'the present author's perceived truth of or about the past'. Or, to be succinct, historians create histories and claim that they discovered them.

The contrast to non-*factive* mental states can very easily link an agent, which includes author-historians, to either truths *or* falsehoods. Historians invariably draw a sharp line between their capacities to attribute accurate states of the mind of past agents, which appear thanks to the author's available data/sources as 'reality-incongruent states of mind' aka false/true belief. Historians then, should be aware of the distinction between the *factive* and the non-*factive*. Conventionally, historians believe that 'the historical truth' is defined as the correspondence between discoverable and verifiable truths, i.e., facts *as* events under a description. The upshot of this is plainly that the past only exists in our present when it is historied into an existence—and unavoidably— 'history' thus becomes 'the past'.

The problem with this situation then is that far too many historians still do not understand the nature of the concept of the *factive*. Most historians, perhaps the majority, accept that facts—the *factive*—are what is attested and known. However, and unfortunately, there are those (happily only a very tiny group) of historians who wish to offer false propositions and beliefs about events in the past. Such 'pseudo-historians' will also deploy the *factive*. Of course, not having the supporting data that will evidence and support the historian's analysis is worrying because the probabilities will support all kinds of bizarre propositional interpretations. Unfortunately, a few historians continue to accept what is the truly strange situation whereby the past is assumed to be history and history is assumed to be the past.

Plainly, this is nonsense in much the same way that facts are taken to be fragments and pieces of truth. Today, historians are plainly still associated with the facts following in the way of the German historian Leopold von Ranke. His belief was that history could, should, and must hold up a mirror to the past. Obviously this is nonsense because the past would be back to front. Obviously, the thought of historians suddenly 'telling it like it was' would be too much to deal with, given that historians change their minds far too often despite the constant supply of fresh new *factive* sources and meanings. Or, if they prefer (and yet again ironically), our historical knowledge will recede as the past expands.

Now, it also remains a surprise to me that so many academic historians continue to invest in the rhetorical device of mimesis aka art imitating (in this situation) past life. But, it is much worse of course, because and as I have noted before the past is not history and history is not the past. Thus, conflating the past with the historian's notion of what they believe was the past is a prime example of cultivating a beach after a high tide. So, the most noteworthy feature of engaging with history is that it must always change and be amended, adjusted, attuned, adapted, tailored, and above all made-to-order to fit in with the historian's ideological, ethical, and philosophical desires. So, all histories are not only driven by the authenticity of the past but also by its form and narrative content as shaped by the author-historian.

Throughout this chapter, then, the *reality* effect in writing history is the central feature of the processing of turning the past into a history. Now, forgive me, I have to be blunt. The most striking and significant development in the history of the philosophy of history of late is its demise. The rapid growing interest in historiography of late has now just as swiftly disappeared. Ironically, writing about the nature of the past is hardly transparent. What this means is that in engaging with the past, historians have to offer a past, which can be 'see-through' in their historical text. To be blunt again, historians have to recognise that the first postulate of 'doing history' is to work their way through the text that they have themselves created.

Arguably, then, the past puts all historians in a double bind. The first 'problem part' is that historians have to explain their intentions, as regard to the nature of what they believe was the nature of the past. The second 'problem part' is that historians are also expected to allow the past to speak for itself. Obviously this is impossible. The past cannot speak for itself through its own process of historying. All histories are like puddings but peculiar ones because they expected to cook themselves. But that, obviously, is nonsense because the ingredients of the past do not create their own cakes. However, then the history text is somehow expected to speak for itself. But that is impossible as we know because *the* past is turned by the historian into *their* version of the past. To be clear then, the reality of the past can only exist through the text of the history. And so, the past is only accessible through the intervention of the historian.

The past, then, does not present much less represent itself to the historian as it was because only the rough and ready 'reconstructionist' historian desires and expects to escape the most likely past. Unhappily, there are always variations on the nature of 'the past' in terms of the historian's preferred form and content. Now, all historians lay claim to know what actually happened in the past and the consumer can choose which version of 'what actually happened' they want. However and anyway, the *factive* nature of 'history form and content' shapes the past only in the mind of the historian. As I have suggested, the problem of the concept of the *factive* always faces historians. Ironically, then, the historian's history is always both prior to its content and its meaning. Historians form the past through the structural design of the historian's *factive* 'ontological history' which is never discovered but is made to meet the needs of the individual historian (and the consumer then pays their money and they are always left to decide if the money was well spent).

Today most historians still endeavour to reconstruct/construct the reality of the past according to the evidence as found. Hence, most historians thus remain empiricists and realists and thus they deploy their version of common sense which they believe makes them open to the 'truth-conditional' and obviously the attested 'referential nature' of the past. Given this, it seems reasonable for such historians to continue to believe that the past can be (again and constantly) reanimated and hence 'the-past-*as*-history' is a reasonable pursuit. But, that remains nonsense (even if it is a comfortable nonsense) because while knowing what happened in the past may be a form of knowledge, it is both rarely useful because knowing what happened in the past is always 'truth-conditional', which, of course, can only be constituted and delivered through the deployment of the historian's *factive* thinking and language. The nature of the *factive* is the engine of the historian's reality effect.

Nonetheless, the real problem with history is historians. They have invested both their minds and lives to the very dubious belief that they can engage meaningfully with that which no longer exists—the past. To make up for this unavoidably ontic and epistemic 'crash' and 'clash' the majority of historians insist that the past possesses its own in-built reality. This only seems like common sense. Surely, knowing what actually happened in the past is an absolute? Hence, there is no point in denying the reality of the past as demonstrated by the overwhelming weight of 'the evidence'. Hence, the vast majority of historians make extraordinary efforts to reconstruct and/or construct 'the-past-*as*-history' which means we can reject and deny the irreality of the past. Only the worst kind of pernicious fool would deny the reality of the past. However, what the past meant is the issue. All historians have to accept that like everyone else, they exist in a 'historical meta-aesthetic' situation. By that somewhat clumsy description, I mean that in the absence of the past all we have are authored histories and they seem to work because of the reality of the *factive* effect.

The irony of the *factive* effect is simple. Historians rarely believe that the past 'does not exist in their minds' because it was (and still is) 'evidentially back there and then awaiting discovery'. Hence, historians feel they can and are right to demand access to 'the most likely past reality' in the same way they believe they have access to the perpetual present. Historians thus subscribe to the belief that the contents of their minds concerning the nature of the past unavoidably exist both dispassionately and impassively. Unfortunately, historians rarely adopt any other stance as to the existing nature of the past apart from sneaking at the efforts of their contemporary interventionists. Thus, historians invest most of their time and effort in rethinking 'the past' of 'our history' rather than 'rethinking the *factive* nature of all histories'. So, knowing what happened in the past is crucial.

Beyond that, historians expend much *factive* mental effort with the curious notion that they can directly engage with the past. This belief is, of course, nonsense given that the time before now is simply 'the-past-*as*-history' as created by the minds of historians. Historians and everyone else then (with the exception of hardcore laboratory bound scientists) should accept that turning the past into history is jacketed by the deployment of the concepts of 'causality', 'truth', 'ultimate beliefs', and invariably everything else that can be regarded as the unavoidably 'abstruse'. Historying, then, depends on the moral, aesthetic, and intellectual qualities of the historian given that they are paid up 'realists', 'objectivists', and 'cognitivists'. Hence, historians find it difficult to deny 'the facts' but as we now know, the *factive* is a very slippery if significant notion. Unhappily, of course, most historians do not deploy this description. Historians rarely define the past—in their hands and minds—as being slippery and untrustworthy. Well, at least that past they select to engage with.

Now, historians are quite often (self-)assured as to the nature and security of the past. Throw enough sources and data at the past and enough of it will stick and become history. Now, (as I have often intimated so far) historians are usually told and then eventually forget that they should never intervene in the reality of the past. This notion is obviously very silly. By offering a history the historians have intellectually already re-enacted the past as they perceive it. When engaging with the past the first requirement is to sort out their authorial stance. By 'stance' I mean their prejudices, intolerances, chauvinisms, bigotries, and so forth. The past sooner or later turns out the historian's own personal reading of the past. This is hardly a problem of course, because for every historian there is always a good, bad, or indifferent version of the past, which they have authored into existence.

Historians—quite clearly—have a mental menu from which they choose their preferred plate of the day, i.e., the tastiest available interpretation. Unfortunately, historians are not trained to recognise the *factive* and so most also fail to understand that there is—of course—an 'aesthetic' objectivism in 'doing history' or, for that matter, in any other way. Therefore, the hardest of hard social science historian's remain inured or probably just ignorant as to the unavoidable *factive* association between *the* reality of the past and its 'aesthetic description' *as* a history. Knowing what happened in 'the past' only has 'meaning' and 'explanation' when it is 'aestheticised'. To be as clear as I can, there is aesthesis in all representations as in correlation coefficients, and/or trigonometry, and/or mathematical induction. For all I know, doing history can be reasonably regarded, like any human endeavour, as possessing its own aesthetic dimension.

This situation is unfortunate but unavoidable. It is luckless for historians (like every other human being I assume) that not only do historians debate the nature and meaning of the past but also they do it through the mechanism of aesthesis *as* knowledge. Perhaps the most problematic situation that historians confront is the reality effect of engaging with the past while endeavouring to engage aesthetic truth. Unfortunately, then, far too many historians rely on some very crude thinking and writing. For a start there is the issue of chronology—'this happened then that'—and then historians are also required to 'imagine and envision' themselves as actors in the past. Hence, historians are expected to 'imagine as actors in the past' so they can evaluate 'the past' in respect of 'what might of/and/or what did (or did not) happen for what reasons'. Hence, the significance of 'cause and effect' is central to 'doing history'. Moreover, and obviously, historians are required to acquire a range of 'research skills' among of which are engaging with the sources. And not least of all—and embarrassingly obvious—historians have to engage with what happened in the past by opening up the *factive* so they can resolve problematic 'outstanding and unresolved historical issues'.

So, the historian's factive state of mind demands that they are self-conscious of the inaccessibility of the past while allowing them to be linked as directly as possible to the reality of the past. This bizarre process demands that the historian discover the so-called historical truths, which exist back there and then by reconstructing and/or constructing and/or deconstructing the 'historical imagination'. Historians, of course, have a choice of these positions although most will take/make the common sense choice, which is to reconstruct the past; but, obviously, this makes no sense at all. The famous reconstructionist philosophical doctrine of R.G. Collingwood is hard to accept (although the majority of historians think it is common sense) because 'the past' can only 'be engaged with' when it has been historied. A history is somewhat like a soufflé: it takes a lot of work to make, but it very rarely lasts.

Historians, then, invest a great deal of their time and effort in honing and deploying the(ir) historical imagination. This invariably leads to a consideration (again and again) of the history philosopher R.G. Collingwood's contention that, besides requiring the interpretation of evidence, historians must invest a great deal of effort in nurturing and thus then sustaining their belief in the historical concepts of continuity and coherence. These concepts are thus then supposed and presumed to lead to the reality of the past by the nurturing of their historical imagination. Happily, this notion is not hard to figure out and even easier to deploy. Basically, historians simply imagine that which they cannot tangibly engage with. No sources mean that there is no past. But that is nonsense because the past is the past and history is immediately construed as 'the history'. Plainly the past and history do not exist in the same ontic environment. Conflating the past with history and history with the past is nonsense in both ontological and epistemological terms.

So, how can we (without laughing out loud) conflate the past with history and history with the past? Happily, most historians find it quite simple. The existence of the past is construed through the 'the historical', which is an act of imagination. This then demonstrates how the historian's factive endeavour 'can bring forth the past' initially in the historian's mind's eye. This ironic process, of course, is at the heart of 'doing history' and hence, the past is an 'inaccessible necessity' that is shaped and wrought as it is by the historian's 'historical imagination'. Like all every other human beings, then, historians believe they can bring forth that which does not exist, i.e., past events. Thus: as soon as 'a history is authored' it exists 'in the past'. To be obvious, the past cannot exist until it is authored. Consequently, all we have is 'the-past-*as*-history' which is 'constituted' and 'turned out' through the historian's 'historical imagination'.

The historical imagination, then, is just another part of how 'the history narrative' is authored into 'the-past-*as*-history'. So, how does this turning of dross (data) into gold (history)? Fortunately it is not complex. Thoughts about the past and also present thoughts about the possible future are created and organised through the application of the human capacity to 'compare, 'contrast', 'analogise', and 'constitute' differences and differentials which then enables and deploys the historian's capacity to turn the past into that convenient thing we call history. Of course, the belief in 'history recreation' in itself is nonsense. While it may annoy most historians, engaging with the past is an effort to recreate that which does not exist except as an elaborate 'treatment' and 'dressing' or 'preparation' in order to make sense of the time before now. This does not mean the past can just be invented at the pleasure of the historian (or politician or any other ne'er-do-well) but it is a process of a convenient clever 'creation-discovery'.

To be clear on all of this, then, like everyone else historians can only engage with the time before now through their figurative representational descriptions of what they take to be the structure and configuration of the past. The nature and logic of history, then, is that of an authored 'version' of a preferred past narrative. This is why the past should always be defined as 'the-past-*as*-history'. Accordingly, then, it should not be a surprise to know that the historian's narrative is the 'authorial delivery' of varieties of meanings and explanations of whatever the historian wants to offer as the(ir) history. Now, what all this means (or might mean) is that we should recognize that 'the-past-*as*-history' is never fixed even if most historians think 'her or his' history is the closest to the reality of the past in terms of the empirical and what it might have meant.

Accordingly, then, historians cannot avoid creating their 'historical imaginations' as shaped by their 'preferred inferences' and all other matters that may shape the historian's engagement with the past. This, I suspect, that the factive dimensions of historying requires that historians and their consumers have to accept that the past is not history and history is not the past. Unfortunately or fortunately (take your choice) my analysis does not define the nature of 'doing history' because, as I have argued, the past is not to be (con)fused with history and history is not to be (con)fused with the past. However, of course, there are other further awkward problems that I suggest can and shape and constrain the nature of 'doing history' and not least the 'history reality effect' or, as I have already suggested, the factive reality of the past as a verb that assigns knowledge.

So, our knowledge of the past is simply the reality effect of what historians do—or do not do—when they wish to create their histories. Reduced somewhat in meaning, then, the past is sustained by the historian's ontological addiction to the past. Now, and reduced considerably, the historian assumes that they are uncontaminated by the past and so they can see through their history text to a past reality which lurks behind the past. Now, a historically uncontaminated and thus transcendently pure past, demands the historian's ability to conjure up not just a plausible past reality, but the actual past and hence the 'half-way sensible' historian may well feel it is reasonable to engage with the past. Hence, the historian can see through the historical texts at a past reality that lies behind the past.

Historians, then, have to accept that their once previous frameworks for 'fresh' and 'new history(ing)' sooner or later generate a wholly fresh factive concentration of 'history (un)decidability' in the historian's historical text. What this leads to is an underdetermined and (un)decidable past. For every historian, then, there is always going to be a fresh history. Now, these constantly new histories may have been around for some time. The Ph.D. is the ironic and classic instance of this situation where every Ph.D. (or M.A. or undergraduate thesis) has to be decidable. The Ph.D. (and which sooner or later turns unto a new book or series of articles) lies behind the apparently independent revelation of the nature of the past. In engaging the past that past is merely a textual means for engaging that past.

Traditionally, then, engaging with the past has been blind to the opaqueness of the past. That is why we have histories so we can blame the historical text when the past somehow never quite works out. So, how can historians overcome the problem of turning the past into a convincing narrative (or narratives). Well, they cannot. Historians are—obviously—in an impossible situation. Knowing what (they think) happened in the past, historians have been fortunate in asking more and more questions of the past. But these days, thanks to the brief postmodern upheaval in the past 20 or so years, there are—or there should be—far more uncertainties as to the nature of the past than ever before. New statistical mechanisms, psychoanalysis approaches, group, and troupe methods are novel ways to engage with the past. Unhappily, the past remains the past until it is recovered, recouped, retrieved, and reclaimed by individual historians.

In the first two decades or so of this century, 'doing academic history' has unwillingly but increasingly emphasised the limits of the historian and the utility of 'the-past-*as*-history'. Increasingly, then, there has been a growing vacuum among contemporary academic historians and 'the history reality effect' has rarely been less acknowledged and less employed. The notion of 'historical reality' today is 'mashed together' with all kinds of 'reality effects'. It is useful then, to acknowledge that history is little more these days than a factive reality effect of the historian. Today, the aim of the historian (even if they do not realise it) is that the reality of the past is simply a reality that is created by largely irrelevant details and minutiae scattered about in the historical narrative. So, still today there is no differentiating between history (language) and the factive past.

So, as the French philosopher Roland Barthes argued a generation or more ago, the 'referent' (that which is referred to in the past) is unavoidably detached from 'discourse' and the 'signifier' (the description) is just a reality effect. So, historians exist in a problematic situation and so most of them simply ignore their unavoidable collapse into their process of historying. The truth of 'historical statements' in histories is simply located. Of course, it is possible to create a history narrative, which is entirely 'made up' and/or 'invented' and (apart from high end professional historians) will in all likelihood never realize the distinction between the past and history.

However, the real problem is the distinction between historical writing and past reality. Historians tend to author historical texts in the belief that they are writing and thus creating the reality of the past. Now, while most historians insist they are discoverers of the past there is an insuperable problem. It is the problem of connecting 'historical writing' with 'past reality' and vice versa. The common sense of most historians remains that there is a past reality that is made up of historical events, actions, and happenings. This means most historians can only offer what they think is their fair representation of the past. Unhappily, all that historians can do is provide a factive reality effect. Unhappily, then, there is far too much history already spread all over the past. Hence, and happily, there is a history for every historian.

Now, and this might be regarded as the central failure of 'doing history', in order to engage with the reality of the past, historians have to create their own past history. This does not mean inventing the past because all that historians can offer is a 'fair representation of the past'. But, of course, the historian's 'fair representation' is just another 'fair representation'. Hence, then, all histories are at best guides and attendants in their delivery of the birth of the(ir) preferred history. Plainly, this does not mean that all historians are unreliable witnesses, although they often are. Thus, all that historians can hope to offer is to acknowledge that 'historical reality' is chunks of diverse data that is eventually delivered as 'a history'.

So, history then, is no more than a reality effect of the historian (or anyone else). Thus, knowing what actually happened in the past is plainly not the same as its history and at best all histories are simply 'contrived historical realities', which, directly, have very little to do with the past. History is thus simply a reality effect of the past, as construed by the individual historian. What this means is that for every historian there is always a different past. The notion of 'the past', then, is simply a process of discovered shards of records, archives, and sources that conveniently turns the past into a reality effect. Thus, historical reality is never simply chunks of statistics, indicators, markers, signs, and so forth. It is the factive creation of the individual historian's engagement with the(ir) history.

So, what this means is that 'historical reality' is not the same as 'past reality'. Past reality is not a datum but is a convention construed by the historian's descriptive (re)presentation of the 'history reality effect'. What this means, is that the past is plainly not history and history is not the past in either content and form. All histories, then, are factive analogies and histories, both arts and impressions. What this suggests, then, is that all histories are both illusion and art and which are presumed to be real. Unfortunately, for historians and their consumers, a realistic history representation can only be that which the historian has promised.

So—and obviously—both the concepts of reality and the factive reinforce each other. Indeed, without each other there would be no notion of reality deployed by the historian and invariably aided by the rest of the academic history publishing industry. Writing history can be believed to be a reconstruction, construction, or deconstruction. These three simple designations (which your author has deployed over several decades) bring into very sharp understanding the nonsense of conflating the past with history. If you want a history, write a history. If you want the past, then write another history. The reality effect, of course, is the most misdirected notion that any historian can endorse. The best the historian can have in seeking out the nature of the time before now is to create her or his own 'historical past'.

Now, the foundational and unavoidable problem with history is historical writing. Getting at the reality of the past demands their preferred self-guided narrative. The writing of 'the-past-*as*-history' is a major problem, which no historian can resolve and so they forget about it. As I have suggested, turning the 'factive past' into a history is simply an exercise in acknowledging the reality effect. Hence, the realism of the past (aka history) is just another text. It is essential then, for both the historian and the history consumer to acknowledge that the factive reality of the past is all we can have in accessing the past. This is the possible/probable situation that the reality of the past is an effect created by the historian's historical text. Hence, there is no engagement with the past beyond the historical text.

Now, 'historical reality' is not discovered. Indeed, there is no such thing as 'historical reality'. There are the beliefs of historians about the nature of the past but that does not mean it is history. Indeed, there is, of course, no such thing as history in that history 'writes itself'. The past, then, is only an existential imprint that historians impose on the past. That is self-evident given the multiple versions of the past. If you do not like the history you are presently reading, then get a different book. Now, this may seem to be a dangerous belief. Surely, the whole point of history is to (in)scribe the history of the past in a lecture, seminar, book, journal article, and/or chat in a bar or pub? To be clear, then, the reality of the past is an effect created by historical texts.

The problem for so many historians and among politicians, firemen/firewomen, academics, airline pilots, waiters, tree fellers, retired magicians, and so on and so forth is their insistence that there is only one history when of course there is no definitive past. I appreciate this thought will upset many folks. How can anyone deny the factive nature of past reality? Well, obviously denying the reality of the empirical past is just plain crazy and pernicious. The past is what the past was. But that does not apply to the process of 'historying'. The reality effect is the reality effect. Nonetheless, 'the historical reality' remains the intervention/invention of the historian'. This may not be pernicious sets of lies but every history is, well, just another history. Historical reality, then, may exist where preexisting historical realities once existed and/or a new historical engagement may be filled by a previously nonexistent vacuum of explanation, which is acknowledged and hitherto has not been filled.

So, the situation of factive reality is an effect of the beliefs (and/or denials) of historians. Historians can only create their own historical realities where and when there is a presumed vacuum. Obviously, the ideal situation in engaging with the past for historians is when they discover a hitherto source which suggests there must be 'the revisioning' of the past. Hence, history is a process of rereading, revisiting, reassessing, re-evaluating, reconsidering, and reviewing the nature of all or most extant past historying. Now, for the non-historian the question may arise: why should a more recent factive reality be any better than a previous one? Historical reality is crafted in the situation 'when and where' the historian has decided they have to offer a more recent 'reality effect' of 'again (re-)processing the past'.

Now, we have to acknowledge that the process of 'doing history' is foundational to the constant processing and re-processing of 'the history of . . .'. So, it seems not unreasonable to create new forms of history. After all, why should not have a more recent 'history reality effect' and have a fresh, crisp, and garden-fresh version of the Battle of Waterloo or the ascent of Everest? Now, what is the problem with history then? It is simply that the factive foundation of 'doing history' is just another 'reality effect'. If the historian falls down stairs and breaks their hip, they have a straightforward (hopefully) ten days in hospital and then they get a hip replacement. Ditto with history. The old and faulty historical analysis is extracted and replaced.

Now, some four decades ago a few Anglophone historians had a brief encounter with that Continental invention called postmodernism following the work of the American philosopher Hayden White. I was one of those happy philosophers of history who deconstructed history. History was obviously not a reconstruction because history was invariably and perpetually a deconstruction of the past, as in reconstructing and/or constructing the past as it actually was. However, for the postmodern historian such as me (who wrote several books on deconstructing past reality and co-edited a journal entitled Rethinking History) the certainties of the modernist historians seemed to be a mindless effort. It still is as far as I am concerned.

Anyway, I rejected the notion of 'getting the history narrative straight'. Fortunately, most academic historians continue to sail happily along, dredging the old waters of 'what they see is what want to see'. Hence, the notion of the factive returned around the time that postmodernism started to decline. However, and regardless as to whether historians are happy again, 'past reality' remains what it is—past reality is past reality and language remains language. Now, factive verbs are especially significant to historians whether they realise it or not. Indeed, and arguably, factive verbs are central to what historians do when endeavouring to sort out what probably happened in the past. Historians deploy the factive to denote the state of some past situation. Illustrations of factive verbs include notions such as 'selection', 'determination', 'assignment', 'judge to be', and/or, for example, 'Hitler was a madman' and 'President Trump was for many electors and remains a person of high quality' and your author 'remains unsure as to where the past ends and history starts'.

Unhappily, far too many historians take it as simple common sense that there is a narrative back there in the past which is 'the most likely history of . . .'. Now, I have often deployed the notion of 'the (hi)story' for what I believe is a good reason. However, now it is essential in my view that 'history' is long overdue for its displacement by the emergence of 'historical reality'. But, and this notion is hardly new, far too many historians still have very little grasp on the distinction between the past and history. The reality of the past, then, can only be engaged through the histories that historians create. So, history instead of being the past, it is very long overdue for historians (and again everyone else) to accept the demise (as I have already noted) of the 'the-past-*as*-history'.

The nature of the past is thus a factive hyperreality which can only be accessed via that proffered representation we call history. Now, most historians will—if they have read this far—be extremely upset. Conventionally, historians offer the(ir) available versions of the past but despite that, 'historical reality' is obviously a constant simulacrum. The past is simply the (con)fusion of the past with the historian's chosen (selected and elected) history. The central failing of history is embarrassingly obvious. History is not the past. History, then, is simply a mix of language and the historian's drive to reach their preferred reality effect, which is a factive hyperreality. Obviously, most academic historians—if they have got this far—will reject the consequence of all this.

The truth of the past, then, has to be historied in some form or another. As I have already noted, the past is entirely different to the factive history. Plainly, then, the truth of the past is that it is different and distanced from the historian's histories. Knowing what happened in the past and the reasons for those happenings is entirely the consequence of the historian's choices and decisions. The depthless experience of the past can only be engaged by experiencing the past. But—unfortunately—we cannot experience the past. Nostalgia (in whatever form it comes) is not a re-enactment of the time before our perpetual present.

Now, there is a view that all histories cannot be the same. This is obvious. There would be no point in being taught precisely the same 'past history'. Obviously, in certain intellectual circumstances the past is constantly construed and constrained. But, despite the factitive nature of the past, in most circumstances historians insist that they experience the reality of the past. Hence, the historical experience is an essential part of the anticipated (and hoped for) history. What is all too often a peeved engagement with the past turns out to be the historian's recreating and restyling of the past. Conflating the past with history and history with the past is nonsense in both ontological and epistemological terms.

Now, most historians accept that their job is to engage and discover the nature of the past. Unhappily, language is not up to the job. Indeed, all descriptions of the past ultimately fail. All knowledge is inherently figurative somewhere along the line. Of course, all historians have an 'in-built' inclination to being some sort of scientific engagement with the past. Unhappily, as the philosopher Ludwig Wittgenstein implied, every sentence is a picture of reality. Unfortunately, no historian can see through the past into its history. To be blunt then, historians always fail to engage with the reality of the past. But, if we think about it, all that historians can offer are good, bad, or indifferent (while hopefully obliging) figures of speech.

The persistent foundational failure of history lies in its constancy. This is thanks to the historian's steadfastness in representing the past through their 'historians histories'. Histories, obviously, have very little to do with the past because they are created by historians who insist that their narrative substance is the past. Unfortunately, all histories are dummies, which means that animating the past is an ontological impossibility. The ultimate irony for any historian, then, is the(ir) impossibility of creating a convincing factive history. Now, then, all histories are ultimately—and obviously—deconstructions of the past. No histories last forever. Historians can never adequately reconstruct and/or construct the past. The only certainty a historian can offer is their preferred certainty of a catastrophic/deconstructive failure. The evidence of and for this situation is the constancy that every historian fails. Revisioning, revising, and previsioning that which no longer exists mean accepting the dissolution of all histories. This does not mean not knowing what actually happened in the past. It simply means that historians, along with everyone else, have to accept that the past has very little to do with history.

Now, as I have indicated, most jobbing historians have very little to do with how language hooks onto the world and/or how the world hooks onto the historian's language. And so, epistemology (the study of knowledge and justified belief) is an unavoidable figurative language undertaking. To be clear, however, most historians fail to engage with the most basic element of what they do. By that I mean how the words that most historians use to relate to and inherently describe things in the past usually deploy via figures of speech such as alliteration, assonance, analogy, anaphora, hyperbole, irony, metaphor, metonymy, onomatopoeia, oxymoron, paradox, pun, simile, synecdoche, and several others. Hence, language both allows and permits and eventually demands that historians (and everyone else) must engage with the richness of 'description'. So, the past is the past, however, engaging with the past remains inherently factive, but as we shall see, it is also unavoidably factualist, fictitious, fictive, and figurative.

Now, the foundational and unavoidable problem with history is historical writing. Acquiring the reality of the past demands their preferred self-guided narrative. The writing of 'the-past-*as*-history' is not a major problem. It is not a problem that no historian can resolve. Turning the factive past into a history is hardly complex. The only problem is that jobbing historians fail to acknowledge and understand that eventually all their statements are untrue. Or, to be more accurate, all histories are fundamentally ironic. The logic of this is embarrassingly simple. So, it is hardly difficult to deny past reality but historians still demonstrate an embarrassing ignorance of how they turn the past into history. Engaging with the past is a very simple engagement. All histories like all narratives (real or invented) offer the illusion of a reality whether factive or genuine.

So, the art of the historian is a mimetic faux act. This does not mean they invent and contrive a history for the past for their own pernicious wishes. Of course a few will deliver the past for their own wishes. Now, historians are subject to the content of the past. However, the historical experience is shaped and formed in manner and style, and the factive content of the past is unavoidably derivative in terms of, well, the style, which the historian creates and shapes. Historians do not discover 'past reality', they form, shape, contour, and sustain it. That process is usually (invariably?) called 'the historian's interpretation'. The content of the past then is unavoidably subject to the historian's factive engagements with the time before our perpetual present.

So, content and form is shaped by the historian's individual wants, desires, and aspirations for the past. The notion of the individual historian discovering the reality of the past is at best silly and at worst they believe it. The problem that all historians face is their unavoidable and irresolvable consolation of the(ir) preferred past and which eventually they will insist is the actuality of the past that they prefer. They do this most often not by denying or inventing past reality but by choosing their preferred words through which they (in)vent their judgments as to the nature of the past. Of course, historical writing is as obscure and impervious as any other aesthetic undertaking.

Happily, historians have a very simple intellectual life. The historian seeks out the(ir) sources/evidence which leads them to a (hopefully) hitherto hidden past and then they can debate with their colleagues as to the nature of the past and its (possible/least possible) meaning(s). Now, being a historian is hardly back-breaking work (or mental). Obviously, the past only has an internal reality when the historian has injected it with the history they prefer. This does not mean historians are liars and/or dissemblers but all historians have their own interpretations as to meanings and thus 'historical explanations'. So, the historian's evidence concerning the nature of the past does not carry the historians back to the past (much less the future). The reason for this is because historians create 'the-past-*as*-history' rather than discover it. By that, of course, I do not mean they invent the past.

However, I would suggest it is very long overdue for historians and their consumers to accept that they do not discover the past. Indeed, it is necessary to acknowledge the ontological status of the past as an aesthetic object, which requires historians to accept that the past is not a substitution for the past. To be blunt, then, all historical narratives—paintings, journal articles, lectures, tutorials, and in many other forms—are created and constituted to see through all historical exemplifications. In this chapter I have already—severally—noted that the past is simply irreality, and hence 'doing history' is nothing more than a series of factive cultural expressions of pastness.

The use of a detailed description of the past is a literary device that enables historians to produce and reproduce the varnish of past reality. The past is thus just another example of the reality effect that is created by historians. Conventionally, then, 'historical writing' is deployed to evoke the reality of the past. But when historians endeavour to engage with the 'realist past', all they are doing is offering both an art and illusion. When historians endeavour to offer as close a resemblance to the original past as they can, there is no condition for a realistic interpretation. So, where does the real past come from? All historical realism is entirely relativist because it is historical realism.

Now, the writing of a history has no workable frame of reference as organised and construed by the individual historian (whether they know it or not). So, the past is always and only engaged through the historian's hopeful representation. The past is thus shaped by the historian's intellectual frame. The reality of the past is simply engaged by the historian's preferred history/histories, which always differ in interpretation. All historical interpretations are thus effects that are offered and formed by the historian. All histories demonstrate the pseudo-reality of history. Differentiating the histories provided by historians for the past only exists in interpretations. All histories are freighted with shifts between the extremes of reconstruction and deconstruction. The factive boundary between the history and past reality, that which is usually called history, lurks somewhere.

What this suggests (well, in my view) is that the authenticity of the past is simply an effect that is created by the nature of the historian's historical text construal. Now, the past—the referent—is simply a typescript and a variety of symbols and then the past is simply a construction (and/or a reconstruction or deconstruction if you prefer) upon which historians insist is their preferred view of historical reality. The notion of 'chronological reality' is thus (re)formed and (re)fashioned and which are also inserted between meaningful interpretive significance and the marginal footnote. Moreover, now, the majority of historians have largely refused to move on from their thinking about the past to trying to figure out how the past can be turned into new narratives.

In the now soggy wake of postmodernism, most historians have now returned (straightforwardly) to how they can connect the present with the past. The bodies of knowledge about the past produced by historians together with everything that is involved about the past, again suggests that historical reality has a gap between 'historical reality' and its 'representation'. The disappearance of the brief postmodern engagement has now disappeared. Today, then, historians have returned to the pre-postmodern age when and where historians again believed in past lucid reality. However, even though postmodernism has gone out of fashion, historians remain again happy to believe and insist that the past remains the site of past reality.

7 Factualist

For the substantial majority of historians as well as non-academic consumers, 'the past' and 'history' are assumed to be the same thing. Unfortunately, though, that common sense notion is inappropriately inept. The reason for this odd understanding is because the truth of our perpetual present is revealed in 'authored texts' such as books, TV scripts, lectures, seminars, chats on the bus, and similar. The nature of the past, aka history, is 'attested to' by reference to 'the sources' that are scattered about and then 'selected' by the historian for their attested service to the present. So, all histories and historians are continuously in a discussion and/or debate with other histories and historians. This situation cannot be avoided because there are almost as many varieties of 'historical pasts' as there are historians willing to authorially engage with them. This means historians who may be amateur and professional happily engage with the past through the(ir) process of their 'common sense' notion that 'what we see is what we get'. Unfortunately, that common sense makes no sense of any kind. When we think about history 'the history narrative' is assumed/presumed/anticipated to be back there and which then is awaiting discovery.

This simple common sense is, of course, nonsense. The reason it makes no sense is because the reality of the past—and I have to say 'obviously'—is beyond the limited realm of the historian's forms. The past is shaped, fashioned, and formed through 'the literary', or 'the filmic', or the 'stage theatre', or the 'seminar', or the 'lecture', or the 'speech', or any other representational form of artifice. The upshot of this simple situation, then, is that the past is plainly not history and history is not the past. To avoid this problem, and a problem it certainly is, historians by and large accept that histories are *factualist*, i.e., concerned with the evidentially sustained 'facts'. Historians, then, are simply (yes, it is simple) undertaking their equivalence of history sheepherding. Ironically, then, the historical experience is not a process of discovery because it is a construction and/or deconstruction of the past.

Unfortunately, 'the historical experience' is not a discovery that can be offered as *the* narrative. The fortunate situation in 'doing history' is that the past is highly amenable and elastic to being the processes of being 'discovered', 'shaped', 'formed', and 'designed'. The obvious description for our engagement with the past, then, is that 'histories' are 'events under a description'. Now, and again unfortunately, most historians are constantly surprised to learn that when it comes to writing 'the history of whatever' they begin with the *factualist* dimension of the past. Now, somewhat bizarrely, it has to be quickly admitted that the historian's 'history narrative' can be regarded and accepted to be the 'real narrative of the past for all we can *tell*'. Now, then, the past is what the past was as dressed and arrayed by the individual historian. But, the foundational problem all historians have to cope with is that historians are always endeavouring to change the meaning of the past.

So, the unavoidable and inevitable problem at the heart of all historying is that the historian's presumed narrative is invariably not *the* reality of the past because while it may be delivered given by the available data and sources, all histories are subject to the stress test of aesthetic truth. The belief that the 'empirical past speaks for itself' and 'the truth and nothing but the truth' always emerges is embarrassing nonsense. Historians acknowledge, being very sensible folk by and large, the notion that the delivery of 'the real history narrative' is always subject to various kinds of 'artistic truth', not to mention ideology, dogma, doctrine, and word limits. Now, no matter how diligent, industrious, and hard working, no historian can 'escape into the past' to bring 'the past back again'. Getting the data straight is not very difficult or awkward in many/most instances. But, there is also the problem of 'getting the data straight' and, of course, what 'the past means' is the perennial and permanent problem. There are no 'evidential narrative truths' in the past until historians authorially constitute them as their preferred history descriptions. Histories, then, are measured by the stress test of 'this seems to true in accord with the sources' and then the historian can claim the past gives up its meanings and explanations. Unhappily, (or happily depending on how you read it) the historian's 'stress test' eventually always fails.

Yes, all histories fail. We have the past to argue about, but we always make a mashup of that past we call 'doing history'. While we think that we can probably know the reality of the past given the presently available sources, we always have to cope with the ultimately unknowable pastness. Obviously, all historians (along with everyone else) can never escape their cultural existence, and/or their preferred 'past reality' is the one they presently have. The past always defeats our hopes about history. Hence historians, along with everyone else, can never conquer past reality simply because it changes in and through the minds of historians. This is both fortunate of course and also providential because 'the history' of 'the past' always turns out to be some sort of a workable narrative creation. Happily, however, all histories end up being ontological and epistemological failures. All histories eventually collapse. So, and it is a full-size problem, where exactly does history come from? This is where historians lean on the *factualist* nature of the past.

So, the ultimate stress test for 'doing history' is entirely established and sustained by the historian's own 'historical imagination'. Now, that notion of 'historical imagination' is at once illusory and an imaginary processing of that which no longer exists, which is also presumed to be 'common sense' and formed (and then understood) *as* a composition. Histories, then, always come in many different prefabricated forms. They can be delivered *as* a school essay, or *as* an answer to an examination question, or *as* a novel, or *as* a stage production, or *as* a film, or *as* whatever other form or forms the historian chooses. Thus: you are reading my preferred form now through which I am endeavouring to be '(re-in)formed', '(re)engineered', '(de)constructed', and '(re)compiled' in anyway way I want. Let me be as clear as I can then. The-past-*as*-history is whatever the historian wants it to be and in as many differential forms as the historian desires, and ultimately then their preferred past is—obviously—what they want the past to be whether it is as construed and certified as the individual historian wants.

To be clear, then, historians do not discover the past. That notion is silly, senseless, vain, and pointless. This does not mean I want to get rid of the past. It is, after all, very important that, in our perpetual present, historians must endeavour to reconstitute, reconstruct, construct, or deconstruct a form of and for the past which they choose to believe is the most likely 'past-*as*-history'. But it gets worse. In addition, historians engage with multiple histories that are nothing more than a range of descriptions of 'what happened according to the evidence which the individual historian has selected'. Hence, all histories are incomplete, piecemeal, and predisposed, because the past is nothing more than 'a collection of events under (the historian's preferred) description(s)'. By now, it should be clear that the past—as offered by the historian—is simply the historian's preferred (hi)story. But it has to be clear, of course, that the past can only be experienced as a past. So, the majority of historians sooner or later recognize that their act of 'authoring the history narrative' can be offered in several legitimate forms.

The historical past can and is always incarnated as something that it is not. It is not the past because it is a journal article, or a seminar, or a lecture, or (for the lucky few) a film script, or a stage play, or a book, or a chat with a taxi driver and wherever and/or for whatever desire the historian (or anyone else) wants to create even if they claim it is a discovery. Moreover, and now regardless of the form the historian selects, the history narrative can be legitimately defined as either a 'reconstruction' or a 'construction' or some kind of 'deconstruction' of 'the-past-*as*-history'. Accordingly, each form of 'the history as created' by 'the author-historian' demands and requires interpretational claims on the *factualist* past. So and then, every historian can and usually will insist that they have discovered 'the most likely historical narrative of the . . . whatever'. This claim, of course, is the worst kind of nonsense.

It may seem reasonable, but every history is intentionally designed. Every history is calculated. Every history is planned. Every history is devised. And every history is entirely contrived. The notion of discovering *the* narrative(s) in the past is at best wishful thinking. Indeed, the notion of discovering the history of 'whatever in the past the historian wants to discover' does not mean there may be 'given histories in the past to be found', but still the sole aim in turning the past into a history (hopefully *the* history) necessitates aligning 'the past' with 'its history' in the fond hope that the past and history are the same thing. Happily, then, while there may be just one 'past time' there are always many, many, and many more histories to be constituted by historians. The ultimate irony in all this is that the past is never discovered *as* history. And while this is plainly obvious, most historians (probably all of them) still insist that they efface her or himself from the history they are writing or telling.

Perhaps the most obvious nonsense in the process of turning the past into a history or worse, believing they can discover the reality of the meaning of the past, the past has to be drenched by the historian's preferred reality of the past because they have to (happily?) believe that they can re-enact the past in and through her/his writing (or screen play or in any other form). Now, there is a thought, which far too many historians continue to believe in, that the absolute *ultima thule* situation is that they can efface themselves and thus the past itself offers its own *factualist* self. Hence, historians are somewhat like self-effaced and silent servants who can be called on to sort out a problem in the servant's quarters as required. The latest historical interpretation then comes on a plate. Unfortunately, some of these recent dishes (new histories) are all too often tasteless and/or tactless and even worse thoughtless.

So, in all this, what 'the evidence suggests' is invariably always selected and winnowed by the historian and unsurprisingly every historian prefers her or his narrative(s) of the past. Historians then, always hope their 'historical choice' turns out to be the(ir) preferred history and not 'another historian's history'. Ironically then, and this is seriously incongruous and ironic if not absurd, all 'historying' starts out as 'a *factualist* process' of imaginative construal. Although the data from and of the past is what the historian discovers and then chooses to deploy in their history(ies), the deeply ironic act of 'doing history' remains a *factualist* process of imaginative construal. Historians then, never fully discover the emplotment of the(ir) history. Historians, thus, research the past in order to turn the past into a history, rather than the vice versa of turning history into the past. Of course it is never quite that simple. Historians herd and quite often they all fall over the same cliff.

Historians, of course, devote a substantial investment of their time in terms of 'being objective' in their defence of their *factualist* undertaking.

This notion usually means not only that the historian's evidence/sources support their theories and explanations but also that there is no possible room for a contrary analysis as to the reality of the past and what it meant. Unhappily, every historian has a position (political, gendered, economic, and so on) on just about everything when it comes to the *factualist* meanings and explanations as to the attested environment of the past. Now, there is a serious problem that all historians (like everyone else) have and which they cannot avoid.

Now, what I have just described is a process that is dependent on two foundational philosophical concepts. They are those of epistemology and ontology. Epistemology concerns the process of knowledge acquisition through the discovery of 'the evidence' via the sources that are assumed to refer to and validate the 'ontological reality content' of past events. Processing this is the 'nature', 'form', 'procedures', and 'methods' that yield the nature of the nature of 'history as a reference to past reality'. The notion of 'discovering the history' of the past is nonsense of course because history is an act of authorship. Getting the data straight has very little to do with authoring 'the history' and with which there is a very well known problem. This is the processing or turning of 'the past' into 'history' and, of course, its degree of complexity is measured by the extent to which the past *is* history and history *is* the past. That problem, of course, is impossible to resolve.

The implication of this apparent 'applied common sense' then, is the central feature of the *factualist* in all histories. Unhappily, there is a depthless irony in the deployment of the *factualist* past because while history is (in a common sense fashion) assumed to be a 'meaningful *factualist* message from the past' it actually remains only the historian's narrative account of that message from the past. So, 'the history' or 'any history' is never more nor less than an act of irony in that 'the *factualist* past construal' can only have its own narrative existence when it is supplied by the historian. To be plain then: the past is not history and history is not the past. While each element connects with each other, neither is interchangeable. Obviously then, the *factualist* nature of the past then is plainly concerned with facts. However, there is a serious and awkward problem in connecting the past with history and *vice versa* and there is a real problem with 'the past' and that is 'history'.

History, then, is obviously 'authorially created'. And so it is not surprising that there are always lots of different versions of 'history' or 'histories', which are 'made' available. Now, the foundational problem with 'the past' and 'history' is obviously that there is presumed to be just one 'past reality'. But that is plainly nonsense. Just pick up a history text on the same subject. In ontic terms (in respect of existence) there can only be one past reality but—as we are aware—there can be and there are many different versions of 'the past'. The evidence for 'this past' claim is readily available in the debates between historians. Now, the perpetual difficulty with history is its subjectivity and that generates many histories. While historians try to be 'objective in their engagement with the past' they cannot be objective with history. To be very clear again, history is not the past and the past is not history. In engaging with the past then, there are substantial quantities of 'historical unavoidable problems'. In engaging with the past, historians are unavoidably subject to their 'predispositions', 'prejudgments', 'preconceptions', 'partialities', and their preferred 'penchants' in 'doing history'. Without historical bias, of course, we would only have one (the historical) past. Now, and of course, historians do not occupy a position-less situation just like every other human being when it comes to the past.

Now, then, I suggest the historian's understanding of the evidence of 'the past' remains as a fairly unproblematic act of 'finding out the data' and turning it into a 'sensible narrative description' is simple. Happily, the essentials of 'doing history' (aka historying) are disconcertingly straightforward. The 'uncovering of the *factualist* evidence' thus produces an interpretation of the most likely meaning of that evidence. This conclusion is then turned out to be either the most convenient and/or unfortunately the most awkward representation of 'the history narrative'. The history narrative, then, is what results from the historian's individual or occasionally collective authorial engagement with the attested events of the past. Nevertheless, it can be impossible to know if any (or all) histories as authored by the historian are 'in reality' the most likely (hi)story back there and then. However, and happily for historians, 'getting the data straight' is a largely guileless undertaking in that they select the data that fits their 'preferred judgments' and the only serious problem is 'figuring out' aka 'interpreting' what the past meant or what it could mean. Happily, given the nature of history as a *factualist* and interpretative undertaking, historians are happily 'required' to both address and infer the form and function of 'their authorship' as much as the past can be. The key problem in doing history, then, is figuring out the 'sensible historical meanings and explanations' that seem appropriate for the past as the historian.

In the process of 'doing history', then, it is usually anticipated and expected that historians infer the most likely meaning of past events. This is obviously useful but most often purposeless given that historians deploy their *factualist* imagination as they make the effort to construe the meanings of past events. The historian, along with everyone else, invariably employs the simple imagined 'counterfactual'. The 'historical imagination', then, offers an interpretation and/or construal and/or analysis of what is a rendering of the available evidence, which thereby enables the reasonable and sensible most likely 'historical' meaning. Consequently, the reference to the 'historical sources' is expected to be the groundwork of both the 'suspected' and the ideally 'preferred' history. Now, historians quite often want to rethink the past by linking and juxtaposing sources insisting that 'the past now most likely (hi)story'. However, this simple practice increases the inevitable glitches concerning the 'practical common sense' belief that 'the past' and 'history' must be the same thing. This, of course, is nonsense. Histories can be reflections *on* the past but they cannot be conflated with *the* past.

However, there is an extremely awkward problem with rethinking the nature of 'the-past-*as*-history'. This is the notion of the 'historical fact' alternatively known as the *factualist* certainty. The reason for this awkward and embarrassing if simple problem is because all *factualist*, i.e., 'historical facts' are merely 'events under a description' of yet 'another historical fact' of yet 'another historical fact' and so on. Happily or unhappily if you don't like a particular 'historical fact' or 'facts' which slip from the tongue or into the book of another historian, you can create your own 'historical facts' fashioned from scratch. Facts, then, are usually 'redefined' as 'fresh descriptions of the past' and/or the other way around. Understandably, and one way or the other, 'historical facts' (events under descriptions) are sustained by a consensus (even if only by a few historians) until that particular consensus collapses as—of course—they eventually do. Plainly, all of this is very useful for historians. Most historians and probably everyone else take certain 'useful descriptions of events' as being 'convenient facts'. However, to be useful, a 'historical fact' has to have the weight of a consensus behind it. Nonetheless, and when brought down to basics, a historical truth is a matter of the correspondence between a description and (yet another) set of verifiable facts.

Possibly, the historian most associated with the concept of the *factualist* 'historical facts school' was Leopold von Ranke (1795–1886). Ranke was determined in his effort to make history 'empiricist-scientific-objective' and the legacy of his desire remains today with 'social science history'. Hence, 'historical facts' have to be supported by 'the evidence'. Now, and as I have suggested interminably in many other books apart from this, 'history' is a 'narrative making' activity. What follows is that the nature of 'historying' is permanently subject to the constraints of those authorial literary forms I have already referred to in the first three chapters of this book. Every historian, like every other human being, runs the gamut of 'factualist explanations' as to the nature of 'the past' and, of course, the historian inevitably turns not into 'a history' but is 'the history'. Subsequently, then, the really awkward problem with 'doing history' is 'interpreting the nature of the past' by 'getting the (hi)story straight' which sustains 'doing history'. As I have suggested, then, the meaning and/or explanation of the past simply depends on the historian's preferred interpretation(s). Unhappily and awkwardly, discovering 'the real meaning and/or understanding of the past' is impossible.

Now, this is very awkward especially for trainee historians and, of course, the established employee historian who just tends to ignore it (and simply take the pay). Nevertheless, 'the historical explanation' cannot be avoided eventually. Now, and understandably, without a history our culture would collapse. It would break down because without a permanent engagement with the past we would never be able to connect time and place. Now—for good or ill—history is not a science. It is true that historians endeavour to 'find out' what happened in the past and this notion is assisted by varieties of 'social science' mediations. History, then, is that 'academic discipline' which enables historians (and especially social science historians) to engage with 'the-past-*as*-history'. Now, without that connection all we would have is a very unstable past. A rickety past is the worst kind of historying. But then, history has always been/being reimagined, rethought, reconsidered, and reorganised and is still wobbly. This happens every generation or so.

Consequently, then, if historians fail to ignore the *factualist* bedrock of 'doing history' and very rarely do they want to escape it, neither can they circumvent the deployment of the(ir) 'historical imagination' which, of course, is an artificial, i.e., *factualist* creation. Unhappily and obviously, historians have to accept that a 'history' is not that to which it refers. In one sense this is understandable given that histories, whether they are literary or some other sort of text, permits historians to 'imagine', 'evoke', 'infer', and 'surmise' in terms of 'this' and 'that' and 'so forth' about the possibilities in 'the-past-*as*-history'. Nevertheless, while facts and the *factualist* 'events under a description' are the bread and butter of 'doing history', ironically, the past has very little to do with history and much more to do with the historian. Hence, there are as many different pasts along with their meanings as there are explanations.

Now, engaging with 'a *factualist* historical explanation and representation' is as easy or as hard as the historian wants it to be. Obviously, then, most historians choose what *they* think is probably sensible at least for them given their preferred engagement with the past. As I have already noted, and fortunately for historians, the nature of 'the representation of the historical' is no more nor less than a 'narrative symbolic representation' that is invariably plucked from the recesses of the historian's mind. Now and nevertheless, the foundational problem in 'doing history', and which cannot be removed and/or denied, is that 'historical theory' is 'stiffened' by appropriately quantities of the *factualist*.

Now, and all too often, the nature of the *factualist* 'facts' is simply 'events under a description'. Thus, the founding phenomenology of history is, simply, the recognition that the past is no longer the 'real object' of doing history. The reality of the past is what the historian injects into 'the processing of the past' when they endeavour to engage with the past. Disarming the past then leaves us with a very serious problem with the concept of the *factualist*. Turning the process of 'past reality' into a *factualist* understanding of the past is extremely difficult. The phenomenology of historical experience is, arguably, the most significant feature of 'doing history' with its study of structures of experience and consciousness. Now, most academic historians would leave well alone at this point. Now, and unavoidably, the distinction between 'fact' and 'theory' is always compromised, as they cannot exist without each other. Anyway, the nature of a 'historical description' *aka* a representation of what the historian wishes to engage with, is obviously defined by 'the facts' that are the structures which shape and form the reality of the past as the historian 'sees the past'.

Unfortunately, 'the facts' are simply events under a description (as I noted before). Hence, 'the history text', and whether historians like it or not, the meaning of the past is never the same because all histories are always events under descriptions. Hence, the past is always changing. This, then, is perhaps the central tragedy all historians have to deal with. Now, and unfortunately, most historians are earnestly and sincerely naïve in that they wrongly assume that 'by writing about the attested (evidential) past' they can establish 'what actually happened in the past and what it most probably meant'. But unfortunately their accounts of the past will present them and their consumers with (more or less) non-copies of what actually happened in the time before our perpetual now. Historians like to believe they are realists but—unfortunately—there is no commensurability between the past and history and *vice versa*. Hence, the myriad concepts deployed by historians to assist them in 'figuring out what happened in the past and what it might possibly/probability meant' usually cannot make sense. But, then, that is not the historian's problem. Like every other human being all historians are constant in believing they can access the past 'for what it actually was' even though that belief makes no sense of any possible kind.

Many (most?) historians will not agree with my analysis, which is a phenomenological study and through which I approach the frameworks of 'awareness' as experienced from the historian's first-person point of view. Now, when historians want to save their preferred historical analysis on which they may have expended substantial amounts of time and effort, they endeavour to seek out 'content' and 'meaning' and which then almost certainly may also mean they have to cover 'ethics', 'agent intentionality', appropriate 'logics', 'ontology', 'consciousness', 'epistemology', and the 'philosophy of mind'. Now, and again, most historians will pass over my list for engaging with the simple *factualist*.

What historians can do and most of them make a very good job of it, is shifting between kaleidoscopes of conceivable and promising *factualist* historical representations. This enables them in turn to constantly revise the past by 'finding' new sources/data, which leads to new fresh 'interpretation avalanches'. The unending fear in the historian's mind is, of course, the thought and, what is possibly worse, the reality of running out of sources that will further endorse their pet/preferred (and ironically fresh) interpretations as to meaning and explanation. Happily, however, there is very little horror lurking at the heart of 'doing history' as long as historians can and continue and constitute fresh 'slants' on the one time new history. But this fear is hardly a problem as there is no worry about running out of 'the stuff' that supports and generates constant avalanches of 'fresh virgin pasts'.

Now, there is another useful *factualist* inspired situation, which is of immense help for historians who are always made well aware of it early in their careers. It is that there is no shortage of the 'empirical past', which can be 'turned into fresh history'. To my knowledge, no historian has ever lost the ability to reconstruct and/or construct and/or deconstruct the past. The mechanism for this 'flow of historying' emanates from a very fortunate situation. This is that the historian's representations of 'events under accounts' which they have created (discovered?). However and happily, their representations are always 'authorially guided', 'nurtured with care', 'generously attended to', and 'carefully steered' in the effort to recoup the (hopefully) hitherto unknown reality of the past.

Now, and unhappily, history will not offer up its nature to the historian 'to discover and narrate into some sort of past reality'. Clearly, then, 'historical writing' is created to offer a 'historical meaning'. Unhappily, of course, it cannot offer up the 'correspondence truth', which historians and everyone else always hope for. Now, then, the serious and ironic problem that all historians have along with their consumers are that they believe they have *discovered* the relationship which *they* believe they have found between *the* past and *their* history. This means that, along with everyone else, historians are forced to accept that the past is nothing more than 'the-past-*as*-history'. Thus: although 'the history representation' is sensibly presumed to have a *factualist* basis, the truth of the past can only exist in the process of authoring a history.

Now, and as I have already noted, we have again come across (what is possibly?) the single and most problematic situation all historians eventually have to face. What most academic historians and amateurs alike have to deal with is the phenomenology of the historical experience. Happily, all historians manage to engage with the past without engaging with the concept of phenomenology. Phenomenology is commonly understood in either of two ways: as a disciplinary field in philosophy or as a movement in the history of philosophy. Now, then, for most historians the concept of phenomenology is almost certainly unwelcome and almost certainly pointless in their pursuit of the nature of 'the history of the past'. Hence, then, history is a discipline the function of which is to 'discover the most likely *factualist* (hi)story of the past'.

Unhappily, of course, the notion of a phenomenology of 'the historical experience' is going to make most jobbing historians unhappy, worried, anxious, and fretful. And, of course, they should be unhappy, worried, anxious, and fretful when they come across several other associated concepts of 'history aesthetics' and the 'artistic truth of past reality'. The discipline of phenomenology, then, is the study of constructions of 'experience' or 'realisation' such as history, which was once real and now is transmuted into a past reality (by the historian and then the publisher and finally the student). Literally, then, phenomenology is the study of phenomena such as the 'appearances of past things', or 'things as they appear in our past experience'. Moreover, history is always experienced and offered from the idiosyncratic or first-person point of view. Most historians, then, veer away from concepts like ontology which is the study of 'being' or what 'is', and then they may also feel queasy when other unpleasant concepts and notions such as epistemology (study of knowledge), logic (study of reasoning), ethics (study of right and wrong), and possibly worse of all, what the publisher will think when they are not really sure that the book will sell.

The historical movement of phenomenology is that philosophical/metaphysical tradition that was launched in the first half of the twentieth century by theorists such as Jean-Paul Sartre, Maurice Merleau-Ponty, Edmund Husserl, and Martin Heidegger.

However, Anglophone-American historians (by and large) endeavoured to escape from what was generally regarded as tainted and bizarre Continental thinking. And so, phenomenology studies—engaging with structures of conscious experience as experienced from the first-person point of view—never caught on in the Anglophone intellectual world. And the result of this was the fear that 'past *factualist* reality' would simply disappear among shrouds of incense(d) Continental thinking.

Anyway, phenomenology developed a multifaceted account of temporal awareness in the forms of stream of consciousness, perception awareness of one's own self experience (self-consciousness, in one sense), kinaesthetic cognisance, the sentience of other persons, meanings, language, communication, and social and cultural interaction, intentionality, embodiment, bodily skills, and thus phenomenology lead into conscious experience and further understandings of our experience. Happily or unhappily as you read it, 'the-past-*as*-history' became a form of hyperreality. Now, for most 'straight historians' the notions of phenomenology and postmodernism were once nonsenses. The best that historians again can offer is now yet again simply 'telling it like it was'. Now, once again defending the notion of 'the *factualist*' in doing history was all historians once again had to know was the (re)presentation of the past as it was in accord with the available data again. The postmodern 'effort to offer' a (re)presentation of the past meant that the truth of the past was never straightforward. So, the past is no longer the 'real thing'. However, for 'proper historians', i.e., non-postmodernists, all was back in kilter (order was restored).

Happily, for 'straight' historians, the notion of *the* historical experience as it was in the past 'was today' getting back into its stride and the past was returned to being the past and history was past. Unhappily, despite the return to 'the history of the past', history remains a seriously whimsical past and whether most historians like it or not, history is history and the past is the past. The past, then, remains the 'real object' of the aim of historians. But, there is no denying that the past is 'the past' and 'history' is still at best a construction and/or a deconstruction which is a reified past. Brought down to earth, then, history is never to be found in the past. It only comes from the historian. This, of course, is embarrassingly obvious given that most historians are clear in their certificated belief that they have reconstituted the past they believe they have revealed as a *factualist* figure that is wrapped up as a 'narrativist piece of the past'.

While most historians rarely think about the phenomenology of what they do, i.e., describing the past as it is (was?). This process is in accord with the present available past, which, of course, is assumed to be 'simply awaiting its realisation' it is 'conceived' in their/our contemporaneous existence. Now, and obviously, the residue and detritus of the past has at some point, to be 'made *factualist*'. The facts of the past are, of course, largely useless to historians because the object of the past of 'historical experience' is, at best, the evidence that the past has left to us but not the past itself. And, of course, in this (actually rather simple process), the historian's constant engagement with the past is simply those bits and pieces of the past that the historian believes to be useful to their preferred and pet analysis but which, and understandably, is not the past itself.

Now, when engaging with the phenomenology of the historical experience, it opens up the very awkward situation—and which I briefly suggested previously—that the past is not history and history is not the past. No matter how *factualist* 'the historian's history' is claimed to be the reality of the past, the historian's evidential experience of the past can only offer the(ir) presumed reality of the past and for whatever reasons they want. Hence, for all the engagement of the nostalgic past, it cannot be argued to be a re-enactment of *the* past. Whether historians like it or not, then, no amount of nostalgia can reconstruct the past as it probably was. Hence, those historians who want to engage with the past 'as it actually was' are whistling down the wind. Knowing what actually happened in the past does not carry within it the past. Obviously, what happened in the past unavoidably casts its shadows on our perpetual past. However, that perpetual past is always with us in our constant present for us to use or forget, as we deem right.

Now, then, in our 'perpetual *factualist* present', for all historians, along with everyone else whether they know it or not, the nature of our historical experience is our choice as we prefer shaped as a reconstruction, construction, and/or deconstruction or some kind of mix. In expressing the nature of the past, every historian creates and constitutes the past, as they believe it was like. And there is the nub and absolute failure of the problem of history. As I have already noted, the past is not the past and the history is simply just another history. This does not mean all historians tell lies, but they are often close to 'defamations' and 'smears' of historical actors by historians. This where historians invariably offer their experience of the(ir) past. Now, this situation is the nub of the ultimate failure of all historians, which includes me as well. Turning 'past reality' into 'a history narrative' or what is far more likely 'several many different history narratives' is the process of 'rethinking history' and that means the notion of 'historical interpretation(s)'.

Now, all historians have the identical problem with the *factualist* past and the same difficulty with (hi)story. If there is one primary problem with 'doing history' it is that historians experience the reality of the unreality of the past. This sounds dangerous and it is. No single history can experience the unreality of the experience of the unreality of reality. This somewhat awkward situation is always manifested in the historian's nostalgia for the past as they like it. Or want it. Or desire it. Or demand it. Or believe it. And this is where the *factualist* past is all that the historian can offer to her/his colleagues who (sooner or later) will be forced to stab them in the intellectual back with a new interpretation. Eventually, at some point, historical interpretation will always wreck (or make for a while) a career. It is the nature of historians, then to collapse into the black hole that is always history.

The deathless certainty that awaits all historians (yes, all of them including your author, and also, you dear reader) is to be told in a book revue or lecture or chat over a dinner at a conference is that you just 'got it wrong'. But, now, at this point I recommend that every historian reading this book should recognise that they all fetishise the past *as* their preferred emplotment narrative—tragic, comedic, romance, and comedy. At this point I strongly recommend Hayden White's (infamous) analysis of the historical imagination *Metahistory* (1973) and the ways that he suggested individual historians create their histories through their rhetorical language.

Now, most historians today just as they have for the past couple of centuries and to do it today (wilfully), the past is history thanks to their authorial expertise, knowledge, comprehension, conceptualisation and usually fall in with the publisher. But yet, while the essence of doing history remains the garnering of appropriate data and collating it and then the past—obviously—becomes the realistic *factualist* past and which can then be regarded as 'the history of . . .'. In this chapter I have already engaged with the concept of epistemology while most academic historians see very little reason to engage with that central philosophical concept. But at this juncture it is necessary again to note briefly its nature again for one particular reason.

While I have briefly already noted the significance of the concept of epistemology to 'doing history', most jobbing historians still see no point in engaging with it. Nevertheless, it is indisputably necessary for historians because epistemology is foundational if historians wish to investigate the problem of how 'language' hooks onto the world so we can possess reliable knowledge of the past (as well as the future). Now, epistemology is the theory of knowledge and particularly in terms of engaging with justified belief, judgment, and opinion. Now, for most historians (and probably everyone else) all epistemology is innately figurative. Thus, if I offer a metaphor and/or a simile and/or a symbol to describe 'some thing' then you, my reader, and I understand how reality and language work together. To be clear then, and ironically, the *factualist* can only be demonstrated through both language and science (equations for example). Ultimately, then, the past is always subject to language and science through both the scientific and the linguistic together.

Now, today, scientists still insist that figurative language is a perversion. But there is a bridge—it is called history. Hence, every history is a protracted figure of speech in which a word or phrase or chapter is linguistically applied to a past object or action to which it is not literally applicable. The ultimate failure of history emerges, then, when historians (and everyone else) have to eventually ask of themselves who and/or what makes a historical text possible? So, what makes this text you are now reading of any utility? Presumably, what makes the historical text possible is because the historian has turned the past into a narrative? The historian can claim that they found *the* narrative but it is only the author-historian's narrative. So, just what is it that makes the historical typescript possible?

So, it is the authorial efforts of the historian that makes the historical text rather than its 'historical' *factualist* nature. Thus, acquiring the reality of the past is straightforward through the historian's creating and processing of their historical experience. Now, and obviously, the past cannot speak for itself even if too many historians insist they have discovered the reality of the past's history, when it is actually the historian's history. Now this notion is ridiculous because all histories are the deconstructions of the historian's apparently *factualist* reconstruction. Thus, all histories, like everything else that human beings inscribe as 'reality past', they see it as they see it. This means that the significance of the past is entirely in the hands and minds of authors, let alone historians. The notion that the past speaks for itself, then, is nonsense. And, further, this is why for every history there are multiple pasts, which are entirely subject to the authorial impress of the historian. Now, then, the unfortunate thing in all this is that every history is 'made up' through the historian's construed contextual historicality, i.e., *the* reality of the past is never agreed upon between the hardest of hardhat historians.

Now, and obviously, historical thinking is entirely subject to its own account through the individual historians sense of their historicity and by that historicity I mean the inherent reality of the past. This means that there are always multiple 'pasts' even if only in small details especially thanks to individual historians in terms of their inferences, connotations, references, meanings, implications, denotations, and so forth. Thus, all histories have their own historicality—their nature as inherent past narratives recreated as and by historians whether sitting on a bus, busking, or acquiring prizes for skating which, of course, might be their history of ice skating. Perhaps the most obvious element in engaging with the past is the historian's impulse to turn the past into a history and/or multiple histories (to be clearer) through their 'historicisations' by which they 'turn the past' into their preferred histories.

Thus, all histories are unavoidably reconstructed and/or constructed and/or deconstructed by the historian in some way or another. This makes a nonsense of deploying metaphor as a comparison and/or symbolism and/or representation and allegory through which 'the past' is made to be 'history' by the historian. History, then, is simply a series of figures of speech in which expressions or phrases are deployed to either construe the reality of the past as an 'object' or an 'action' to which it is not literally applicable. Plainly, then, the logic behind 'doing history' is to accept that the past is certainly not history despite the efforts of virtually every one academic historian.

Now, then, the reification of 'the time before' *as* 'history' is obviously very, very silly. History is history and the past is the past or and/or history is a figure of speech in which an apparent contradiction is presumed to make *factualist* sense. As a *factualist* situation, then, the conjoining of the past with history and history with the past is simply an authorial indulgence. So, and unavoidably, 'historying' makes no sense. It is similar to the notion of long shadows at noon. In their efforts to experience and recoup the past, historians have to transmute the past into a series of differential histories. Thus, to experience the nostalgic past means accepting that the past is always beyond the past while historians insist that there is always a possibility of going back to 'the future of the past' or 'the past before the future'.

The depth of the conflation of 'the past' with 'history' among historians, who thus maintain the notion that history must be the past and the past must be history, sustains the bizarre belief in the notion of the historical representation of the past. Now, the past is formed and/or hypothesised by all historians, trained as they are. In most circumstances this training does relatively little harm because historians are sustained by the belief that history is the past and past is history. While this seems straightforward, all there is for anyone who wishes to engage with the past means creating a historical representation in pursuit of the past.

What this means is those historians, who usually engage with 'past reality', write history that emerges from the view of the *factualist* rather than the view of aesthetics. While for very few historians, the matter of representation in 'doing history' is and remains somewhere down the list of essentials when they turn the past into a history. To be blunt, then, historians today engage with the past in terms of the criticism of previous (re)thinking. A 'breakthrough', a new *factualist* analysis of the past, has also always needed a creative independent mind, while every historian living in the data sources also has to have some sense of the poeticisation of the past. History is a narrative but to be good and largely blameless, the empirical data has to be offered in the form of a poeticisation. Loads of 'statistics and facts' and offerings of 'likely meanings and explanations' will never (re)produce the past. But then, of course, there is no means to revivify the past as it actually was.

Now, in respect of all histories, denotation is at the heart. However, and unfortunately, all historical representations are at best vague in every respect. So, all histories are simply mere linguistic symbols (representations) for what the historian wants to embody after they have sieved through the *factualist* detritus of the past. Only the dimmest of historians will insist that their historical representation is nothing more than a mere symbol for what the historian wants to represent. Now, no history can seriously claim that a representation of the American President George Washington is George Washington. Like all histories, then, all histories are fabricated representations. Every history is just another dummy version of the past.

Thus, like all *factualist* representations, histories are aesthetic demonstrations and depictions of what they ought to be what they were. All *factualist* histories as exercises in *mimesis* are what they are and not what they are presumed to be. All histories, like all representations, are (f)acts of aesthesis and artistic endeavours. So, all histories are more and/or less than they are. All histories, then, are substitutes for past (historical) reality. Historians have a very serious problem (among many others) when it comes to differentiating between the innocent eye and the given absolute. Now, what this adds up to (sort of) is the historian's individual preferred interpretation *as* shaped and formed via ideology, gender, spatial location, publisher's insistence that the contract will be foreclosed if the historian hangs about, and so on and forth. History, then, as an interpretative processing of the past, can only give us 'as illusions of a reality that cannot be again engaged? History, then, is not the past, indeed, it is not even a weak and glassy-eyed version of the past.

History then is no more than an insubstantial substitute for the past. But, of course, it is all we have and that, of course, is merely an aesthetic representation. To be clear then at this point: something in the past is 'genuine' when it satisfies historical representations, which are regularly demonstrated, when more than one historian 'proves' the ontological and epistemological nature and status of their engagement with the past. It is at this juncture that the smart historian manages to offer what they believe to be the attested and most likely *narrative substance* aka 'historical narrative'. The bad news (again) with the narratives created by historians is that historians create them. So, which is the representation of Napoleon—the tomb or the book on his life that takes a year to read? Well, neither I suspect, because both are differentially created *factualist* representations. Just like all histories, then, I have suggested that the *factualist* dimension to history meets much less than the eye suggests.

8   Fictitious

Unfortunately, and by accident, while writing this book the present American President has deployed the concept of 'fake news'. Now, this is entirely coincidental and has nothing to do with my writing of this book. However, the concept of the adjective fictitious summarises the situation of the now 'fake' and 'non-reality' of the past and the tried present. And so, the only way to conflate 'the past' with its presumed 'history' is to deploy the well-known process of 'discovering the history of the past according to the individual historian'. However, this widespread notion deployed by historians (and all too often everyone else) makes very little sense. However, the really bad news for historians is that when engaging with the past they cannot avoid their 'historical imagination'. This concept of the 'historical imagination' means the historian's (or anyone else's) interpretation through to 'the explanation of whatever the historian wants to engage with'. To be clear then: the past is the past and history is *fictitious*.

Obviously, histories are those fictitious narratives constituted and offered by historians along with, well, everyone else. Hence, I have written this book to point out the aestheticised nature of how historians construe the nature of the past through their authorial engagement, which is called history as I have suggested. Plainly, then, the past requires histories in terms of the key concepts I am offering in this book. Now, as I said at the start of this chapter, those historians who read this book will, in all probability, have been somewhat worried by now, to be told (by me) that when they write 'their history book or journal article or read from their lecture notes' what they are offering is fictitious. Normally, of course, the concept of the fictitious is defined as that which is an invention and/or untrue. So, the thought of buying a history book or watching a TV documentary or sitting and listening through a seminar or lecture is a fictitious undertaking.

Now, dear reader, I expended two decades from 1997 to 2017 as one of the editors of the journal Rethinking History. This journal created a space for—literally—rethinking the nature of history and its relationship with the past. This 'rethinking' undertaking challenged in many different ways engaging with the past by deploying innovative and creative forms of experimental meetings with the past. Anyway, the brief 'postmodern condition' with which far too many historians failed to engage meant that a minority of historians accepted incredulity toward 'metanarratives'. By that, (in my view) was meant not to accept any narrative that confronted not simply 'the content' but also the rethinking of 'the form' and thus the nature of 'doing history'. Hence, rescuing and resuscitating the most likely narrative from the past achieved turning the past into the most likely history.

The nature of the historian's engagement with the past, then, was undertaken through a revivified 'historying process' through which the past as one might imagine certainly does not extinguish the variety of engaging with the past. Thus, today, the central relationship between the *'factualist'* and the *'fictitious'* is certainly less worrying than it might be if only because the vast majority of historians (and their readers) have no understanding of not just those two concepts but also their highly complex relationship. Now, and of course, most historians are comfortable with the notion of the factualist but not the *fictitious*. For the majority of historians the concept of the fictitious does not exist in their vocabulary. This is because the concept of the fictitious means 'invented', 'not true', or 'non-existent'. Plainly, then, most paid up historians do not need to come to terms with this concept because the fictitious is assumed to be in the same camp as 'pretense' and 'sham' and historians have very little use for those concepts.

Now, and happily for most academic historians, they continue to insist that all 'historical representations of the past' are not just a 'historical representation of the past' but they can bring history to life. That notion is nonsense of course given that 'the past' is not 'history' and 'history' is not 'the past'. The past and history exist in entirely different ontic and epistemic universes. Conflating the past with history for most historians and their (far too many) unthinking consumers, the concept of the fictitious has no function. But this is both an ontic and epistemic error of substantial size. Or, to be clear then, it is one of the most stilly foundational beliefs of and in 'doing history'. Historians then, both 'deny' and 'dismiss' any and all forms, which they insist 'misrepresent the past'. Surely, this must be simply common sense? Unfortunately, it is not simple and certainly it is not common sense.

The reason for this is that history is a language construal and that means we cannot ignore the aesthetics—the fictitious nature—of the historian's use of common sense language. Hence, historians can only access their chosen past through their 'designed and created aesthetic representation' of the past. The past, then, does not supply its own history in the form of a discovery or accessing that, which has hitherto never been scaled. All histories, then, are what the historian creates in terms of 'the(ir) deployment of 'the(ir) historical imagination'. Without 'the(ir) historical imagination' historians would be left with the deployment of the 'mirror effect' that sustains what they process of 'the-past-*as*-history'. Unfortunately, the process of 'historying the past' is not that of a discovery. Plainly, much knowledge can be discovered in an archive, but when defined as 'a discovery' the historian's representation of the past is simply their formation and composition.

All historying then, is a very simple fictitious process of writing as a play, or as a film, or as a history documentary, or as a news programme, or as a history textbook, and so forth. Somewhat awkwardly, however, engaging with the past always—yes always—fails to recognise the nature of history as a representation which is construed and understood as that mechanism through which everyone (including historians) (re)create the past. So far so good, but unhappily, and to repeat, what the vast majority of historians fail to acknowledge is that 'the past' is not a 'history' and 'a history' is not 'the past'. What this means is that historians (like everyone else) have to cope with the slippery but very 'common sense' belief that each and every 'past period of time' or 'epoch' or 'age' or 'past place' has its own peculiar nature because it is always 'a narrative authorial creation' even if it is claimed to be at one time the reality of the past.

So, surgeons can 'save patients' and airline pilots can 'land planes' safely and even politicians can 'put things right'. But, historians do not have the ability to discover and save is the(ir) possession of the past. The best that historians can do is to offer their 'preferred history narrative'. But, and unfortunately, the best most historians can do is offer their *fictitious* 'history territories of knowledge'. Hence, all historians are destined to collapse into a process of 're-describing' or 'redefining' or 'further explaining' or 'rethinking the nature of 'the-past-*as*-history'. This does not mean inventing or reinventing the past because the notion of the fictitious is rarely openly deployed by historians engaged in and with their presumed 'historical reality of the past'.

But, what kind of engagement with the past would there be, if there was no fictitious disposition among historians whether they know it or not? The logic, then, of what historians do is embarrassingly simple. Historians, along with their consumers, expect to deal with 'the real past' through 'the factual'. Unfortunately, that belief is desperately embarrassing. It is nonsense. All we have is 'history' because the past no longer exists to be constituted sustained by the carapace of 'times gone'. Or, if you prefer, and more accurately perhaps, all we have and all we can have in engaging with the past is the invention of fictitious historying. Every history, then, is not what it purports to be. By that I do not mean historians can elect to describe the past just as they want it to have been. The short or long story of 'a history' is not the same as the past and, obviously, the past is not the same as history.

So, what is the reality of a history if it is not the same as the past? Well, to start with historians can only engage with the past through the(ir)

Fictitious 135

deployment of their fictitious 'historical imaginations'. Even though historians insist that their histories are facsimiles and/or duplicates and/or reproductions that notion makes no sense. In engaging with the past all that historians can hope for are the historian's narrative interpretations of the past. Thus, when historians talk about the Second World War or the Renaissance or the presidency of Donald Trump there is always a 'looseness' or 'indeterminacy' between 'past reality' and 'history'. The depthless irony that all historians have to live with is that the historical narrative is the only reality. The past is the past and history is our authored claim to be, well, the past. To be blunt: the past is the past and history is history and there is no epistemic or ontic connection. This notion may seem odd, but the only reality in doing history is the historian's authorial intervention.

Now, if we accept this argument (and the substantial of historians will not of course) history is little more than a fictitious 'reality effect'. Accordingly, the concept of the fictitious, which at first blush seems to have no useful role in 'doing history' is, arguably, the foundational feature of 'doing history'. When engaging with the past the substantial majority of historians entirely fail to acknowledge the role of their mediation in the process of turning the past into a history and invariably, at some point, rejecting a history they dislike. History, then, should never to regarded as the same as the attested past because it is an 'authorial inert mirror' of the past. The past, then, comes to us all only through our historying. In 'processing history', then, we have to both acknowledge and accept that the historical narrative has its own substance. 'The past' is 'the past' while history is, well, a shadowy reality effect of 'the history of whatever the historian wants to deploy'. This does not mean our grasp on the attested reality of the past is lost or should be denied. The past was the past and no historying can deny that. However, 'acquiring the reality of the past' is invariably and constantly and relentlessly compromised through the unavoidable nature of the 'history reality effect'.

Many social science historians continue to try to overcome the problem that there is no epistemological (theory of knowledge) connection between history and the past. Nevertheless, historians have plenty of choice when it comes to reconstructing, constructing and/or deconstructing 'the-past-*as*-history'. Plainly, historians cannot access the past as a tourist might visit an exotic foreign country, equally historians cannot send a postcard from the past to the present although most historians think they can (they call them lectures, seminars, books, and so forth). Perhaps the silliest (and strongest) belief held among historians is that they can recapture the past for what it was and what it meant. This, after all, is what historians are surely supposed to do and obviously, knowing what happened in the past cannot be denied. However, all historians have their preferred 'past narratives' but rarely do they confront the notion of the *fictitious*.

What relationship do most historians have (if any at all) with the connection between literature and history? I suggest that historians have very little connection (in my experience) between the 'past-*as*-history' and literature. However, the irony in this will come with some surprise to most historians and their readers. Yes, historians write about the past but rarely does the term 'history' signify a concept apart from a reference to a thing or process in the past. Yes, there are residues of the past (traces?) but most histories are just references to places and/or processes in the past which are impressed by the historian. The past, then, is solely the historian's past and for every historian there is always a differential conjectural past. The past, then again, will invariably remain a fictitious undertaking.

This is hardly news of course as historians engage with the past in order to make sense of the past but, and obviously, for their purposes. The notion of the objective historian is, of course, nonsense. The immeasurable majority of historians still believe that the past is a force in our perpetual present. It seems like the plainest of common sense to assume that 'the past' remains the opposite of a fictitious undertaking. But this is nonsense because there is much more to the past than its history. History is a poor stand in for the past because when engaging with the past 'the past' is unavoidably constituted, created, generated, shaped, and fashioned and hence the fictitious history never existed in the past. History only exists, then, as a lecture, book, journal article, radio presentation, argument on a train, and so forth but all those forms exist briefly in our perpetual present. Historians, subsequently, commend, purge, dispute, and domesticate the past in order to serve our present and possible future needs.

By fictitious, then, historians, happily but if customarily and unwittingly, seek out a fictitious nostalgia (and often a legacy and/or heritage) that saturates every aspect of our popular culture. History, thus, sustains the past through its re-enactments, reminiscences, commemorations, academic classes, and so forth. History, then, is the context for our culture. The foundational problem with 'doing history', however, is 'undoing history'. The notion of a unified past makes no sense because there are always 'new insights into history' as delivered through '*fictitious* memory', '*fictitious* ideological bias', '*fictitious* subjectivity/objectivity', *fictitious* artifacts', '*fictitious* monuments', '*fictitious* identities', '*fictitious* remorse and contrition', 'this book is *fictitious*', '*fictitious* authenticity', and for sure no history can be believed to be 'the essential guide to the past that we inherit and/or reshape and bequeath to the future'. Getting the data straight is always useful but 'getting the past straight' is an endeavour, which is more often than not a largely fictitious undertaking because the author-historian has no alternative.

Now, dear reader, if my analysis annoys or worries you, then you will have to get used to it. Whatever you do, never say 'get real'. The notions of 'empathy', 're-enactment', 'memory studies', 'commemorations', 'schools of historying', 'revised book editions', 'turning the past into digital dots and dashes' all add up to the creation of an overwhelming historical scholarship which (and seriously) cannot claim to engage with the past. The central failure of 'statements of new certainties about the past' by historians today increasingly give way to fictitious messages from the past (ironically) that they shape and in large part by the untutored general public. Revisiting the past then is the worst kind of tutored nonsense. This does not mean denying past reality. The past was what was the past. Unfortunately, history is also claimed to be 'the history'.

So, in the fictitious universe of historying there is no given symmetry in the connections between the general statement of 'what happened in the past' and what it becomes 'as the history'. But, there is no commensurability between 'the past' and 'history'. Historians (along with everyone else) have the inescapable ontic and epistemological situation that all they have are the pasts that historians create through for themselves for other historians. What does this or may this mean? Historians always have a multitude of reasons for preferring one 'history narrative' to another. The in-built contradiction in this process of turning the past into a particular/preferred history demonstrates the vast range of narrative interpretations that are inventible and/or available to historians.

Thus, figuring out what the fictitious past meant, or possibly might have meant, is fortunately very simple. Once they have done their time in the archives, by and large historians (re)create their 'narrative proposals' for 'the past' and which, of course, they claim is the(ir) 'discovered history' which they then trust what they have 'made out of the past' which (happily and usefully) throws 'a new light' on whatever it is the historian, well, wants to illuminate in the past. The historian kick-starts this embarrassingly simple process by coming up with a new narrative proposal—aka a new interpretation to test run—and to do that they have to work out 'the form' and 'the nature of the language' they want to 'deploy' and to 'invoke' and 'shed a light on' that part of 'past reality' they have somehow bumped into in the archives and/or the library, and/the lecture, and/or the chat with a colleague, and so on and so forth.

Now, and presumably along with all other human beings, historians in their varying ways create and impose a structure on the chaos of the past although most historians will say it is their discovery of what hitherto was in the hidden structure of past reality. Thus, with a magnificent irony, the historian 'discovers' and/or 'creates' and 'imposes' a structure both and/or for the past. This is structured through notions of 'cohesion', 'coherence', 'consistency', 'unity', and 'organisation', which are imposed on the past through their claim to have hitherto discovered new histories for old data. The historian thus supplies cohesion for the past by their narrative proposals, which they have (conveniently) 'discovered' and/or 'revealed' and/or 'disclosed' and/or 'realised' and so on and so forth. Unfortunately, discovering 'the history narrative' unavoidably and always upsets the balance between the past and history. The result of the logic here is embarrassingly simple. So, there is always incommensurability between the past and history and then, in addition to the classic triad of (historical) representation, explanation, and interpretation, we always have to cope with the fictitious.

So, what is the nature of the relationship between literature and the fictitious nature of history in term of its fictitious nature? Sadly, the connection between historical 'meaning' and historical 'interpretation' is worryingly murky. In all histories there are 'meanings', 'significances', and 'interpretations' that never go away. Histories continue to lurk. Of course, then, only historians could come up with the perpetual conundrum of historiographical disagreements. While acknowledging that the past and history are not directly connected in either epistemic or ontic terms, there are three more other foundational problems that shape and form the meaning and interpretation of the past. These are the unavoidable notions of 'description', 'representation', and 'explanation'.

Now, most historians do not think about this when they expend all their efforts in investigating, exploring, and studying in the archive. Nonetheless, and in any way, historians engage 'the past' not only through the detritus of the past (aka the sources) but also with 'the aesthetics' of 'their representations' of the past. 'The past' then is obviously elemental to the creation of that aesthetic representation called 'history' and this claim has solid and irrefutable logic on its side. Historians tend to ask themselves what is the nature of 'the history' to be found 'in the past'. To be blunt, history always 'creates', 'builds', 'fashions', and 'forms' the past through the historian's subjective engagement. Put briefly, then, history always comes before the past.

This odd arrangement of history before the past may seem to be dangerous nonsense because it apparently admits space for telling 'lies about history'. However, that precept is entirely wrong because the past always comes pre-owned and hence there are many multiple 'ready-made histories' for both the historian and consumer. Unsurprisingly, then, our 'historical representations of the past' are indifferent to 'the process of historying' because the time before now is always construed as the historian's preferred histories. Now, if we accept that the past has no history until the historian provides it, we are forced to think about the art of turning the past into the process of historying. To repeat, then, at the centre of our representations of 'the-past-*as*-history' there is an unavoidable fictitious irony because the past is utterly useless, pointless, and worthless until historians (and lots of other non-historians as well) turn it into some form of preferred narrative that is usually known as a history. So: there is no (hi)story in the past until it is emplotted into existence by the historian. The past, then, does not produce 'the history' because history produces 'the past'. This may seem an odd and even dangerous judgment.

However, all histories start sooner or later to die as meta-histories that constantly lurked behind the historian's preferred differential histories.

'The past', then, is not accessible until it is authored into existence in the form of a preferred, selected, and desired history narrative and hence it is never 'stumbled on' nor is it 'discovered'. This judgment on my part may annoy some historians but it is hardly my fault that historians need to get a grip on what they are actually doing when engaging with the past. The historian, then, affiances the past but only when 'what happened in the past' is emplotted by the historian. The past, then, only has value as the historian's preferred narrative model of the past. Historians, then, cannot escape the fictitious irony of their condition. The past, then, 'is not back there and awaiting' to be aesthetically acquired so that the historian can 'attain', 'manage' and 'understood' when it is shaped and offered as a history because the preferred history is a fictitious undertaking. The time before now, then, cannot yield the past beyond suggesting 'what happened' and what 'the past might have meant'.

So, in the situation of the perpetual absence of the past all historians can do is note the range of the 'history possibilities in the past that they want to deploy'. So, all the historian can do is fall back on their very weak knowledge of 'what happened' by selecting the sources and data, which supports the historian's preferred 'historical past'. So, there is a central failure in aligning the past with history. There is no effort worth the effort of the historian to seek out the resemblance they hope can be found between the past and history. This does not mean ignoring the attested past. However, past events no longer exist and hence all historians can do with the nonexistent past of assertion, which is based on their preferred sources and their readings of their meaning.

So, engaging with the past, all the emplotments, arguments, and ideological positions that historians choose to deploy in order to access the past for what it was by 'getting the data straight', unhappily the historian's endeavour to figure out 'what the past meant' always fail. This is the profound irony in doing history. Despite the historian's efforts to gain access to the past 'as it actually was' they cannot access 'the past' through 'their historying'. Historians cannot escape their state of aporia (doubt) in their constant 'fictitious ironic state'. This, of course, is (quite possibly?) very bad news for historians. If 'getting the data straight' is not bad enough, the past is constantly moving. Yes, the past is rarely fixed. Now, this is not necessarily a bad thing. Historians would have a bad time if the past were 'sorted out' for once and always. Happily, then, language cannot escape from both its own linguistic failures and all the other unavoidable empirical relativisms. Hence, it is hardly surprising that all historians permanently fail to get the (hi)story straight. They cannot be blamed for this. Indeed, neither human beings nor historians can be freed from 'what is expected' of the past. That is why there are as many 'historical pasts' as there are histories.

Historians, then, are in a constant bind, which is the situation that they have to present the reality of the past according to 'their evidence' and 'their inferences' and so they also have to live with never quite knowing enough about the past. Obviously then, historians always—yes always—fail when faced with the past. Hence, historians are always in permanent denial as to the real nature of the past. Fortunately, the historian's constant failure to understand the past always eventually collapses into the deployment of the fictitious even if they do not recognise it as that, i.e., to be artificial and/or fake or an imitation or a 'failed replication'. Happily, this is not a serious problem. All human beings—including historians—sooner or later collapse into 'the universe of the fictitious' every day and/or every hour and/or minute. This is usually revealed when (along with everyone else) historians 'escape' into 'metaphor', or 'litotes', or some other 'imagery', and so forth.

Now, most historians today are well aware that 'doing history' means making a living out of not being sure as to what was/has been going on in the past. Happily, history is never fixed. But historians (like everyone else) eventually bellyflop and have to admit that figurative metaphor, symbol, representation, and/or image is so flexible that it can 'realistically' serve as a 'representation or image' that will do well enough in lieu of a concept.

Now, then, the concept of the *'factualist'* and the *'fictitious'* at first blush appear to be opposites. However, they work together even if the substantial number of author-historians is ignorant of that relationship. There is an unavoidable irony in 'doing history'. There is no objectivity in engaging with the past and so there cannot be any closure (and I have said this before) and hence the past is an endless space because it can only exist in the historian's mind. The facts of the past are endless which means there cannot be any objectivity in the past. The past is a construal of historians and—frankly—anyone else who wishes to engage with the perpetual time before now. Because of this situation 'the facts of the past' are simply occurrences under a narrative description. To be clear then, 'the past' is always made into many different varieties of pasts.

This does not mean historians or anyone else can contentedly invent the past for their leisure and pleasure and/or for some, of course, it is a convenient invention in terms of what happened or did not. There is always a fundamental partiality in the construction, production, and deconstruction of historical knowledge. The past is invariably constituted through the historian's preferred history. The notion of 'bringing the past into the present', then, is arguably the simplest nonsense that historians come across. The process of turning the past into a history cannot recapture past reality. We can know 'the events of the past' but it is only through the sinews of 'historical reality' that we can make any sense of the time before our constant present. It is clear (or it should be) that 'history' is not a natural process.

I suspect that it is useful for historians to accept, along with everyone else—and whether they know it or not—that they are subject to an art technique that deploys the 'realistic' and/or 'lifelike' description which is 'authentic imagery'. This is better known as the trompe l'œil art technique of visual illusion through which the viewer is tricked into a visual illusion. This representationalist form uses 'lifelike' and 'accurate realistic imaginary' to create reality. Historians obviously know that the narrative they create about past reality can be 'devised' in three dimensions but rarely is. All histories, then, are obviously 'shaped', 'wrought', and 'fashioned' but when it all comes down to basics, history is simply 'made' by the historians through their authorial 'perspective on the past'. While histories are not inventions in the sense that they are 'made up', all histories are 'realistic imageries'.

History then, is not 'the past' and so historians and their consumers have to deal with 'an ersatz past reality'. Now, historians are always keen to get the (hi)story straight. However, and as I have described elsewhere in this book, 'the-past-*as*-history' demands that historians, along with consumers of history, unavoidably attend far less than to the content of the forms of 'historying' than they should. Unhappily (in many ways), histories are rather mundane in their form with the usual book chapters, indexes, and occasional glossary. However, 'the history book' is a largely hopeless means of communication especially given that the content of the form is at least as significant as the empirical content.

Now, I was taught at school and it was reinforced when I took a degree in history that historians are supposed to discover 'the most likely (hi)story'. Now, later and unfortunately and with substantial irony, the concept of the 'fictitious' works in tandem when it comes to authoring 'the-past-*as*-history'. So, when historians and their consumers offer the past or engage with the past or deliver the reality of the past they also and unavoidably engage with another notion. This is their claim that they have discovered (fortuitously?) the reality of the past. Now, in this situation, historians have to face the awkward situation that history is not necessarily real and honest because the 'historical imagination' is 'fabricated'. This does not mean denying the 'empirical past as it actually was', but all historying—along with its other features—is nothing more than the historian's preferred 'fictitious' narrative.

For most historians (and probably their consumers) there is an unavoidable 'connect' between history and literature. The logic in this is as simple and as extremely awkward if the historian assumes (presuming common sense?) that the past and history are conflatable. Plainly, then, this conflation makes no sense of any kind. The past is the past and history is a narrative. Of course, it is awkward that the past and history are constantly glued together by far too many academic historians who assume the past and history go together. Far too many historians, of course, choose to conflate the past with history and vice versa. But this notion is nonsense. So, what is the nature of the relationship between literature and history?

To begin with 'history' and also all those other histories that abound do not and cannot signify 'past reality as it actually was'. History can refer but it cannot be the warp and weft of what it constitutes because the past is formed by the historian through their efforts to 'recreate' what they choose to believe about 'the nature of the past's reality'. Unfortunately, the concept of 'history' is simply a weak and frail signifier/reference of 'the past' as described by the individual historian. Individual historians who turn that past into history determine what signifies the past. These (most likely called) 'traces of the past' or more likely 'facts' are simply events under a description and so they have the status as being a fictitious construal.

Now, when I was planning and writing this book I deliberately ignored the crude concept of fiction. Obviously, fiction has no utility for historians and hence I rejected that concept because the concept of fiction is simply a pointless and purposeless conjecture of and/or about the 'past'. Now, engaging with the past means that historians create and construe the nature of the historical past. The past is the past and history is the past dressed up by the historian. The irony in all of this is that far too many historians continue to insist that there is always the possibility of a scientific knowledge of the 'historical past'. This makes no sense of course. Being able to resurrect the past as it actually was and for what it was is, frankly, nonsensical.

Now, as I have suggested, knowing what happened in the past is not the same as history. To be blunt then, I hope that 'the history' (my history) will correspond to 'the past', which is obviously both ontic and epistemic nonsense if you, dear reader, have to decide if my history (this book) makes any sense at all. The ontic and the epistemic, of course, relates to 'entities' and 'the realities' as I have just written this sentence, which (I hope) relates to the reality of my writing of this sentence, as opposed to my phenomenal existence, which is perceivable by my senses and/or through my immediate experience. Unhappily things get seriously worse because historians cannot exist in history—historians cannot exist in their own books. Happily, all those historians who seemingly never agree as to the nature and meaning of the past demonstrate this awkward situation.

Fortunately, there are four straightforward ways to address the irony of 'the truth of the reality of the fictitious past'. These are the four 'truth concepts' of correspondence, correlation, constructivism, and consensus which have to be deployed by historians (like every human being) whether they know it or not. So, how can historians engage with 'the pasts' that no longer exist thanks to all those historians who will insist that their history is the history? Ironically, then, there is no escape from this situation. Now, fortunately or unfortunately for historians and their

Fictitious 143

consumers, there is never any certainty which 'truth form' will do the job better than the other three forms.

Now, dear reader, you will have to make up your own mind as to which of the four truth forms is better than the other three when faced with the problem of the fictitious past that you want to believe. Now then, we have to accept the subjective nature of that 'authored narrative history making undertaking' when it comes to which history you choose to believe. When this situation arises (and it always does) 'the history of the past' is entirely dependent upon the written narratives individual historians prefer. The really awkward problem with history not to be confused with the past is that there is no absolute past. As the French theorist Jacques Derrida once suggested, there is no authority beyond the text. Or to be as blunt as I can, all histories are substitutions for the past. This is embarrassingly obvious if you think about it. History is the past and the past is history.

Now, historians always deploy the concepts of correspondence, correlation, constructivism, and consensus whether they know it or not, and, to be frank, most historians do not know it. This is unfortunate because if there were more attention paid to the nature of history rather than the past, there would be more consideration paid to the unavoidable fictitious nature of the truth of the past construed as history. This may appear to be a rather odd opinion; yet, the notion of truth more often than not is rarely up front in histories because it is assumed that 'history' is always delivered as a truthful undertaking. However, historians are always in a double bind situation.

Now, this is a condition in which opposing burdensome meanings are transferred in the same message that is often a referred and a preferred historical judgment. A history teacher, for example, may urge a student (or a whole class) to read one historian over another because that is the teacher's preferred historian rather than another. Now, then there is often (usually!) the application of 'the law of the history jungle', when historians prefer some historians to others because of ideological reasons or just because they do not like one historian over another. Or the novitiate historian may end up in a double bind fictitious situation? The irony here is at the heart of the process of turning the past into a history. And, obviously, there is no straightforwardly manageable and intellectual authority beyond the history text. Thus, the 'single fact' is invariably elevated 'to the truth of the . . .' or whatever the historian wants to be correct about.

Now, the *fictitious* nature of history is deeply ironic because of the subjective character of history, given that historians unavoidably and intentionally create the 'the-past-*as*-history'. The foundational 'errors' and 'deficiencies' of 'doing history' then are obvious when it comes to 'the proposed truth of the reality of the past'. Plainly, then, there is no possibility of conflating 'the past' with 'its history' because all that historians can do is offer an ersatz access to the past through the historian's authored historical text. Unfortunately, then, no individual historian's historical text can claim to be 'the reality of the past'. This is unavoidable because all that the historian can do is assume there must be versions of the past 'back there and then' from which the historian can choose.

Historians, then, can insist interminably that there is 'the history back there and then'. But, at some point, historians will have to accept (whether they like it or not) that there is no definitive history available in the past. Obviously, a few historians will insist that there is only one past, which is legitimate, truthful, and correct. But that is plainly nonsense. The past is the past while history is history and there is no way out of that dilemma. Consequently, in the absence of the past, which no longer exists, all we have is the historian's 'multiplicity of what is for them their historical truths'. The simple job of the historian then is to choose which 'fictitious historical past' they prefer.

Now, for me I choose a relativist position on 'the history and the past' debate. Now, this is hardly a dilemma of course. I suggest, then, that the truth of the historian's acquaintance with the past is what the individual historian insists it is. As I noted earlier, the choice always put before the historian is to choose from the list I noted before—the four 'truth concepts' of correspondence, correlation, constructivism, and consensus. Now, as a relativist I do not see that the past can be open to all of the four 'truth concepts'. Now, the silliest situation that historians can get into is to worry about which form of truth they want. I suspect any or all of the four forms of 'truth concepts' will do as the historian wishes. So, historians can ignore everything I have said so far given that my position is that of a relativist. I do not see how the historian's engagement with the past can be other than relativist despite the existence of the four truth forms I mentioned.

Thus, all historians and their readers can choose which 'truth form' they want. Plainly, then, both historians and consumers will assume history is 'realist writing' which means it is (p)referential when it comes to the past. Historians, then, quite rightly accept that the past is made up of events, which no longer exist. However, and obviously, the past can be accessed through the traces of the past (as the attested past) in our perpetual present. This is obvious and straightforward given the range of referents that are readily representable and which are formed and shaped by the historian. So, in the absence of the past what we have is what the historian 'construes', 'constructs', 'reconstructs', and 'deconstructs' and then we end up with some kind of 'historicised' past.

Beyond all this, there is yet 'more' and 'less' to it as the historian wants or desires. Again then, what really is the point of 'doing history'? Well, it is valuable for one thing, because the historical past is at once both useful and unhappily entirely nonsensical. To be clear, then, the historical past has utility but only when historians insist it does. So, one historian's fictitious inference is another's complete waste of time and the accounts and descriptions of the past as offered by academic historians are merely illustrations of what is the irreal. So, all histories are no more than very weak efforts at gathering 'data' which can be offered as a means for yet another set of meanings and possible significations. So, which is the real past and which is the practical past? So, that depends on which kind and form of history you want. So, which is the real history? Obviously, then, every historian agrees that on November 10th, 1966 Her Majesty Queen Elizabeth began the start of her tour of Ghana but as to the rest of that activity it is entirely a historical construal. So, where, when, and why does the notion of that event become the fictitious history of that event?

So, when does the historian or all historians, or no historians, agree that the past was imprinted on their 'fictitious historical analysis' of the event/s? So, when does the empirical past become the real(istic) history? The really awkward problem that all historians have—along with their consumers—is their conflation of the empirical and documentable that is invariably presumed to be 'the historical'. To be clear then, when does a history become a history? All 'past histories' then are simply fictitious and thus asserted and historical referents carry their own in-built 'historical reality'. Thus, the reality of the past is unavoidably a 'made' historical referent. This does not mean historians invent what they want about the past, but insist that they will offer their access to what they take to be the real, historical referent. But, obviously of course, the past is always reconstituted figuratively (again and again and again . . .) and thus reengaging with the past is a fictitious endeavour.

What this adds up to (in my judgment) is that all historians have to determine what is the past and what is history. Historians, of course, always have their own ways of distinguishing between the past and history. This may seem to be common sense and obvious but that belief is invariably impractical and meaningless. What, dear reader, you are now reading my in(ter)vention in the nature of the 'historical'. This means that this book is a dip into my history of history and also other historians whom I have chosen because I think they make sense. Now, most academic historians are genuinely honest and earnest in their seeking out of the reality and meaning of the past. So, why are there so many historians who cannot agree with the explanation and nature of their closest colleagues? Well, it comes down for most historians to engage with the non-fictitious reality of the practical past.

Unhappily then, and invariably awkwardly like everyone else, historians can only engage with the past through their authorial intervention in terms of what will be their 'preferred history'. Obviously, then, that 'preferred past' is a practical past. This notion, as described by the history theorists Michael Oakeshott and Hayden White, means looking back to the past to see how our 'preferred history' makes sense for our perpetual present. So, 'the historical past' is a theoretical, speculative, and conjectural environment through which historians guide their consumers through the complexities of the time before now. The historical past then (is there anything else?) is a construed, constructed, and deconstructed history. The 'historical past' then is an 'authorial motivated space' of and for historians. No historians ever lived or experienced the past (unless it was in their lifetime) and so their engagement of the past is constantly evolving.

Hence, nobody actually experiences the past because there is no 'constant present or presence' of the past unless they believe that they can experience the past. Ironically, historians constantly observe the past from a (their) privileged view in a way that no 'historical agent' could have possessed. Historians, then, can never win when they engage with the past because all they can have is the(ir) historical reality of the past. So, historians observing the time before now can claim knowledge of the past but it is always tenuous. And here is the central problem with history. It is that no historian can lay a claim to a knowledge of the 'past present' that no person in the past in their present could have ever possessed.

Historians then are constantly surrounded with *fictitious* problems that cannot be obviated. For example, then, the notion that historians can discover the meaning of the (presumed?) reality of the past and acknowledging at best history is always an uncooperative undertaking. Thus, all that the 'historical past' can do for us, given that it is created by historians in our perpetual present, historians along with everyone else can only sit back and watch the backwash of the receding past. This is why we have history of course even though it is always a flawed intellectual engagement with a constantly revisioned past. So, the past is practical and so is history. Now, this notion emerged in the nineteenth century as new 'content' and 'forms' of history emerged. Hence, 'nineteenth historical reality' is what the historian wanted and still wants from the past.

With a deep and abiding irony, history is what the historian presumably either 'discovers' and/or 'wants' or both. Hence, the notion that history is some kind of detective undertaking is simply nonsense. Knowing the reality of the past is always an excursion into a quagmire where the stepping stones constantly disappear. Hence, there is no singular past awaiting discovery, but, unfortunately, historians are usually wilful in their pursuit of the history they want. Admittedly, some historians 'find what they want in the past' while others do not and hence they move their aspirations into different directions. When I was pursuing my PhD. in the 1970s and I eventually secured it in 1979, I created a social science research design (with cargos of coefficients of elasticity and regression equations the deployment of which I thought could discover how European urban immigrants, between 1870 and 1920, politically assimilated into the large urban cities of the United States). I think four people eventually read my PhD—me, my wife Jane (who typed it) my supervisor, and the external examiner. Such is often the nature of 'doing history'.

Eventually, I engaged with the far more interesting process of how the historian turned the past into a (or the?) history. So, I started out as a hardcore social science historian who eventually collapsed into the gravity hole of postmodernism. In that hole I soon noticed that 'my history' of 'my knowledge' of the past was an unavoidable deconstruction of history rather than that of the past. My engagement with the past had soon become a process of 'my take' on the fictitious nature of the past. So, my knowledge of the past could not be of any utility at all. As the history theorist Hayden White once insisted (and he was right in my judgment), the 'historical past' as they see it is all that the historian can offer simply because all history is unavoidably the historian's *fictitious* past.

The historical past then is that past which is engaged by historians. Thus, the practical past is rarely (for all we can know) either or neither what we want out of the past. Now, most historians (like everyone else) swim in a pool of both past and (likely) future realities. Most historians certainly want to engage with 'the facts' prior to moving and shaping the past. Historians thus live in a universe of pastness secreted into our present where they can claim the facts first and then the interpretation. Historians today insist on neutrality and disinterestedness. But that is nonsense of course. Neutrality and disinterestedness is always soaked in the historian's fictitious weak defiance of the interpretations of other historians whose judgments they disagree with.

All histories, then, are sceptical essays or, perhaps more accurately, 'rationality' in 'opinion'. Historians, by and large, will contentedly swim in shoals of 'probabilities' and 'the facts' but, unfortunately, probabilities and facts rarely make good companions. Nevertheless, facts and probabilities are primal when it comes to engaging with the past. And so, historians, then, are hopeless (like everyone else) when it comes to 'truths about the past'. The legal nonsense of 'the truth and nothing but the truth' should be avoided among historians unless it is when the historian is run over by a truck. That is not *fictitious*?

9 Fictive

In this penultimate chapter I will address another 'narrative' concept that enables the historian to turn the past into history, and this is the concept of the *fictive*. Derived directly from Medieval Latin, 'the *fictive*' describes and defines the concepts of the 'imaginative' and/or 'imaginary'. Now the *fictive* is, more often than not, a rather peculiar notion but one which is essential to 'doing history' (like the other concepts I have described thus far). Among the concepts I have addressed thus far, historians invariably deploy the concept of the *fictive* most commonly, whether they realize it or not. This terminology, like the others I have offered so far, enables historians to deploy the notion of the 'historical imagination' most clearly. I first came across the notion of 'the historical imagination' when I was an undergraduate history student and for some considerable time could not figure out what the notion of the historical imagination was. Surely, history was all about the nature of past reality?

Sooner rather than later, I was told firmly by one of my history tutors what he thought was the definition of 'the historical imagination'. He told me that history is a conduit through which historians can process the most likely nature of the past and eventually extend their truthful knowledge of the time before our perpetual present. Now, when I was about to pack in 'doing history' because it was primarily all about what so many historians on my reading lists disagreed, I came across the notion of 'the historical imagination'. The historical imagination, then, was as close as possible to being the past as historians could get. And just when I was getting a handle on history, 'the historical imagination' was rapidly followed by 'wie es eigentlich gewesen', or in translation, to show what actually happened'?

My reaction to this was to believe that history was/is just 'finding out the reality of the past'. Unhappily, 'the past' turned out to be 'history' and it still does. To be generous at best, then, history is a detective story. Who did what, who thought that, why did they do that, why did they not make that obvious choice or a different range of choices? Figuring out the reality of the past, then, always means rubbing up against the intellectual clashes of so many historians. Now, 'doing history' is actually really simple. The historian decides what they want to engage with in the past. This demands a 'history methodology', which invariably has postulates and procedures some of which work out splendidly but most do not.

In my engagement with the past I start out with the framing of a topic, which is sustained by a list of questions as formed in my brain by a utilitarian methodology that is *fictive* (obviously). It begins by my framing of a topic as a question that centres on a particular issue. For instance, this book is an engagement with the nature of how historians turn the past into a history. To begin with, why would anyone want to engage with the past at all? Then, if the context permits, the author-historian engages and construes how they turn the past into a suitable (probable?) process for engaging with and explaining the meaning of the past. This simple notion applies to all histories and that includes texts such as the one you are presently reading.

Now, like just about every other human being, historians constantly judge not just their own engagement with the past by their own benchmarks and especially the present state of her/his knowledge. Unhappily, the observable truth of the past has all too often prevented even the most sophisticated of historians from using contemporary values and knowledge to characterise the past. The *fictive* past, of course, is created as history in our endless present. Now, all historians are told at some point in their training to be aware of their own biases. Now, historians always claim to be objective but that belief is nonsense. The belief in objectivity is a cherished trait for all historians—a 'noble dream' as the American historian Charles Beard once asserted. Unhappily, no historian is blameless when it comes to his or her interpretation of the nature of the past. Of course, the silliest notion that any historian can offer is their insistence that they know the nature of the past as they have 'found it'.

The *fictive* processing of the past then, is 'crafted' entirely by the historian's 'historical imagination'. The deployment of the *fictive*, along with the other aesthetic engagements I have addressed, is central to all forms of 'historical representation'. Given the purposes of this book, by now I assume it is clear that history is not to be found in the past. To be blunt then: all histories exist in the past but only at the behest of the historian. Hence, as I have noted throughout this book, it is the historian—and only the historian—who undertakes to lift the burden of the past and the authorial responsibility of 'historying' the past. It is not only historians but also their readers who should be aware of the literary and other myriad forms of aesthetic representations in 'doing history', not least the historian's 'timing of the text' as they author their narratives.

Now, because 'the past is the past' and 'history is history' the notion of 'historicity' is central to the process of turning the past by 'doing history'. To be clear then the foundation of 'doing history' is for the historian (and everyone else) to have to engage with the notion of 'historical authenticity'. By this then, I mean the historian's along with everyone else's state of 'experiencing', 'imagining', and 'expressing' 'the-past-*as*-history' through her or his *fictive* understanding of the nature of change over time. To be blunt, then, and like everyone else, historians always 'look back' to the past to know what it was and what it meant *as* history in our perpetual present.

I am well aware that despite the demise of the brief postmodern insurrection, which confronted the nature of history as a narrative form in the late last century, many if not the very substantial majority of historians, still struggle to grasp with what they are actually doing. I appreciate that many historians will disagree with that thought and such historians will continue to insist that by deploying 'common sense', the 'empirical', the 'analytically self-informed', and their dutiful 'processing of the past', historians are enabled to 'discover the nature of the past' and thereby find the most likely probable 'meaning' and/or 'explanation' and/or 'implication' that can be discovered in the past.

Now, this 'plain common sense' allows historians to compare and contrast the historian's 'preferred sources' and which then is also followed by a shrewd analysis of the yet to be discovered most probable 'historical meanings and explanations' in 'the-past-*as*-history'? Given this simple procedure, most historians remain content to render the most likely interpretations of what the past most probably could/should sensibly mean in their judgment. Of course, this *fictive* process is at best naïve and at worst a catastrophic display of seriously bad logic. This bizarre notion can only be sustained (and it is) because far too many historians constantly and wilfully and failingly continue to understand the nature of the(ir) representation of 'the-past-*as*-history'. To be clear then: there is no history in the past until the historian injects their beliefs about the past. The past is not history until historians provide it.

The idea that historians discover 'the past' is an obviously and embarrassingly 'nonsense' given that the past does not exist until historians along with everyone else (in some way) seek it out in order to provide it for our wants in our perpetual present. Happily, then, the past is a depository, which can be raided as and when the needs of our perpetual present determine to cash it in. Historians, then, are rational in proportion as to their belief in respect of the(ir) presumed understanding(s) of the *fictive* past. Now, at this point a majority of historians both professional and amateur are highly unlikely to have agreed with my analysis (so far) and, as a secondary source (a book), it can easily be rejected as a seriously disarranged understanding of what history is.

However, I was taught (for good or ill) that consumers of history and history authors alike are lead to the so-called primary and secondary sources through which they can endeavour 'to figure out' what did and did not happen in the past and what it meant for the past and also our present and future. Now, a primary source is more often than not a written (or some other figurative form) such as diaries, speeches, letters, images, artifacts, buildings, and so forth. But, and as we know, in addition to primary sources, historians deploy secondary sources, which are usually defined as what other historians have chosen to 'say about' and/or 'author their history into existence'. However, and ironically, it is well known that historians invariably quote other historians in order to support each other's *fictive* understandings of the past. And, of course, the opposite also happens.

Now, all this discovering of the nature of 'the-past-*as*-history' seems to be a very simple process but it is not. Somewhat more realistically, historians (and everyone else) can only exist in what they believe to be 'their construction of the past' which they believe is the(ir) 'discovered past'. Including academic historians, all human beings invent a convenient past for a variety of reasons. This is where aesthetics emerges. Obviously, telling lies about the evidenced reality of the past is stupid and irresponsible. However, in 'doing history' it is impossible to avoid the situation that 'the history' is not the past because—quite simply—it is that aesthetic *fictive* construal we designate as the (hi)story. The reality of this situation means that all histories are the result of the historian's preferred authorial decisions as they choose to suppose that they can reconstruct and/or construct and even deconstruct it if they wish. In my judgment, this situation is plainly unavoidable.

So, how do historians cope with the nature of their *fictive* historying by turning the past into a/the history? Well, to start with, the vast majority of historians are entirely ignorant as to the concept of the *fictive* so there is nothing to worry about. However, should they inadvertently come across the(ir) 'historical imagination' they have to engage (if only briefly) with the historian theorist R.G. Collingwood. Collingwood suggested that 'doing history' was akin to 're-enacting the past' which was a significant element in the historian's historical imagination and which is unavoidably threaded throughout all histories. Critics of R.G. Collingwood (and there have been many) have claimed that his historical thinking requires 'an historical imagination' which is the ability to form and shape new thoughts about the nature of the reality of the past. This means there are lots and lots of legitimate pasts to be discovered as fresh histories.

Thus, Collingwood's conception of the historical imagination is an instinctive *fictive* element that 'all good historians' deploy whether they know it or not. Unfortunately it never works. This is because 'the historical imagination' sooner or later collapses into a bizarre situation. That is the state of the historian's deep down and sure ability to 'reconstruct the-past-*as*-history'. The notion of 'acquiring the sources and then getting data straight' is, of course, a reasonable undertaking. Unhappily, there is very little intellectual effort required in 'figuring out what happened in the past' and 'what it might mean' although historians always make much of comparing and contrasting each other's judgments and interpretations. Apart from those few madcap historians who deny the reality of the past, all other sensible and rational historians eventually figure out a suitable interpretation given the available sources they have consulted, which they have 'sifted and chosen' to fit into the historian's preferred history.

Now, by and large, historian practitioners are generally not philosophers. Of course there are a small coterie of historians who will dabble with 'the nature of history' as opposed to 'figuring what happened in the past' but the real problem—yes the real problem—that all historians face is 'reality' over the 'appearance' of the time before now. Historians, sooner or later, eventually face up to their classic problem, which is 'present appearance' and 'past reality'. Now, 'history is a 'thing' which is three-faced. It faces the past, the present, and (hopefully for the historian) the future. Now, if there is one singular element that defines history it is its situation of both 'uncertainty' and 'surety' in equal measure. The past varies as historians change their minds, especially those who have had particularly good reviews for their latest engagement with the(ir) past.

Now, the vast majority of historians attend to the process of 'doing history' through their 'historical imagination' which is controlled by 'learning and scholarship'. This notion was never better described by the (sometime history theorist) R.G. Collingwood's doctrine, which has often been seen as closely related to that of re-enactment or rethinking the past through the historian's historical imagination. Detractors of R.G. Collingwood have repeatedly associated these two ideas—re-enactment and/or rethinking—and many have suggested that his view of historical thinking depends on 'the historical imagination' which, in my view I suggest invariably turns out to be their own choice of either their 'reconstruction' and/or 'construction' and/or 'deconstruction' of the past. This does not mean the historian creates a convenient past where some events did or did not happen, as the historian wants. Telling lies about the evidenced reality of the past is plainly stupid, irresponsible, and outrageously negligent. However, the fundamental problem that (ironically) 'doing history' cannot avoid is that history is not the past (and the past is not history). The past—among many other things—remains a *fictive* (hi)story, and hence all histories are the result of the historian's preferred authorial decisions which are imaginative interventions even as they cope with getting the sources and data precise.

Thus, the concept of the *fictive* relates to what is at once an extremely complex process of 'imaginative historical in(ter)vention'. Now, that difficult processing of the past by turning it into history is unfortunate for the majority of historians who continue to insist that their function is to discover 'the truthful (hi)story' of the past. Unhappily, all of this makes no sense. Getting 'the data straight' and thereby investigating 'the reality of the past' is clearly an indispensable cultural undertaking. And so, plainly denying, repudiating, and/or disclaiming the 'evidentially attested past reality' is at least unwise and at worst stupid. But, historians are expected to deploy their authorial and technical skills in discovering 'the nature of change over time' in accord with 'the available sources' that they have 'discovered' and 'sorted out' in the archives. Unhappily, of course, some of the sources do not 'fit' into the historian's understanding of the past as based on other sources they have engaged with. Therefore, there is an unfortunate situation, which historians cannot avoid. 'The past' remains 'the past' while history stays what it is—an authored narrative about the past created by the historian.

Now, as I have noted in the previous chapters of this book, history is not the past and historians have to substitute something for it aka history. However, the notion of the '*fictive* historical imagination' is not news. Some 50 years ago the theorist Hayden White suggested that all histories and philosophies of history contain not merely 'data' but also deploy 'theoretical concepts' for explaining these data. Now, in addition historians create a 'historical narrative', which is unavoidably 'poetic' and 'linguistic', through which they can conveniently present 'the-past-*as*-history'. Unhappily the vast majority of academic historians have studiously ignored White's analysis and, in my judgment, all histories are *fictive* realities. Plainly, the substantial majority of academic historians today (as I write now) have failed to recognise White's argument that there is no 'proper history' that is not also a 'philosophy of history'. Hence, in this book I am offering my analysis of how the past is turned into history. So: I am suggesting that historians are constantly creating *fictive* 'realities' whether they know it or not.

Now, I suggest that most historians are (by and large) unmindful that when they create their histories they are creating *fictive* past realities. Thus, 'historical characters' from and/in the past are 'authorially developed' by 'the history author' and 'once lived' characters are unavoidably *fictive* creations. This does not mean they are presented by the historian-author as 'formed' thanks to the available evidence and the historian's interpretation of the meaning of the detritus of the past. Ironically, the *fictive* embellishment of the past is the historian's own a priori imagination. Now, the obvious problem with history, and which cannot be resolved, is that there are always several histories somewhere wedged in the past. As the author of this book I am swayed toward an ironic mode of analysis because, well, that is my personal inclination, but my ironic intervention assists me to create and shape 'a history of history' as a 'romance', 'tragedy', 'comedy', and/or satirical 'emplotment'.

While sticking to the evidence of what they hope will turn out to be the most likely 'narrative reality of the past', historians—along with everyone else for that matter—create *fictive* realities. This is not invention. All historians and their readers constantly create *fictive* 'realities' for the past even if they do not know it. Thus: the 'past historical character' is shaped and formed by the historian's understanding of the 'past *fictive* reality' through which the historian 'forms the past'. The *fictive* is not a 'take it' or 'leave it' add-on to the historian's conception of the(ir) history. All historians can engage with the reality of the past but only ironically given the substantial numbers of historians who are not aware that 'turning the past into a history' is entirely their responsibility. Historians, then, are constantly creating 'historical *fictive* realities', which the historian emplots.

Happily, getting the data straight is usually very simple for historians. However, most historians elide the really tricky part of what they do which is figuring out whether they are an 'extra-diegetic' or 'intra-diegetic' author which means they have to choose to be 'outside' and/or 'inside' of the 'historical world' that is construed as delivered to the reader. The 'extra-diegetic' history narrator is 'above' or 'superior' to the story she/he chooses to invent or devise, while the 'intra-diegetic' narrator is inside the *fictive* universe as with an autobiography. Moreover, the author-historian has a choice of 'reconstructing', 'constructing', or 'deconstructing' the past. Unhappily most historians fail to acknowledge they have that choice.

Accordingly, historians—to be very clear—are first and foremost authors. As I have already noted they engage with the past hoping to 'discover' past reality and its meaning; however, historians cannot 'authorially recreate' a complex duplicate of past events and what they (in probability) mean. Thus, both 'the novel' as well as 'the history' is self-justifying and self-authorising and hence it is expected that 'the history' aims to be true. But, unhappily, this belief cannot work out because the past is not history and history is not the past. All histories are supposed and presumed to be truthful in a correspondence sense. So, what the historian writes about the past is simply what the historian writes about the past.

So, unfortunately for the historian and dependent on their intellectual proclivities, they have to construct and/or reconstruct or deconstruct a coherent picture (as an image, tutorial lecture, book, and so forth) of the past. As I have already argued (at some length) historians concretise the past as a depiction or image of past reality in terms of space and time. So then, all histories are representations and those representations always remain—as I have already noted—as representations. The concept of 'the historical imagination', then, is fashioned only in small part not by the past as such but by the mechanics of the 'historian-as-an-author'. Thus: every history is wrought and created by the historian as an author and not the genuineness of the past. Now, historians must get the data straight, however, inventing the past as a *fictive* undertaking is consistently dangerously self-serving.

Deploying the *fictive* thus means 'figuring out' or more often 'created with the imagination' in order 'to get the (hi)story straight' depends on working out the distinction between 'the past' and 'history'. However, making that distinction requires accepting that (and annoyingly) there are several forms of 'historical realism', which are defined by the emplotments that all authors deploy (including historians) of romance, comedy, tragedy, and satire. The 'stuff of the past' aka 'what actually happened' seems simple enough to grasp, but it is not. Historians can only engage with the past through 'doing history' in terms of 'the-past-*as*-history' as laid down by each individual historian. Regrettably, every 'past time' one engages with is never exactly the same one you engaged with before. The past never stands still. Historians constantly recreate the past. To be clear: the immeasurable range and activity of 'past time' can never be visualised as a whole, or as 'a history'.

As the historian E.H. Carr famously suggested, one should study the historian before beginning to study the facts and he further suggested that facts are what the historian wants in order to interpret the past. This was a worthy effort to summarise what historians do. Unhappily, it makes very little sense in my view. The deployment of figurative language precedes all histories. The typical history narrative as constructed by the historian is intended to represent the past. However, the historian as a series of statements constructs that history narrative. All historical narratives, then, are comprised of statements that add up to being a 'narrative substance'. This narrative substance eventually adds up to being a coherent history. The narrative of a history is thus a series of statements, which eventually add up (hopefully) to a representation of the past. This does not mean such history narratives are the history narratives and so—perhaps awkwardly—there are as many pasts as there are *fictive* histories.

The upshot of this is that turning the past into a history is little more than a 'writing reality effect'. Every history can reference 'what probably happened in the past' but all histories are also unavoidably a morality play. All histories are a series of ethics strung on a string of empirical events shaded by collections of ideological assumptions. All histories are nothing more than the reality-effects through the authorial endeavours of the historian. To be clear, then, the reality of the past is just another 'authenticity' game of figurative language. The historian's engagement with the *fictive* dimension of history is unavoidable because that rendezvous is foundational to the historian's (and everyone else's) *fictive* engagement—a reality effect—with the past.

Perhaps the single major problem with history and which is impossible to resolve, is determining between two histories of the same past. Thus, the Industrial Revolution would be different according to the decisions of two economic historians where one ignored the Spinning Jenny, Bessemer process, interchangeable parts, sewing machine, and so forth, and another did not. Which history is the best and/or appropriate? This is the problem that every historian faces. Which *fictive* past do they want to resuscitate through their 'selective historying'? Remember, historians discover 'the-past-*as*-history' as they create it. By that I do not mean historians 'make up the past' for their personal preference. And, of course, there is the problem that the past always ends up as simply historical 'descriptions' and 'depictions'.

None of this is fresh news. The philosopher Nelson Goodman addressed this problem in his text *Ways of Worldmaking* (1978) but I suspect that, if I am right, most historians will not have read that text. His argument is at once both audacious and iconoclastic and it will strike loathing and fear in the hearts and minds of most historians. His argument is that some true statements—and this applies to all those authorial versions of the past and their meanings—can legitimately conflict. This means there are 'many commensurate histories' (among other things). This does not mean historians tell lies and others do not (although, of course, there might be). That apart, Goodman suggests that many 'true statements' conflict with each other and I suggest there are legitimate competing histories. Hence, there are no unquestionable 'true facts' when it comes to the process of 'doing history' simply because all 'past events' are only *fictive* descriptions.

Consequently, by and large, historians never have very much to do with the concept of the *fictive* because the idea describes that which is not real and is usually feigned. Now, as I have already noted, the historical imagination does not engage with literary fictions, however, the concept of the *fictive* does and it is capable of imaginative invention and/or creation. The American poet Wallace Stevens re-energised the concept in order to represent the making of fictions that do not suspend credulity. This pretty much represents the situation with history. History is generally regarded as the record of what happened in the past but unfortunately history is primarily a *fictive* undertaking.

Thus, historians assume that they can engage with time and space and interpret both at the same time. This is impossible of course although historians try to achieve that impossibility. This is why, along with everyone else, historians are blessed with 'imagination' plus 'reason' and hence they also believe they can reconcile both without diminishing either. All historians then are always engaged with and by the 'objective correlative'. In other words, historians always have a set of aims in respect of the nature of the past. However, history always gets in the way of the past as much as it gets in the way of the historian. One of the major problems that get in the way of the past is history.

The reality of the 'historical past' is simply a somewhat crude rethinking and/or reinventing of the past in our perpetual present. Historians, thus, interpret, reinterpret, enact, reenact, decode, unravel, unstitch, disentangle, and untangle 'the past' so that in 'the future' history will simply generate a host of more uncertainties about the past. Now, not unlike novelists, historians manage in some way to deconstruct and/or construct and/or reconstruct that which they have already created. But what is always difficult for historians (and their consumers) is that their histories are at best a very crude analogue and referent for the past. Now, the problem that most historians ought to worry about is that in 'doing history' their very best 'analogue' of the past—the *fictive*—invariably deposits the 'historical detritus' (the past) which the historian unavoidably trails behind them.

Now, as far too many historians insist, their job is to reconstruct the 'real reality' of the historical past. Obviously then, historians will always insist that history is the treasure trove of 'the past'. Unfortunately, while the past is what the past was in both empirical and ontic terms, all that historians can do with the past is hope they can reconstruct it. Obviously—in both epistemic and ontic terms—the past cannot in any shape or form be reconstructed as it was. Hence, the best that historians can hope for is some sort of crude 'trace reconstruction' of the past. History, then, is a (very basic) crude description of the historian's preferred past. Knowing what probably happened in the preferred past is about all historians can do and then mop up any shallow *fictive* pools of meaning that seems useful to the historian.

So, when engaging with the reality of the past all that historians can do with the(ir) preferred past is to offer a universe of possible past likelihoods. So, along with everyone else, all that historians can do with the past (defined as the time before now) is to constitute the past as a *fictive* past. So, as the historian R.G. Collingwood argued, doing history was always—in some form or another—a re-enactment of the past. Unlike historical novelists, historians have to reconstruct and/or construct a coherent representation of the past that seems to make sense of events as they really happened. This is where historians severally rethink the past diligently, assiduously, and unremittingly in order to align their understanding of the *fictive* reality of the past as it likely was. Anyway, whether most historians understand it or not, they soak the past, as they understand it, in 'the sea of representation' and 'language ornamentation'.

So, those historians who insist that they have 'discovered the reality of the past' (or have stumbled over it or fell into it) have to accept that the historical text is a literary artifact as White insisted—correctly—some 40 or more years ago. White argued then although historians continue a reluctance to accept that histories are as much invented as found. As the theorist Northrop Frye argued, every work of literature, and that certainly includes history, has both a *fictive* and a realist thematic aspect. Obviously, of course, no honest historian invents the past, but it must be reiterated that every historian when they produce their literature cannot avoid the *fictive*.

As I noted earlier in this chapter, all histories, even the most scrupulously construed by the author-historian, possess the *fictive* elements of the comic, tragic, ironic, and comedic in various shades. Thus, when the historian engages with the past by creating their preferred historical text of or for the past—and that is the only way even if it turns out to be a lecture, or seminar, or article or book—it is deeply ironic that the historian who has collected and collated the detritus of the past still has to turn the reality of the past into a literary artifact and vice versa. What most historians still forget (well, far too many still do) is that the events of the past are 'made into a preferred story (history)' by the historian.

All *fictive* histories, then, are narratives that are made by the suppressing and/or the subordination of other elements of the preferred narrative. These obviously include emplotments, characterisations, and themes. As literary artifacts, all histories can be created as the historian wants. Thus, as I noted just now, every event in the past can be intrinsically authored in the forms of the comedic, tragic, ironic, and the romantic. Now, if the historian decides to transform a comedic emplotment into a tragedy that is their choice. Hence, all historical narratives are not simply models of past processes and practices and events and occurrences. But whatever the content of past, these processes and practices and events and occurrences that I just noted are culturally sanctioned and understood.

So, given that the past no longer exists, just what are historical 'representations' of? Well, as the history theorist Hayden White suggested in 1978, historical texts are nothing more than literary artifacts that refer to or at best are simply representations of the past. Now, history is obviously not a science even though 'social science historians' will insist otherwise. I was one such historian as attested by my social science Ph.D. which was packed with regression equations and coefficients of elasticity through which I could connect the voting patterns of European immigrants in the USA between 1870 and 1920. But history can also be set against literature by its interest in the reality of the past rather than the *fictive* possibilities in the past.

As the history theorist Hayden White suggested, human beings impose stories on the past as we read them. The historian manages to impose those events in which they are interested (for whatever reason) and which then are recognised as 'the most likely past'. Writing the past blooms on the discovery of myriad emplotments in and imposed on the past and which can be offered as differentially 'plotted histories'. Histories and historians, then, are not simply lazing and lying about in 'the past' waiting to be discovered, because all past events are proto-histories that engage the minds of historians. As I have already noted, I am persuaded toward an incongruous mode of analysis because my tongue-in-cheek intervention assists me to create, structure and restructure 'a history of history' as I want as a 'tragedy', 'romance', 'satire' and 'comedic' emplotment.

So, what is 'the reality' of 'the *fictive* historical past'? Well, and most significantly, the French philosopher Paul Ricoeur like all historians addressed the notion of their narrative identity through their preferred cast 'of the historian's preferred characters' in the past 'who is allowed to say this and that' and 'who did not say' and thus and thereby constitute the past as the historian's preferred past. Hence, all historians are detectives but seriously bad ones. Historian's then, constantly offer counterfactual narrative explanations for what (probably) happened or did not in the past.

'The-past-*as*-history' is a product of the historian's personality (devious or otherwise) along with their political stances, moral principles, that distressing failure to get that book published they had been working on for the last decade, and so forth. So, what is it to be a historian? More often than not, it is invariably a 'wounded cogito'. Thus, all historians have to take responsibility for their actions. So, historians can speak—by their nature—to travel through a sequence of *fictive* stages in their pursuit of seeking out of their conflation of the past with history. Historians thus identify 'characters' and 'things'. All historians then, have their own personalised narrative identities in terms of the question of the ethical aim of engaging with the past. Unhappily, all historians cannot deny their problematic issue of 'hermeneutics', aka interpretation. Historians may seem to be detectives but their foundational problem is that of interpreting their own 'intellectual selfishness', which eventually culminates in 'the conclusion' that is always attested through the testimony of others. So, all historians (like all human beings?) cannot avoid their 'selfhood', which is entwined in a '*fictive* historical discourse' that the historian believes must be back there in the past.

Now, it should by obvious that no historian fears 'forgetting the past'. This is because they selectively choose those 'bits' and 'parts' of the past that they think are essential to their ends of interpreting the nature of the past. Thus, historians always choose those 'things' and 'processes' and 'events' and 'occurrences' and 'occasions' and 'peoples' and 'nations' and 'political decisions' and most commonly those other histories that they do not like for whatever reasons. Historians, then, will omit and/or insert varieties of all other elements in their histories, which they believe are necessary to their 'appropriate historical interpretation'. Hence, historians deploy 'memory and also forgetting', as they want. So, it is with a certain irony, then, that the historian Paul Ricoeur's last book (*Memory, History and Forgetting*, 2004) summarised the central intellectual failure of most historians, which is thus the unavoidable failure of most 'history'.

All these threads in Ricoeur's philosophy came together in his last substantial book *Memory, History, Forgetting* (2004). This book took up the question of memory in answer to questions about memory in our present-day society. Ricoeur lists these—memory, history, and forgetting as occurring on a pathological-therapeutic level as the problem of blocked memory, and, on a practical level as manipulated memory and on an ethical-political level as 'obligated memory'. So, Ricoeur asks whether history is a remedy for or a hindrance to these problems. This apparently leads him back to the question of both the epistemology and the ontology of historical research and writing but, of course, there remains the perpetual problem of memory. So, the central problem with the past is perpetually its 'history'.

As I have suggested, then, historians are incapable of escaping what must be back there in the past but which is impossible for them to access. Understandably, then, historians cannot approach 'the practical past' because historians can only fall back on their own preferred past reality and which then, of course, becomes that 'understanding of the past' that crudely conflates the historian's 'historical imagination' and 'the reality of the practical past'. The foundational problem that underpins all historical analyses then is the historian's practical past, which is shaped out of the historian's all too often vague 'understanding' of the nature of the past as they conceive it. Unhappily, this process of 'discovering the history of the past' is simply that all too crude and constantly unfinished process of not merely knowing what happened but also what it meant.

So, the past is no more than a crude and rude repository for information, which is 'understood' and 'read' through beliefs, dogmas, doctrines, codes, constraints, restrains, confines, and so forth. This very practical past, which is turned into a history, as the author-historian wants also, has another element to it. Thus, the past is a site, which is excavated (constantly) for what the historian hopes that the past can offer up. That excavation process is usually known as 'the historian's insights' into the past; however, there is 'the past' and then there is 'the *fictive* historical past'. The *fictive* historical past is not just lying about until the historian constitutes it. The past, then, is never a discovery.

The historical past then as I have already noted, is that theoretically inspired intervention (in the past) by the historian. Now, and again it must be clear, the past is not a discovery. As I have noted already, there is no discovery in rummaging through the detritus of the 'history junk' of the past. Knowing what actually happened in the past is foundational to any engagement with 'the reality of the past'. But, as I have suggested several times, that 'past actuality' is always shaped and formed by the historian, not 'the past'. The historical past is so obviously what it is—the creation of the historian in terms of explanations—that the past is all too often presumed to be 'the past'. But there is no past to be 'excavated into a past reality' as it actually was. Knowing what happened is knowing what happened, but history is not history because it is a *fictive* (hi)story.

As the history theorist Hayden White insisted (and I think he was right), the historical past is a theoretically driven reality of historians. That is why we have so many different and indifferent versions of the past and its meaning(s) as provided by so many competing historians. All histories are a construal, and/or a construction, and/or a deconstruction, and/or a reconstruction. The only history the historian has is the one they want. No historian experienced the past unless it was their autobiography and most of those are shady undertakings. No historian lived or experienced the past for what it was. Historians can only engage with the past from the vantage point of their perpetual present. And so, the historical past is useless because it is inaccessible. Plainly, and as I have suggested, we can know what happened but what it meant is an intellectual lottery.

So, when engaging with 'historical reality' it is impossible to avoid the *fictive* past. Obviously, most historians will have very little knowledge of the *fictive* past, but all the key concepts I am describing in this text are useful in terms of acknowledging what actually happened in the past. Nevertheless, as I have already noted, the meanings and explanations that historians can offer in their efforts to imagine the nature of the past demonstrates how malleable is the 'the-past-*as*-history'. As is well known, as soon as a history is authored into existence, all histories are soon morphed differentially. So, like lava flows, history is shaped by the geography of the volcanic past. The historian's imagined past is, well, simply history. However, knowledge of the past all too often buckles and error.

Now, historians always have to distinguish between what I assume is 'the practical past' and 'the historical past'. As to the nature of the 'practical past' that is simply the collective evidential material(s) that are available that the historian can acquire and disperse in their effort to constitute the(ir) *fictive* past, which obviously is 'the historical past' as the historians infer. Historians still tend to look for the facts of the past and then they seek out their imaginative interpretation of those preferred facts. So, historians cannot fail (at some point) to come up with the(ir) preferred interpretation as to the nature of the past. But this is obviously nonsense given that for every historian there is always a different, dissimilar, divergent, and deviating 'historical interpretation'.

Now, all historians (to my knowledge) always take very seriously both the form and content of the past because it is the(ir) form and content that produces their histories. Now, there is no given history in-built into the past. That is simply plain common sense. So, all histories are metafictions whether historians and their consumers like it or not. All histories refer to themselves. All histories are classic examples of self-referencing. Thus: all history texts are by definition *fictive* in the sense that all histories are unavoidably self-referential. Obviously, for every history there is an in-built philosophy of history and its unavoidable aestheticising of the past.

What all historians should be interested in is 'getting the data straight' through which the past can be regarded as some form of truth. I have already noted this situation, however, when dealing with facts we must never forget that all facts are descriptions. All histories then should be to be accurate but they remain the descriptions of historians. Historians cannot escape—as Hayden White argued—the pairing of truth and circumstance. However, if we conflate 'the past' with 'history' we unavoidably create (or discover?) a historical past. So, historical narratives constantly tidy up the past but, and ironically, they always leave the past open-ended. Sooner or later, every history metamorphoses into a new past.

But, as I have noted, this process of differentiation is always 'formed' as a reconstruction, construction, or a deconstruction of the past. This is why there is no certainty or certification in the nature of the past. And, of course, most historians unfortunately and invariably talk about 'history' when they actually mean the past. So, the knowledge of history as a *fictive* construal is always patchy, constrained, curtailed, and constantly unfinished even though the impossible and unresolvable problem with history remains. The central problem with history, then, is that it never ends and hence all histories are constantly supplements or, worse, a complete rethinking of our existent history. So, 'historical events with meanings and explanations' cannot exist before the historian creates their version of the past.

So, the *fictive* nature of history means there are so many—and unavoidable—differential pasts. Now, this does not mean 'anything goes' in the past. Thus, when it comes to James Buchanan, the 15th President of the United States, many historians claim it was his failure to stop the southern states' secession which probably led to the American Civil War—or not depending on which 'historical analysis' you prefer. Thus, 'the historical event' only exists in the individual historian's range of their *fictive* history. Today, most historians tend to think there is no emplotment in the past until they have discovered it.

So, for every historian there is always a 'simulacra' and 'simulation' as the philosopher Jean Baudrillard suggested, and he might be right. The 'simulacrum' then (as quoted by Baudrillard) is never what hides the truth, and it is the truth that hides the *fictive*. So, the simulacrum is most likely true but, unfortunately, most historians herd in the direction of the archives that are invariably located in a very tacky and boggy location of the mind. The central problem with history, then, is that it is supposed 'to be discovered for what it was' when it is of course a simulacrum—exaggerated in comparison to reality. Thus, because all histories are *fictive* simulacra it is dangerous to put too much into them if you want the kind of truth you prefer.

Now, the really bad news for historians is that history is a very weak mechanism if all historians want *the* reality of the past. So, all that historians can hope for (yet again) is the(ir) image of the past. The doppelgänger of the past that all historians can hope for is *their* history. Because the past cannot be captured for what it was, historians have to do with their reflection of a profound past reality. So, all history can provide is some sort of reality that can be regarded as a reflection of the past. But, as a *fictive* construal, history is more likely to be a denaturing of a profound past reality or, more likely, it masks the absence of the perpetual past that cannot be engaged with. So, all that histories can do is mask the situation that there is no profound 'now reality' in the past that can be captured.

Fictive 163

History, then, is just another simulacrum of a once profound reality but which is no more.

History, then, may appear to be simulacra but, in reality, it is a procession of simulacra constantly marching on. The past never stands still because the past is constantly recycled, re-vivified, re-verified, de-verified, re-demonstrated, re-certified, re-denied, re-polarised, and so forth. History, of course, is also a Mobius strip. And, of course, the past has its own engine but which is one that is metamorphosed into its *fictive* opposite. Far too many historians thus lean far too dangerously toward the real. Obviously, historians insist they must get the reality of the past, however, the past is constantly metamorphosed at the same time. Historians (well, most of them) know that it is impossible to rediscover *the* reality of *the* past. While it is a rather clumsy notion, all histories are hyper-simulations. Of course, most historians will hardly brook this language to describe past reality. But that is their problem.

Plainly, then, all 'histories' are unavoidably substitutes for the *fictive* past. This means all histories are hyper-theorised so that the past can be reconstructed as it really was. Unhappily (or happily if you prefer) the past never stands still because all histories are delivered on continuous conveyor belts. Happily, neither historians nor their consumers worry too much about the historical procession of 'the-past-*as*-history'. Now, no history can be definitive because no history is an apotheosis because it is always morphing. What this adds up to is that history is a constantly lost (retro) referential. This *fictive* past is pretty much the same as a dose of hyperreality. So, to be clear, history is a process for strong myths to be discovered and made.

Now, no single history corresponds with the past and most histories usually miss the intended target entirely. This, nevertheless, means even if history is a very strong mythic purgative for the truth of the past we cannot do without our histories. However, 'the past' and 'histories' are not clones. As I have suggested already, history can be regarded as a replication of the past but it is certainly not a 'clone story'. The real problem with history is, of course, historians who will insist that they regularly rediscover the nature and meaning of *the* past. This is a problem of course, because far too many historians will still insist that their *fictive* history is '*the* history' even though they insist that their histories are not mirrors of the past while trying to make sure they are. In the next and final chapter, then, I will engage with the unavoidable and obligatory classic problem of the *figurative*. So I will conclude with histories—that are not holograms—but they are certainly *figurative*.

10 Figurative

In this final chapter I will address the narrative concept of the *figurative* that enables the obvious turning of 'the past' into 'a history'. Plainly, the deployment of the concept of the *figurative* is central to all forms of representation especially when engaging with history. Given the purposes of this book the concept of the *figurative* describes the author's turning of 'past reality' into a 'history'. They do this by deploying the so-called common sense concepts of 'analogy', 'correspondence', 'resemblance', and 'likeness'. The past is inaccessible for obvious reasons. The past is the past but histories are invariably crude efforts at engaging that past or pasts that no longer exist apart from the historian's descriptions of the past.

So, just what is the past and how can the historian (or anyone else) engage with it? Well, the only way is by the historian 'authoring the past' as a *figurative* history. History, of course is not the past and the past is not history. Accordingly, history is plainly not to be found lying about in the past (in archives for example) except through the detritus and debris of the historian's *figurative* language. To engage usefully with the past then requires that historians, like anyone else, must accept the only vehicle which is *figurative* language. Here's a quick and simple definition. *Figurative* language is language that contains or uses figures of speech. When people use the term '*figurative* language', however, they often do so in a slightly narrower way. In this narrower definition, *figurative* language refers to language that uses words in ways that deviate from their literal interpretation to achieve a more complex or powerful effect. This view of *figurative* language focuses on the use of figures of speech that play with the meaning of words, such as metaphor, simile, personification, and hyperbole.

Now, given that the nature of the past and its meaning can only be carried in language, *figurative* language is common in all sorts of writing, as well as in spoken language. *Figurative* language is of course only one tool to constitute imagery, but imagery does not have to use *figurative* language by the deployment of tropes. Tropes are figures of speech that 'play' with and 'modify' the expected and literal meaning of words. Now, most historians tend not to play with the meaning of words and so they often create almost numberless new meanings. Historians, directly or indirectly, deploy language in their efforts to sustain what they believe was and still is the truth of the past. But the truth of the past is not the same as history, as when historians play with the structure of words, phrases, and sentences and when they also deploy tropes and all kinds of *figurative* language. Turning past reality into an authored history does not mean the past has been captured. But its nature is unavoidably shaped and formed by the employment of historian's *figurative* language.

So, when historians (like everyone else) deploy *figurative* language, they often play—for example, using assonance and alliteration. So, there are many *figurative* forms of speech with which historians deploy in order to shape the 'historical past' by engaging with metaphor, simile, oxymoron, hyperbole, personification, idiom, onomatopoeia, synecdoche, metonymy, alliteration, assonance, and so forth. Now, by noting all this I mean the historian's (and everyone else's) state of experiencing, imagining, and expressing 'the-past-*as*-history' can only be engaged with and through their *figurative* understanding of the nature of change over time. To be blunt then and like everyone else (again) historians constantly 'look back' to the past 'to know what it was' and 'to know what it meant', which becomes the historian's history. Now this is awkward at best. This is because all narratives, regardless of content and form, are simply substitute(s) for the assumed and evidenced reality(ies) of the past. To be clear on this then, everything in the past is entirely dependent on circumstances in the past, but only as the historian constitutes it. There is no history in the past until historians—along with everyone else as well—constitute that narrative known as 'the history'.

I am well aware that despite the demise of the postmodern insurrection in the last decade or so and which confronted the nature of history as a narrative form, many historians continue to struggle to grasp what they are actually doing. The substantial majority of historians continue to insist that by deploying 'common sense' soaked with the past as sustained by the empirically inspired, analytically self-informed, and dutiful processing of the past, the historian is led to the most probably meaning/explanation/story 'that can be discovered in the past'. This, apparently, is sustained by the deployment of simple 'common sense' and which is then followed by a shrewd analysis of the many yet to be discovered most probable meanings. Given this most historians are happy to 'render the most likely interpretations of what the past most probably could sensibly mean'. However, this *figurative* process is at best naïve and at worst a demonstration of a deeply catastrophic bad logic. This bizarre logic can only be sustained (and unhappily it is) because too many historians constantly and wilfully and failingly understand the nature of the(ir) representation of the past.

Now, at this point a substantial majority of historians (both professional and amateur) are unlikely to agree with my analysis of the deployment of the *figurative* and as a secondary source it can easily be rejected. The *figurative*, then, is simple literary decoration. However, consumers of history and history authors are always unavoidably led to the so-called primary and secondary sources, which further leads both historians and consumers to deploy the *figurative* so they can claim that they most likely know what did and did not happen in the past. Now, primary sources are more often than not a written (or some other ersatz *figurative* form) such as diaries, speeches, letters, images, artifacts, buildings, and so forth. And as we know, in addition to primary sources, historians use secondary sources, which are also usually what historians chose to 'author their history into existence'. And so it is well known that historians invariably quote other historians (secondary sources) in order to support each other's *figurative* understanding of the past.

Now, what I have just suggested leads me to a very simple conclusion. Turning the past into a history can only 'make sense' if the historian has their own and truthful construction of the past. So, academic historians and everyone else, of course, all construe a convenient past for what are a variety of reasons. Obviously, of course, telling lies about the substantially evidenced reality of the past is stupid and irresponsible. However, in the process of 'doing history' it is plainly impossible to avoid the situation that history is not the past because it is a *figurative* (hi)story. The reality of this very awkward situation means that all histories are the result of the historian's preferred individual authorial decisions. Many historians can, of course, choose to 'suppose' that they can reconstruct and/or construct and even deconstruct the past if they wish even as they manage to get the sources and data correct if that is actually possible—and I am not at all sure that it is possible. In my judgment, then, this situation is plainly unavoidable given the nature of our existence.

So, how do historians cope with the nature of their *figurative* historying? Well, to start with, the substantial majority of historians are annoyingly and entirely ignorant of the concept of the *figurative* so there is nothing to worry about. However, historians and whether they are fully paid up academics or amateurs, are constantly aware that the(ir) 'historical imagination', especially thanks to the historian theorist R.G. Collingwood is usually just another annoying spoke in the revolving 'history wheel of the past'. Consequently, Collingwood argued that 'doing history' was akin to 're-enacting the past' which, anyway, is always elemental to the historian's 'historical imagination'.

Now, Collingwood's conception of the historical imagination is an instinctive *figurative* element that 'all good historians' deploy whether they know it or not. Unhappily the historical imagination never works because it sooner or later collapses into the truly bizarre notion of the historian's self-attested ability to 'probably reconstruct the-past-*as*-history'. Unfortunately, that belief is nonsense. The notion of 'getting the sources and data straight' is, of course, an honourable undertaking but there is very little intellectual effort required in 'figuring out what happened in the past' and 'what it might mean'—although historians always make much of comparing and contrasting each other's judgments and interpretations. For every history there is another competing history. Of course, apart from those very few crazy historians who deny the reality of the past and thus who choose to exist in their own past, most if not all sensible and rational historians will eventually deploy their preferred *figurative* interpretation. This is not difficult to do of course because historians always sift and filter the(ir) available sources, which they have 'selected and chosen'.

Accordingly, the vast majority of historians attend to the process of 'doing history' through the 'historical imagination' which is in turn controlled by 'learning and scholarship'. This notion was never better described than by the history theorist R.G. Collingwood's doctrine of re-enactment or rethinking the past, which operates via the historian's historical imagination. Detractors of Collingwood have repeatedly associated two ideas—re-enactment and/or rethinking. For this to make any sense historical thinking depends entirely on 'the historical imagination'. Historians then have choice when engaging with the past as 'reconstructions', 'constructions', and/or 'deconstructions' of the past. These notions allow the historian to create a convenient past where some events did or did not happen as they believe it happened, as the historian wants. Telling lies about the evidenced reality of the past is plainly stupid, irresponsible, and outrageously negligent. However, the basic and foundational problem that all historians cannot (ironically) avoid is that history is not the past. History then is a *figurative* (hi)story. This suggests that all histories are the historian's preferred authorial imaginative interventions even as they cope with getting the sources and data precise.

Thus, the concept of the *figurative* relates to what is the somewhat complex process of 'imaginative historical in(ter)vention'. Now, that difficult processing of the past by turning it into history is hopeless for the majority of historians. This is because historians have to insist that their function is to discover 'the truthful (hi)story' of the past. This, of course, is nonsense. Getting the data straight and thereby investigating the reality of the past is clearly an indispensable cultural undertaking. And, plainly, denying, repudiating, and/or disclaiming the 'evidentially attested past reality' is at least unwise and at worst stupid. But, historians are expected to deploy their authorial skills in discovering 'the nature of change over time' in accord with 'the available sources' that they have 'discovered' and 'sorted out' in the archives. And, of course, some of the sources do not 'fit' into the historian's understanding of the past as based on other sources. Therefore, this is an unfortunate situation, which historians cannot avoid. 'The past' remains 'the past' while history stays what it is—an authored *figurative* narrative about the past.

Now, as I have noted in previous chapters, history is not the past and so historians have to substitute something for it. However, the notion of the 'fictive historical imagination' is not news. Now, some 50 years ago the history theorist Hayden White suggested that all histories and philosophies of history contain 'data' and also deploy 'theoretical concepts' for explaining these data. In addition, he noted that historians create a 'historical narrative', which is both a 'poetic' and 'linguistic' construal and which they can present 'the-past-*as*-history'. Unhappily the vast majority of academic historians have studiously ignored his analysis; however, in my judgment, all histories are also *figurative* realities. Plainly, the substantial majority of academic historians today have failed to recognize White's argument that there can be no 'proper history' that is not also a 'philosophy of history'. In this book I have offered a further analysis of how the past is turned into history. Thus, I am suggesting that historians are constantly creating '*figurative*' realities' whether they know it or not.

Unhappily, then, most historians are unaware that when they create their histories they are actually creating *figurative* 'past history realities'. Consequently, 'historical characters' from and/in the past are authorially construed as *figurative* creations. This does not mean 'historical agents' are simply presented by the historian-author and thus authorially 'formed' thanks to the available evidence and the historian's interpretation of the meaning of the detritus of the past. All histories and their emplotments then, are unavoidably *figurative* creations of the historian. Ironically, the *figurative* embellishment on the past is the historian's own a priori imagination. The obvious problem with history and which cannot be resolved is that there is always a history somewhere wedged against the past. Now, as the author of this book I am swayed toward an ironic mode of analysis because, well, that is my personal inclination, but I could create and shape 'a history of history' by choosing a romantic, tragic, or comic emplotment or any conflation.

Now, sticking to the evidence of what they hope will turn out to be the most likely 'narrative reality of the past', historians (and everyone else for that matter) create *figurative* realities. Historians and their readers, then, constantly create fictive 'realities' for the past even if they do not know it. Thus, the historian's selected 'past historical character' is shaped and formed by the historian's understanding 'past *figurative* reality' which they believe 'forms the past'. The *figurative* is not a 'take it' or 'leave it' add-on to the historian's conception of the(ir) history. Ironically, the substantial numbers of historians are not aware that 'turning the past into a history' is entirely their responsibility. Hence, there is no history in the past to be discovered dependent upon the whim of the historian and her/his desires for the past.

Historians, then, are constantly creating 'historical *figurative* realities' in the forms of books, Ph.D.'s, lectures, seminars, and so forth. And all histories, then, exist in some intellectual/mental hologram form or as a trompe l'œil that unavoidably 'deceives the eye'. Historians thus create the mental illusions of a real past 'object' or 'scene' or 'event'. These illusions include the nature of the 'historical actors' with their 'motives', 'engagements', 'purposes', 'reasons', 'intentions', 'goals', 'objectives', and so forth. So, every history is a *figurative* reality that binds the (historian's) preferred past. Now, the historian-authors and their readers invariably expect to produce and/or read 'a *figurative* narrative of the past' but that expectation is unlikely. The reason is because historian-authors always engage a *figurative* history whether they know it or not. So, the historian and 'their history' has very little to do with 'a discovered past for what it actually was' apart from when it is emplotted.

To be clear then, there is no reality in any history apart from its own existence. In brief, there is no reality in the past but that does not mean there is no past reality, yet, everything in the past eventually escapes its own representation. Thus the past always leaks its resemblance in the form of a history. Now, getting the data straight is usually very simple. The tricky part is figuring out whether the historian is an 'extra-diegetic' or 'intra-diegetic' author which means they choose to be 'outside' and/or 'inside' of the 'historical world' that is construed as delivered to the reader. The 'extra-diegetic' narrator is 'above' or 'superior' to the story she/he chooses to invent, while the 'intra-diegetic' narrator is inside the *figurative* universe (as with an autobiography). Whatever the author-historian wants from 'the-past-*as*-history' their choice can only be that of 'reconstructing', 'constructing', or 'deconstructing' the past. So, historians in their desperate effort to align their pasts with their preferred histories as shaped and formed by their 'engagements' with the past have to accept that all histories are holograms.

A hologram is usually construed as some kind of a *figurative* image that appears to be three-dimensional and which can be seen with the naked eye but which is obviously unreal. This is not a bad definition of a history. As for historians, then, they cannot escape their 'history resemblance'. So, although historians constantly race into the past, all they come away with is its resemblance. So, in the race to acquire the past all that historians can hope for a bit more exactitude. But then sooner or later a fresh past turns up which appears to be a bit more exact. And so, nothing resembles itself, least of all histories, and all histories can only exist in some kind of hyperreality.

All histories at some point exist in a universe of either reconstruction and/or deconstruction but invariably manage to fall—or are pushed by historians—into some kind of *figurative* perpetual and/or construction. Historians then—and to be very clear—are first and foremost authors. They may regard themselves as highly qualified, and to be fair they usually are, who can engage with the past with the intention to 'discover' its reality and its meaning. However, decades in the archive more often than not come to naught if the historian cannot 'authorially create' a complex image of past events and what they (in probability) mean. Thus, 'the novel' as well as 'the history' is self-justifying and self-authorising and hence it is expected and anticipated that 'the history' is a complete-in-itself and self-authorising undertaking, which aims to be true. But, unhappily, this cannot work. As I have already suggested, the past is not history and history is not the past. All histories are supposed and presumed to be truthful in correspondence sense. What is written is what happened.

Unfortunately, for the historian and dependent on their intellectual proclivity, they have to construct and/or reconstruct or deconstruct a coherent picture (image, lecture, book, and so forth) of the past. Historians thus have to concretise the past as a picture of past reality in terms of space and time. Plainly, of course, all histories are representations and those representations always remain as representations. The concept of 'the historical imagination', then, is shaped not by the past as such but by the mechanics of the 'historian-*as*-an-author'. Thus: every history is shaped and formed by the historian as an author and thus insists that they have discovered the reality of the past. To be sure, historians must get the data straight, however, inventing the past as a *figurative* undertaking can be dangerously self-serving.

Deploying the *figurative* means 'figuring out' if there was only one past. Where do all those hundreds of deviant other histories come from? This may seem a trite if not puerile comment, however, far too many historians (yes, far, far too many) are extremely shaky when it comes to confronting the notion of bringing past reality into the present, stuffed away for further planning. Unhappily, then, historians might find it useful to engage with simulacra, simulation, and, yes, holograms.

Regardless of my previous judgment, it is apparent (well, it is to me) 'that getting the (hi)story straight' depends on working out the distinction between 'the past' and 'history'. However, making that distinction requires accepting and acknowledging that there are (annoyingly?) several forms of 'historical realism', which are defined and described by the emplotments that all historians can deploy, romance, comedy, tragedy, and satire. Now, the 'stuff of the past' aka 'what actually happened' seems simple enough to grasp but it is not. Historians can only engage with the past through 'doing history' in terms of 'the-past-*as*-history as laid down by each individual historian. Regrettably, the past never stands still. Historians constantly recreate, redefine, reinvent, and remake the past. To be clear then: the immeasurable range and activity of 'past time' can never be visualised as a whole, or as 'the history'.

Now, as the historian E.H. Carr famously suggested, one should study the historian before beginning to study the facts and he further suggested that facts are what the historian wants in order to interpret the past. That sentence was a worthy effort on my part to summarise what historians do. Unhappily, it still makes very little sense in my view. The deployment of *figurative* language precedes all histories. The typical history narrative as constructed by the historian is intended to represent the past.

However, the historian as a series of statements constructs that history narrative. All historical narratives, then, are comprised of statements that add up to being a 'narrative substance'. This narrative substance eventually adds up to being a coherent history. The narrative of a history is thus a series of statements, which eventually add up (hopefully) to an accurate representation of the past. Unhappily, this does not mean such history narratives are the history narratives and so—perhaps awkwardly—there are as many pasts as there are *figurative* histories.

The upshot of this is that turning the past into a history is little more than a 'writing reality effect'. Every history can reference 'what probably happened in the past' but all histories are also unavoidably a morality play. All histories are a series of ethics strung on a string of empirical events shaded by collections of ideological assumptions. All histories are nothing more than the reality-effects through the authorial endeavours of the historian. To be clear, then, the reality of the past is just another 'authenticity' game of *figurative* language. The historian's engagement with the *figurative* dimension of history is unavoidable because that rendezvous is foundational to the historian's (and everyone else's) engagement—a *figurative* reality effect—with the past.

Now, the single major problem with history and which is impossible to resolve, is determining between two histories of the same past. Thus, the Industrial Revolution would be different according to the decisions of two economic historians where one ignored the Spinning Jenny, Bessemer process, interchangeable parts, sewing machine, and so forth, and another historian did not. Which history is the best and/or which is the most appropriate? This is the problem that every historian faces—which *figurative* past do they want through which they believe they can resuscitate through their 'selective historying'? So, then, historians discover 'the-past-*as*-history' but only as they create it. By that I obviously do not mean that historians 'make up the past' for their personal preference or partiality but of course, there is the perpetual problem which is that the past always ends up as a simple historical 'description' and/or some sort of 'depiction'.

Now, none of this is hardly news. The philosopher Nelson Goodman addressed this problem in his classic text *Ways of Worldmaking* (1978) but I suspect that, if I am right, most historians will not have read that text and should any historian read this book email me and we can talk about it. However, Goodman's argument is at once both audacious as well as iconoclastic and if non-philosopher historians actually understood the reality of the past it would strike loathing and fear in the hearts and minds of most of them. However, Goodman's argument is embarrassingly straightforward, which is that some true statements (and it applies to all those authorial versions of the past and their meanings) can produce useful legitimate conflict. This means that there are 'many commensurate histories' available and there is no way to safely distinguish them. This, of course, does not mean historians happily loll about telling lies while others do not (although, of course, there might be some). Anyway, and that aside, Goodman suggests that many 'true statements' conflict with each other and I suggest that there are still many legitimate competing histories. So then, there are no unquestionable 'true facts' when it comes to the process of historying simply because all 'past events' are only the *figurative* descriptions of historians.

As I noted earlier, the French theorist Jean Baudrillard suggested in his classic text *Simulacra and Simulation* (1981) that there is no fixed reality past, present, or future. Historians, of course, tend not to read and/or learn from Baudrillard, and so vast numbers of academic historians do not entertain the belief that their histories are creations even though they insist their 'history creations' are 'discoveries'. Historians tend, then, to ignore the embarrassingly and unavoidable situation that the past no longer exists despite their bizarre intention and purposeful effort to resurrect the past through their histories. Historians thus engage with a past universe that was once 'reality' but which is now irreal despite the historian's imaginary engagement with the time before now except at that resounding distance of the simulacra. To be blunt then: all histories are simulacra. This does not mean all historians should be put out of a job. But the trade of the historian as it presently exists really does need a substantial intellectual overhaul. Get over history and embrace the simulacra?

Well, I assume that is unlikely to happen soon. However, it might be useful for historians to acknowledge that history is not a discovery but it is a serious *figurative* intellectual undertaking. The past, then, has no in-built 'history-awaiting' discovery. Histories, then, are never discovered or uncovered or unearthed or exposed or revealed and so forth. Histories are never discovered because historians author them into existence. In making this challenge for historians does not mean I am a nihilist. However, I have observed several decades of histories and historians who will insist that 'the past is history' and 'history is the past'. Apart from that bizarre notion being embarrassingly silly, all that historians do and all they can do when engaging with what would be the empty past if it were not 'filled' by the historian's preferred narratives. This is evidenced (unfortunately) by the numbers of the really silly or worse, dangerous nonsense of some 'historians'.

Now, the aesthetics of 'historying' still today somehow rarely engage historians but most presume instead to see themselves as spatial 'discoverers', or intellectual 'adventurers', or just 'pioneers', or 'innovators' and so forth. But, most historians, I presume, want to engage with the reality of the past. However, most historians sooner or later (frequently sooner than later) come across their own 'historical consciousness', which is shaped by their ideology, their age, their gender, their understanding of epistemology, their preferred aesthetics, the grant running out, or total ignorance of their choice of their *figurative* aesthetics, and so forth.

Figurative 173

Now, and obviously, all academic historians engage with the past through their *figurative* writing of the past. This (rather simple) authorial process is an engagement in the process of a rather crude metamorphosis in terms of the historian departing from a literal use of words, which is both metaphorical and mimetic. So, historians engage with 'the history of the past' in terms of their reflections on their nominated sources, which are known as 'the evidence' that reflects and mediates 'the veracity of the nature of the past' and which can be accessed through voluminous 'sources'.

For most historians, then, 'the historian's history' reflects a reality of the past as retrieved through 'the historian's sources' and their insistence that the past 'throws up' 'the historian's preferred understanding of the past'. So, the connecting between the past and history is characteristically accounted for by the 'correspondence theory of truth' and fortunately sustains the referential nature of 'the historian's history prose'. So, what this produces, in effect, is the validation of the historian's confidence in the Greek concept mimesis, which means 'imitation'. Now, most historians like to believe that the past delivers itself 'into their hands and minds' after a great deal of effort on their part (or fortuitousness). Anyway, the appliance of engaging the reality of the past 'evidently' not only depends on the process of '*figurative* mimesis' but also expresses the historian's exemplification of what they believe 'happened'. So, the past looks like what it represents as in a trompe-l'œil painting or the art movement of verism and/or a historian's aesthetic turn.

So, all histories are unavoidably imitations of an assumed and accepted past reality. Now, the most substantial problem that all historians have is the clear one, which is that history is the representation of the past in another narrative. Now this is often believed to be a down to earth realist understanding of what is 'the history of the past'. Now, this view assumes the historian is essentially just a cipher in this representation. At the same time and somewhat paradoxically, it is also acknowledged that the historian is the author of the history they assume they have discovered. In other words, he or she is a writer who, through their narrative making/literary constructionism, chooses to imitate the empirical past in a way as they create their history an aesthetic undertaking.

This imitative tradition that (in)forms the pragmatist perception of history can be 'uncovered' in the belief that 'the history' both discovers and (re-)presents the story of what people did in the past. The brief postmodern critique of 'doing history' as laid out by J.F. Lyotard, Jacques Derrida, Hayden White, and Frank R. Ankersmit has, however, provided grounds for the rejection of the *figurative* theory of representation. Once the metanarrative 'that art must imitate reality' is rejected through the casting out of the transcendental signified or the knowable originary past, the consequent elevation of the *figurative* history can no longer be viewed as just simply the product of an act of mimesis.

Arguably, the most detailed analysis of 'change over time', and noting the acknowledgement of support for mimesis, was that provided by the French philosopher Paul Ricoeur who maintained that the essential nature of our engagement with the past exists in the ability of historians to construct and/or deconstruct, that history is itself most appropriately understood as a narrative making. So, explanation through a history is much more than just following a story and this, of course, is at the crux of the debate about what is history. So, the problem is: what is the balance between the empirical-analytical and the narrative-linguistic? Responding to this, then, assumes that history must possess its own narrative consistency rather than that the past is simply and crudely archival research. What this means is that all historians must combine '*figurative* evidence', '*figurative* tropes', and '*figurative* arguments'.

Paul Ricoeur, in his text *Time and Narrative* (1984) suggested that there is an essential and unbreakable link between 'telling the (hi)story as a text' and 'the reality of change over time'. He suggests that as the referential text describes actual action, this makes texts like history realist and so history brings 'past experience' to 'present language'. While acknowledging the significance of emplotment in making history it is not just a poetic/imaginative and semiotic act. Hence it remains possible for historians to view their narrative making as a truthful, candid, and straightforward attempt to represent the nature of past action through cause and effect. This suggests that the historian can thus view the act of narrative making as a complex mime of the intentional acts of historical agents and/or the evidentially revealed structures of change over time through the hands and minds of historians. Ricoeur reinforces this point by assuming that people in the past always constructed their lives as emplotted narratives. So it is that historians, he concludes, can find out the story shape of the past as it appeared to the minds of historical 'actors' and imitate it in the history texts.

Now, I suppose that some historians (and even worse some non-historians) might even suggest that I am unassumingly suggesting that the past is not history and history is not the past. However, and, like most historians I am a historian who wants to know the nature of the reality of the past—well, in probability terms. I obviously want to know 'who' did 'what' and 'why' and 'when' in the past. But I also want to know why every historian has his or her own version of the past and why some historians work at a glacial pace and why some other historians knock out a book every year. Thus, why do so many historians constantly shape and reshape 'their past' through ideological perspectives?

Now, perhaps the basic problem that no historians appear to be capable of resolving is their conflation of the 'ideological' and the 'philosophical' when engaging with 'change over time'. So, most historians simply ignore their central and unavoidable problem. Rendering the nature of the past depends on two notions. These are cogency and authenticity.

How big (or small) does a book or a lecture or a seminar or a journal article or a chat on a bus need to be in order to insist that it is a definitive history? The answer is embarrassingly simple. There is no answer to the nature of the past even if historians depend on the validity and veracity of their sources and data. However, validity and veracity (as Nelson Goodman maintained) guarantee nothing. Both induction and deduction always fail even if historians expend a career of many decades determining the rationality and legitimacy of the past as offered by countless thousands of historians.

Now, the problem that faces historians and everyone else is that no one can escape from the inductive categories that historians invent. Historians, then, are entirely useless (yes, useless) when it comes to the cogency, legitimacy, and reliability of the past. Obviously, as I have suggested already, it is very easy to know what happened in the past but in terms of its meaning, significance, consequence, moment, and substance history is largely useless. Historians can (and do) engage with the past as best they can, but the inductive and deductive aesthetic categories deployed by historians are seriously flawed. Knowing what happened in the past is plainly very important but no histories—because they are narratives—have any truth-values.

So, every historian is in a very sad state from which they cannot escape. To be clear then: deductive and inductive inference cannot project the past onto the ductile wall of history. Plainly then, the nature of the historian's perspective can only be shown on the nature of the wall of 'the history'. The paradox in all this then is that the past is not history and history is not the past. Hence, there is never the right history to represent and/or re-present. A history, then, is true for the *figurative* history description and/or representation for the world it fits, however, this does not mean lying about the attested reality of the past because that would be mindless nonsense. To be clear then: a history is always designed to stand up to constant re-examination and rethinking. This does not mean all *figurative* histories must eventually collapse. But so far all have. And so, all histories are experiments, and all experiments are histories.

Unhappily, then, historians along with almost everyone else generally ignore the aesthetic *figurative* nature of history. Now, for the historian their job is to be true to 'the facts' and hence 'historical accuracy' is what shapes and forms the nature of the past. However, loyalty to 'the facts' does not in itself bestow 'aesthetic excellence' in the form and shape of 'the history'. Now, and obviously, there is always a synonymy between the reality of the past and its (presumed) history. In respect to the connection between the past and history the historian exists in a very awkward situation. So, historical representations are or are not assumed to be counterfactual historical representations. Historians have something in common with painters. Historians have contexts, frameworks, debates, outlines, chronologies, and construals and from a distance a history can be a rabbit and/or a duck.

The way the 'historical mind' works is in the correlation of 'content and form' but also in terms of 'ideology and trope' as well as 'empiricism and *figurative*' style, and the historian unavoidably acknowledges the awkward connections between the past world and the perpetual present word, the knower and the known, fact and fiction, past and present, truth and interpretation, and, hence, history and narrative. The upshot is that the authenticity of the past is characterised and accessed primarily as an empirical undertaking, which is composed as the historian's desired narrative of a reality/realistic effect. Obviously, the content of the past—history—does not speak for itself. The past is what history is as delivered by the historian or anyone else for that matter as a history. Hence, 'doing history' is simply only a reality effect of the historian's preferred 'history narrative'. So, when engaging 'the-past-*as*-history' all the historian can engage is that history they create as a realistic effect of the past they want to offer. Obviously then, the content of the past is engaged with simply a pre-configured narrative as created by the historian.

All histories then, are pre-configured narratives as construed through the historian's belief that there must be an in-built epistemological and ontological shaping of the past (whether the historian realises it or not). The meaning and nature of the past, then, is simply what the historian wants to believe about the past. Obviously, 'historical situations' are not inherently tragic, comedic, satiric, or romantic and all the historian needs to do to transform a tragic into a comic situation is to shift her/his point of view or should they want to change the scope of their perceptions for what reasons only the historian knows. Nevertheless, historians (and everyone else) only think of 'past situations' as tragic, comedic, satiric, or romantic because these concepts are part of our cultural and specifically literary heritage. How a given 'historical situation' is configured depends on the historian's subtlety in matching up a specific plot structure with the set of historical events that the historian wishes to bestow with a meaning of a specific kind.

Now, most academic historians—whether they realize it or not—engage with 'form', 'ideology', and 'empiricism' and also their '*figurative* style' while also connecting 'the historical word' to the present 'history conversation' in terms of the historian as both a knower and the fact (an event under a description) and the *figurative* 'past', 'present', 'truthfulness', 'interpretation' and 'the history narrative'. The upshot of all this is that historians are invariably anxious about the reality of the past which is characterised as an empirical undertaking, but the effect of 'past reality' disavows the study of the content of the past because the past requires historians and their consumers to think about history not only for what it patently is. So, all histories are constituted and pre-configured narratives that are relentlessly shaped and formed through the broader epistemological and ontological implications for what historians want to do with the past.

History, then, is obviously entirely constituted by the individual historian when she or he 'believes' given the nature of their (the historian's) intentions. To be clear then, and as I noted earlier, a central theme of history today is a paradox. While there are increasingly fewer historians who deploy irony, there is unavoidably and invariably a worm in the fruit of the past. Today, in my experience then, histories are increasingly the dependent ironic residues of the past and that means historians most often seek out—but fail to find—the worm in the fruit of virtue. Historians, these days, tend to seek out an ironic vision for their histories and so historians increasingly today like to insist that 'the past' is a developmental 'process of advance'.

Now, today, it may be time for increasing numbers of historians to pursue an ironic vision of the past. Of course, all historying is subject to ideology, power, authority, influence, gender, and the constant change of 'pastness'. What this means (I suggest) is that most historians desire to assuage the(ir) compulsion to discover their *figurative* 'historical reality' but and obviously, there is no such thing as that. Now, all historians and their consumers seek out realism in the past. But this is a hopeless undertaking. The only realism that we have in the past is in 'the narrative history' that the historian creates for the past. The notion of discovering the nature of the past is a very unlikely undertaking because it can only be *figurative*.

When historians want to get into the warp and weft of the past it usually means they have to decide which *figurative* speech to deploy. The obvious choice is that synecdoche, which is a figure of speech in which a term for a part of something refers to the whole of something or vice versa, so, historians either mention a part for the whole or conversely the whole for one of its parts. Thus, 'a history' is simply an elasticated *figurative* representation and so it is that all histories are constantly malleable, pliable, flexible, and workable. This suggests that the past constantly comes round again and again and again. In a comment of the philosopher G.W.F. Hegel, 'what is' is 'in itself'. History, then, is all too often reduced to a simple set of the historian's preferred *figurative* myths.

So, history is simply a contemporary aesthetic literature. Obviously, all histories 'tell (hi)stories' but no given histories constitute the past. What we have, then, in terms of the past are (hi)stories as shaped and formed by the historian's preferred aesthetic. Hence, the notion of 'telling the past like it was' is a worrisome nonsense. To be sure we can know what actually happened in the past (to a very high level) but not what it means. The eccentricity in this is that historians also deploy 'the *figurative* past'. Now, historians cannot have it both ways. There is 'history' or there is 'the past'. So, historians have to make a choice. Historians can 'construe' and/or 'make' their beliefs about the past. This means all historians have

178 *Figurative*

a decision to make about the past in terms of the(ir) preferred past. Further, this means that the process of doing history is never going to have the in-built past waiting to be discovered story.

Now, there is no reality in histories because histories only exist courtesy of the historian. So, while the job of the historian is to explain the past it can only be of any utility if the historian believes they have discovered the(ir) history. So, every history not only tells a story it is assumed every history is the history. So, historians may engage with the notion of mimesis it is a constant illusion. For social science historians the bad news is that there is no realism in history—there is only a 'make see' social science. There are various realisms in history, but there is never sufficient reason to make good on the historian's insistence that what they 'tell' and 'say' is the reality of the past. Now, the foundational problem with historians is, as Oscar Wilde suggested (in another context), that historians very often offer the unspeakable in pursuit of the uneatable. The past is what each solitary historian wants it to be.

However, there is always and obviously a *figurative* void that separates 'the past' from 'history'. Plainly then, the most serious problem that historians encounter is that *figurative* gap. Historians rarely acknowledge that they are 'telling it like it was' simply because they insist that they are always offering 'the reality of the past'. Unfortunately that is simply wrong. Historians deploy simile, metaphor, synecdoche, hyperbole, personification, and puns like everyone else. Indeed, historians tend to deploy *figurative* language more often than most folk do. The oddity in this is that (by and large), historians like to 'tell it like it was'.

Perhaps unfortunately then and far too often (and possibly) inadvertently, historians deploy catchy *figurative* book titles along with a language on both the front cover and the back cover and also in the rest of the book. The common example of the front cover of a book is an image that stands in lieu of a key concept or character. Thus, every 'history' deploys the usual emplotments of romance, comedy, tragedy, or satire and also with the common various forms of academic texts there are catchy images for the covers and having prefaces of various lengths and with the usual introductions, chapters, and, dependent on the nature of the text, a thin or thick index.

Now, I have to briefly refer to that branch of metaphysics of ontology, which deals with the nature of 'being'. Now, the ontological nature of history refers to change over time and also how the historians deal with that which does not exist—the past. Fortunately, however, the ontology of history is embarrassingly simple because history is simply a representation of the past. Now, every history has a form. A history can be an event, an artifact, a tutorial, a lecture, a book, and a chat in when stuck in a lift, as well as a performance, an interpretation, a clarification, an amplification, and so forth, and, of course, every history is an aesthetic and *figurative* art interpretation.

Now, every history is not just yet another interpretation of the past. This is because all histories are at once unique affective endeavours. Thus, the ontological status of 'the history' is unavoidably an aesthetic object in itself and which thus carries within it a momentum to a lost reality. All histories are to some substantial extent ready-made so they can exist within the wake of all histories. All historians, then, take the mundane past and rethink it for the historian's present and presence. The past, then, is constantly engaged for the past the historian wants. The notion of discovering 'the history' is plainly nonsense. If historians want a new past reality for the time before now they simply create a new past out of the old.

Today then, and as I have already noted, all histories are reconstructed, constructed, or deconstructed and hence now the past is lucid as never before. So, in the past generation of postmodern historying I am often told that the past has now revived itself for many academic historians. However, today, then there is no new history. But then there never was. All histories die, then, before they have been born and hence we have so many differential histories. Choosing the past for the past is a creative undertaking akin to creating conceptual art. No one can avoid the situation that all histories today are ready-made histories. History today, as the history theorist Frank Ankersmit suggested, historiography is more artifice than reality. While getting the data straight historians today cannot readily offer the past as an aesthetic.

So, now, what we have today is little more than a *figurative* 'reality effect' of the historian/historians. Now this means it is impossible to erase the historian from their preferred past(s), and also the historian author's intentions, and the uncontrollable text itself, and also the reading into the past of the history consumer. All this is convoluted by the constant 'new insights' of historians along with the demands of publishers and (presumably) the consumers and the insistence that all involved in 'doing history' have innumerable new histories. But, the reality in the writing of 'the-past-*as*-history' is, as is well understood, just another effect of the historian's authorial in(ter)vention. I think I have engaged with the concept of reality something like 50 times in this chapter which I assume means that I think there is a clear and significant connection between the *figurative* and reality. What I think this means is that reality and the *figurative* should have a safe home among historians whether they realise it or not. Unfortunately, however, I suggest that both past reality and the *figurative* unavoidably combine to generate histories that are, well, unlikely to be objective. However, and unfortunately, historians continue to get in the way of the reality of the past despite how copious are their footnotes.

Conclusion

Now, and surely, all histories eventually come to an end, or do they? Well I suspect not, given that all histories eventually reshape the past. However, which came first? Is it the history or is it the past? I suggest it is the history. This may seem to be counter-intuitive because surely there must be 'the past' first before 'the history'? But, that is nonsense because all that we can access is the past is by creating a history for it. To be blunt then, there is no in-built past to be discovered and the belief that we need the past before we can discover its history is nonsensical. The past only exists through the historian's engagement with the past through the histories inserted into the past by historians and anyone else.

To be blunt then: the historian's and anyone else have a preferred narrative for the past. Thus the past exists as a desired history. It is the historian's interpretation of the past, which creates his or her preferred histories and for every historian then there is always another version of the past. Now, the past existed but only through its history/histories. And so, it is only because of our preferred history/histories that we can access the substance and nature of the past. But there is also another problem. Somewhat awkwardly, there are many different 'paradigms', 'hypotheses', 'assumptions', 'postulations', 'ideas about', 'mindsets', 'convictions', and many other beliefs and opinions as to the nature of 'the-past-*as*-history'. And so, the list I put together in this book—with its *factional*, *factitious*, *fabricated*, *factious*, *factitive*, *factive*, *factualist*, *fictitious*, *fictive*, and *figurative* nature of the past—is my preferred engagement with the past.

Now, I suggest, as historians and their consumers know (or they should know), that there is never the definitive history of the past. For every past moment there is always a narrative, either truthful or not, but nonetheless, historians these days are well aware that there are innumerable 'counterfactual pasts', which constantly struggle with the realities of the pasts as preferred by historians. This is why there are so many different histories available in terms of 'contents' and 'meanings' for the past(s). Now, every historian assumes that there is only one past and it happens to be his or her history. Unfortunately that makes no sense of any kind.

Conclusion 181

This is because there are so many 'privileged' and 'ready-made' historical narratives available thanks to each and every historian. Now, historians can usually tell which histories make sense to them and which do not. But while historians debate with each other over what appears to be 'the reality of the past', all historians still have the same residual problem of knowing and unknowing which is true and which is not.

The residues of the past invariably always end up as a substantial (or unsubstantial) trail of detritus which, when the historian has 'cleaned it up' and having dismissed the dross of the past as they believe, the past speaks for itself but differentially for every historian. So, how can historians 'test the truth of the reality of the historical past'? Well, they cannot. And so there is no 'historical past'. The 'historical past' is a creation of each individual historian's past. Now, it is impossible for historians or anyone else to compare the present presentation of the past with its precise past existence. Now then, all historians make the same serious error—and it is a very serious error—which is that they conflate the past with history and history with the past. This ridiculous situation is made worse if historians assume all histories are, well, living histories. That is plainly nonsense. There are history narratives and that is all we have in the perpetual absence of the past. Now, there is another particularly silly belief that all human beings are 'living histories'. Or worse, there is the silly belief that every human being is some sort of unavoidable historian and so histories are often claimed to be 'living histories'. This again is nonsense.

Unfortunately, rethinking the past creates a lot of injury to those human beings and others involved in the process of engaging with the past. Now, and perhaps undeniably, the greatest danger for people is to be told that there is only one history. Or, there were competing histories because there are constantly evolving historical contexts. And then, of course, the detritus of the past has to be sieved. But, knowing what actually happened in the past is never a guarantee of what it means in our present histories—or worse—what it might have been in the past. Now, the notion of 'if only' is the worse problem in engaging with the past because the past has to be construed, reconstructed, constructed, deconstructed, and unavoidably interpreted. And so, knowing facts defined as events under a description have very little utility. Knowing what happened in the past is useless until it is interpreted. But, then that is not very useful because the past is always 'historied' by historians.

Now, 'facts and dates' permit historians to engage with 'events under a description' at some point in time. But, interpreting 'what the past means' is always an imposition (or a range of impositions) on the past by historians and those human beings who want the past to be what they want it to be in terms of their preferred meanings and explanations. The notion of discovering 'the reality of the past with its appropriate meanings' is a desire never to be fulfilled. The reason is because the past is fluid. There are always new 'forms', 'sources', 'data', 'meanings', and 'explanations'. Hence, in this book I decided to offer a nomenclature for both historians and the history laity who (I hoped) might engage more fully with the process of 'doing history'. Now, engaging with the past forces the rejection of the classic notion of 'the facts' and 'nothing but the facts', which is a truly dreadful guide to the nature of the past.

Historians (and students and anyone else if they feel so inclined) study both the original 'sources from the past' and 'learned opinions' or they think of new ways of re-evaluating new 'historical arguments' although such practices are a long, long way from memorising 'lists of facts'. So, students are regularly told that 'History' is not useful apart from learning what happened in the past and also collating, assembling, arranging, ordering, compiling, and so forth—and so the ten chapters in this book offer various forms of engaging with the past. However, knowing what happened in the past is entirely pointless if it is not acknowledged that 'doing history' is sieved through the historian's personal sieve.

In this book I have suggested that the past is not history and history is not the past. Each chapter in this book, obviously, demonstrates, among other things, that there are many different ways to engage with the nature of history. If I have made one central argument in this book it is that the past is not history and history is not the past. So I have not endeavoured to celebrate the many ways it is possible to engage with the past and this book is conventional with chapters, index, and so forth. But no history has to fit into this form. However, while there are many forms for offering the past, this book can only be a representation, which means there are several dimensions to this book.

The main point to this book is to suggest that history is a construal and certainly that history cannot conflate 'the past' with 'history'. Given our perpetual 'present' we cannot recapture the past. So, all historians can have, in the absence of the past, is the history they construe. Now, all we can have in the absence of the past is that history that can be revealed as subjectively chosen, subjectively interpreted, subjectively constructed, and subjectively incorporated within a narrative. All histories then are narratives, and anyone who writes 'a narrative history' is offering their construal.

The historian's function (obviously?) differs substantially from that of the novelist. Authors of fiction—yes, fiction—may examine the historical record in fine detail in their effort to recognize its intricacies, and then use detours, digressions, and detours via footnotes in order to explain and provide authority to their 'findings'.

Now, the novelist, of course, uses their imagination to create characters and emplotments and can leave out details, which might get in the way of the plot. However, the chief task of the historian is to (re)present the past to a reader in their perpetual present. The past then can only be delivered through the construction of meaning through narrative. In one obvious sense, every narrative is a foremost component in the long-lasting and close relationship between the *factional, factitious, fabricated, factious, factitive, factive, factualist, fictitious, fictive,* and *figurative* nature of the historical past. None of the chapters in this book are offered as little more than a possible intellectual landscape for connecting 'the past' with 'history'. Attitudes among most historians lean simply toward a line drawn between 'fiction' and 'history'. But, as I have suggested in this book, the nature of our engagement with the past does not simply pivot on 'history and the past'. The boundary and borderland between the past and history reveals a hitherto problem. This is the dilemma of history and the past and the past and history.

The obvious problem here is the notion of the concept of 'historiographical metafiction', which was created by the Canadian literary theorist Linda Hutcheon in the late 1980s. The term was (if somewhat less used these days) for works of fiction, which may combine the literary devices of historical and literary texts. Now this notion has been discarded somewhat, however, the notion has been around since the birth of historying, although most academic historians will have never heard of it. So, to be clear, there was a brief flirtation with other forms that 'played' with deliberately entangling unreality pasts. Examples were E.L. Doctorow with his *Ragtime* (1975), Salman Rushdie's *Midnight's Children* (1981), and 'historiographic metafiction' in general.

It also notes the distinction between 'events' and 'facts'. Now, 'historians' do not transmute 'past events' into 'facts' and so the claim is that 'historying' turns out to be what the historian Linda Hutcheon describes of 'historiographic metafiction'. Happily, this is a very simple notion that the past undoubtedly once existed, but our 'historical knowledge of the past' is obviously semiotically transmitted as descriptions. Now, this is not really difficult to figure out. Whether they know it or not, historians always end up with a 'historiographic' that depends on the usual 'authority' and 'objectivity' of 'historical sources' and 'explanations' as supported by 'justifications', 'validations', 'confirmations', 'endorsements', 'ratifications', and so forth.

So, the dilemma for historians remains. Their perpetual dilemma is that the past is not history and history is not the past. Consequently, when/then does the past become a history? Well, I assume, as soon as historians decide to frame their (hi)stories by deploying 'causality' and 'subjectivity' and 'probability' and 'credibility' and 'assumptions' and 'suppositions' and 'presumptions' and 'deductions' and so forth. So, when do historians actually turn the past into history? At what juncture do historians start to believe 'in reality' they can capture 'the past world' on 'the present page'? In one sense, of course, all historians fail in rejuvenating the past through their 'discovered history(ies)'. Now, for every historian there is always 'a past'. But there is also always another history lurking in the intellectual undergrowth of the historian and this is because (ironically?)

there are as many histories as there are historians willing to offer. As the history theorist Robert A. Rosenstone once suggested 'people are hungry for the past'. Now, while histories have their strengths and weaknesses, they are targeted at a limited audience in an outdated format. But, of course, today there is a much wider range of forms for staging the past than ever before.

The historian Simon Schama in his text *Dead Certainties (Unwarranted Speculations)* (1992) was criticised for creating dramatic scenes based on dubious historical sources without informing the reader of the historian's 'fabrications'. In this work, Schama questioned notions of factual history and noted the limitations of historians. The title of his book was suggestive in itself, while the afterword to the book is explicit, as historians are painfully aware of their incapacity to reconstruct a past through their selected documentation. Historians, then, are pre-destined to be forever hailing someone of some importance who has just gone around the corner. Again, considered to be 'postmodern' and not acceptable to publishers and agents as the correct way to present history, despite the author's reassurance that nothing was invented and 'it just tells the story a different way'. So, many historians today can if they want to will be willing to engage with the past in their preferred way, while willing to mix the publisher's commercial constraints with the demands of the university.

Today, then, the substantial majority of historians continue (to insist) that history is not an authorial creation (as I suggest it is) but is an exercise in *the* discovery of the past. To be sure we need to know what actually happened in the past, but the ontology of history is in that form the author-historian wants to construe it. Obviously, historians, then, are not discoverers of the past. Historians are also and unavoidably involved in debates as much as they may be worried about what actually happened in the past. However—and obviously—knowing the nature of 'the past' is unavoidably constituted as 'our history'. So, 'our preferred culture' recreates the past thanks to historians and non-historians alike. Ironically for the historian then, knowing that the nature of the past is irregularly shaped so are the futures of histories. This, of course, is understandable given that historians are sustained simply by knowing the(ir) presumed reality of the past existed back there and then, and they are also happy to 'shape', 'form', and 'constitute' their historical future of the past.

Now, apart from historians, most people have a very limited understanding of their own present and the past. And so, why worry about it? Whether 'the past' might be true or not, no one can travel back in time to recover their preferred history or histories. This is where we have to acknowledge that all histories ultimately turn out to be unserviceable and so the notion of 'getting the history straight' almost invariably collapses as historians struggle with the archive, and so it has to be admitted that the past possesses many different histories. Instead of a lengthy glossary, then, I will offer what is my shortlist of essential concepts that historians deploy in order to open up the nature of the past.

Now, apart from the nature of the past—the time before now—I suggest all historians need to engage primarily with their nature of 'doing history'. This may seem odd because historians are assumed only to be concerned with the 'historical reality' of the past. Now, that makes no sense of any kind. My logic, then, is that I start with the nature of history for what I think is a very good reason. Knowing what happened in the past has to be described. This might worry many historians. Surely history is a detective undertaking? Finding out what happened when and why? As in, getting the (hi)story straight. Unfortunately and unhappily that makes very little sense of any kind. This is because all histories are narratives and an author who wants to be engaged with the nature of the time before now.

Now, in the Introduction I suggested that historians, despite their honest faith, believe they can 'discover' the most likely narrative that surely must have existed in the past. So, in our constant 'now' historians continue to be sustained in their endeavours as to the reality of the past as it actually was. Unfortunately that is impossible because history never existed in the past. History only exists as that intellectual pursuit of the historian and/or anyone else who indulges in their naïve belief that the past can be re-acquired. So, all we can have is that concept called 'history' which is, of course, a narrative literature that substitutes for the past.

As I suggested at the start of the Introduction, these concepts are stand-alone inventions on my part. And, like any other 'analysis' it will eventually collapse and be rejected or repaired in some new authorial way. So, I endeavoured to offer some random thoughts on the nature of history and historying. So, I may be 'overegging my pudding', but history is not the past and the past is not history. To understand the environment of 'history' the substantial majority of academic historians have to accept that they cannot know what the past was. By that I do not mean ignoring the events in the past because some historians (or non-historians for that matter) may not like what happened in the past. Hence, a very few historians just tell lies, but most historians—the vast majority—are honest and diligent in getting *the* (hi)story straight.

Now, in this book I have offered my understanding of how the past is engaged through our histories but it is important to acknowledge that history is the historian's literary understanding of the past. Accordingly, and surprisingly, far too many historians fail to understand the nature of history. History is that branch of literature concerned with the theoretical, hypothetical, and conceptual nature of our knowledge of the past. So, then, the past is history, however, history is not the past. So, knowing what happened in 'the time before now' can only be an authorial engagement. To put this simply, every historian unavoidably deconstructs the past to fit it into the needs of our perpetual present.

So, in this book I have offered those key concepts that I believe historians and their consumers might find useful when engaging with the past. To be frank then, the ten concepts that I offer in this book suggest that the past is an authorial intervention in terms of how the past can be construed. Now, every historian construes the(ir) preferred past, so, there is no single given past. But does this make any sense? Surely this cannot be right? Well, that is the way our world works. For every historian there is a history. Many are very similar to each other. Others are not. And, unhappily still today, some of them are dreadfully dangerous nonsense that denies 'past reality'.

So, in the absence of the past, all histories are in some form or another acts of intentional re-creations. Unhappily, of course, every history is a construal and some are much better than others depending on the individual historian and their social circumstances, intellect, and knowledge. But the basic issue remains. What is the connection between the past and that (usually individual) history literature written about it? Well, the plain and obvious connection is reference. As I have already noted, history is not the past and the past is not history. And that is why I offered the concepts I have engaged with in this book (the *factional, factitious, fabricated, factious, factitive, factive, factualist, fictitious, fictive,* and *figurative*). Thus, all histories have their unavoidable aesthetic nature that historians have to acknowledge.

So, and understandably, the past has an unavoidable aesthetic dimension. The past, then, can only be deliverable as a form of literature and so it is only after being processed *into* the historian's preferred history that the past can be made useful. Of course this does not mean the past can be denied (that would be dangerous and stupid) but all histories are permanently deconstructions that undo the assumed and/or presumed past. However, all histories are ready-made. The irony in 'doing history' then, is that there are always many histories which can be—and usually are—claimed to be 'the past'. To deconstruct the past—which historians do constantly—means undercutting all that historians create. So, there are unavoidable inconsistencies among historians in terms not only of what actually happened in the past, but also what the meaning of the past might mean.

Now, all historians have their judgments as to the nature and meaning of the past and so they insist that the past can be retrieved and then made sense of (sort of) by revising the traces of the perpetual past. Now, it has to be admitted that 'the historical past' as opposed to 'the past' is a preferred reconstruction, construction, or deconstruction as determined by every historian. Hence, the historian's history is always a version of 'the past' that they pursue. And so, all histories are deconstructions of the past and that means that the past is not history and history is not the past. To be clear, then, all histories are made into a past as the individual historian wants and/or believes it was 'in reality'.

Conclusion 187

The annoyance in all this is that the past is an unavoidable deconstruction of the past. So, knowing what happened in the past is simple but it is what it means is the difficulty. To be clear then: all histories are in some way or another absurd. By that I do not mean all histories are silly, but historians and everyone else have to engage with the usually incongruous nature of the past. Dear reader, then, you should by now be well aware that there is a substantial absurdity in engaging with the past. To be clear again, the past is not history and history is not the past. The absurdity of 'doing history' is unavoidable for the very simple reason that the past is the past and all we can create is what we believe and insist is its history. Thus, the absurdity of 'history' is the situation that all historians have to 'discover purpose and order' in a nonsense past. The central irony in history, then, is that it is history and not the past.

Thus, and whether historians realize it or not, the intermediate between the past and history is aesthetics. Each of the ten chapters in this book demonstrates that our engagement with the past—I hope—is a demonstration of aesthesis. Obviously, aesthesis is a form of perception of historians (along with everyone else) that permits an engagement with that which can be accessed through interest and/or disinterest or objectivity and/or self-interest. Thus, history is that multifarious authorial 'aesthetic' through which we engage with the past. So, the author-historian has any number of options when it comes to turning the past into a history. Unfortunately and nonsensically, the notion that the past can be discovered through its history makes no sense. This is because 'the past' is always established as 'a deconstructed proposition'. This 'deconstructed proposition' is simply a processing of the meaning of the historian's understanding of the past.

So, all histories are unavoidably 'deconstructions' and/or 'reconstructions' and/or 'constructions'. Either way, all histories may be legitimately regarded as deconstructive 'stand ins' for the past as suggested by the philosopher Jacques Derrida (1930–2004) who proposed that there is no finality if the aim is to rethink the past. However, that is impossible given the chapters in this book. This historical text is also dialogical text. However, the descriptor 'dialogic' is fortunately very simple to explain but which never has held a solid grip on the minds of historians who tend to ignore 'the epic history' which is disconnected with the literary world. While the 'novel' and/or the 'academic text' or the 'lecture' or the 'seminar' intersect with other literary genres, histories remain what they are—histories.

Nevertheless, all histories are interpretations of the past thanks to the foundational concept of hermeneutics, which comprises the practice and theory of textual interpretation. Thus, the historian soon realises that their interpretation of the past is the only game in town. So, what you are reading now you have to interpret so it makes sense for you. Nevertheless, the only really useful notion for the historian (or anyone else) when faced with the past is the deployment of 'theory', 'practice', and 'explanation' and then hopefully 'understanding of the past' will follow. However, the key to understanding the nature of history, in addition to the ten concepts I have noted in this book—the *factional, factitious, fabricated, factious, factitive, factive, factualist, fictitious, fictive*, and *figurative*—there are also all the fairly straightforward concepts of 'epistemology', 'imagination', 'hermeneutics', 'ideology', 'ontology', and 'reality' and happily none of them are difficult to understand.

Dear reader, as you will have 'figured out' by now, my analysis of the nature of turning the past into the most likely history 'of the past' is an exercise of the historian's 'imagination' which, obviously, is an 'aesthetic authorial undertaking' in addition to 'seeking out the nature of the past'. As you, dear reader, will have by now understood the *factional, factitious, fabricated, factious, factitive, factive, factualist, fictitious, fictive,* and *figurative* are my authorial investments in the aesthetic past. Thus, there is 'no history in the past' until the historian 'fills it in' with their preferred 'history'. This, of course, is hardly news. Simply, then, history is not a 'lost past' awaiting discovery, it is a myriad of lost pasts and of which are disclosed or discovered or denied and contradicted. So, it is useful—and with a depthless irony—as the theorist Jean Baudrillard suggested, history is that 'retro scenario invested in' by the historian whether they realize it or not. And most do not of course.

Today, as always in the past, there is nothing but a constant 'retro secretion' of past meanings, explanations, and doubts that invariably turn up in many differential forms. Obviously, the constant deluge of history/histories repetitively washes the pebbles of the 'beached aesthetic past'. In a somewhat less flowery description, eventually the past is worn away but that is not a problem because there are always new pasts. Now, the connection between history and the past is at best awkward. This is because history is a literary creation rather than being the past. All histories are dedicated to the reality of the past thanks to historians. Unfortunately, history exists in a mythic fidelity to a nonexistent past. This may seem something of overkill, but there is no way to recoup the past until the next demand made of the past.

So, I suggest that history is the quintessential cultural myth that can only be understood through the *factional, factitious, fabricated, factious, factitive, factive, factualist, fictitious, fictive*, and *figurative* authorial engagement in the aesthetic past. But, this is hardly news. Because all histories are narratives this does not mean all histories are inventions. However, history is a very powerful cultural myth—possibly the final cultural myth. Now, by this I do not suggest this is the final age of history. History, I suspect, will always exist in some form and it is likely to remain as a very powerful cultural myth simply because all histories are construed as the historian wants.

However, as Jean Baudrillard claimed, all historians are storehouses of strong myths. So, I thought at some length when writing this book whether I should include the concept of *fidelity*. I left that concept to this paragraph because the notion of *fidelity* is the quality of being faithful to the past. Now, most histories are a very strong and capacious 'myth construing' cultural vehicles. However, the line between the past and history is construed as an invention. Now, historians who eventually end up unsure if they have lost their referential grasp on the past have to constitute their new possible past. Today then, the historical reality of the past can only exist in a series of the historian's preferred representations that are thus a hyper-resemblance of the past. This may be a clumsy way to describe it, but all histories are the historian's restitution and reinstatement of the past. All histories, then, are the last 'strong myths' in our Western culture.

Today, everything escapes its 'historical representations' apart from those of historians who insist that they have discovered past reality. Or, that they think so. However, history is not exactly like the past, it is just a bit more exact. So, all that historians can have of the past, then, is some sort of similitude. Unfortunately, historians have to cope with a process of 'historical catharsis and/or purgation'. Happily and however, historians always fail in discovering the reality of the past because historians and their consumers more than often exist in a universe of paradox, paraphrase, parody, pastiche, plot, point of view, postmodernism, poststructuralism, and so forth.

However, and obviously, the key 'to engaging the past' is not only through history but also through its 'performativity' and its semiotic expression of 'past reality' by historians and/or anyone else. Now, historians are taught to engage with the past in the sense that all 'historying' is 'a performativity rendezvous with the past' through that 'retro scenario' called the past. Arguably, then, history is the 'strongest' 'unconscious' myth in our Western culture. So now, all 'historying' is that cultural process through which historians—and everyone else—seek out the truth of the past through the hyperreality of the form and the content of the past.

Now, of all the history prostheses available to historians is the 'history-processing' clone. This is annoyingly common given that there are numberless historians who will 'endorse the same analysis' of the 'same time, same place, same history'. Historians, of course, constantly insist that there is always a new and radical historical interpretation. Of course, most histories are largely duplicated especially in respect of ideology, philosophy, viewpoint, and so forth and hence what we have are numerous duplicated/cloned/reprised and repeated (hi)stories. Now, to be frank, most histories are duplicates in some way or another. Just how many Russian Revolution books have been written, or the American Revolution, or the French Revolution, or the English Glorious Revolution, and so one and so forth? The obvious intellectual shaping and whittling devices for history texts include ideology, gender, geographical location, and the age of the historian and yet another set of confines such as aesthetics, catharsis, and various cleansing purgatives on and so forth.

Now, another problem among historians is the notion of incommensurability which signifies the existence of at least two or more points of an 'historical view'. All historians, then, compete with each other to better them in terms of the best explanation of the nature of the past. Now, then, there is no possibility of a neutral 'past-*as*-history'. Hence, historians can never deny past reality, as they understand it. The logic of this is 'infinite regression'. So, the 'infinite regression' is a never-ending chain of testable propositions as to the nature and meaning of the past and so to be blunt, then, for every historian there is a (or their) preferred history. No historian then can escape any sort of convenient and perpetual past regress, and hence all historians can never resolve the obvious existence of their intentionality and interpretivism. So, without historians, the past would remain a mush and slush of nonsense.

So, the ontology of the 'the-past-*as*-history' expresses the historian's engagement with the past through its myriad authorial forms, which are their imaginative projections of the past. Now, as I have suggested, history is an aesthetic representation of the inconstancy of the past. So, every historian takes the reality of the past very seriously because they will defy the present past. Unfortunately—or fortunately if you prefer—there are many aesthetic means through which historians (like everyone else) can engage with the past in terms of sadness, taste, restraint, balance, insistence, objectivity, the most obvious of which is an existential warrant that the past might—just might—come into some connection with past realism or even the objective truth.

So, the realism/reality of the past is entirely dependent upon the historian's willingness to produce those truth-conditions they believe will engender the reality of the past. But—and obviously—historians entirely depend upon the aesthetic past they want. Hence, there is no discovery in the past apart from that injection of history produced, fashioned, and/or formed by the historian. The notion of the discovery of the history of the past—obviously—is nonsense. Historians can locate the past thanks according to the probabilities that something did or did not exist and in a certain way or not. So, historians are entirely dependent on the principle of aesthetic realism. History, then, is not just a list of what happened in a certain order, but the past is always and unavoidably an aesthetic undertaking.

All that the historian can hope for when engaging with *the* past, is an ersatz aesthetic reality given the unavoidable situation that they constantly assert *the* nature of the past when they have deliberately authored it into their preferred past reality. So, all histories are qualified versions of that reality they prefer. Hence, there is no single history, which is the

Conclusion 191

'actual past'. Knowing what happened in the past and what it meant can only work if historians (a) ignore aesthetic realism or (b) sell beach chairs or some other really useful undertaking. Either way, the reality of the past has to be described. To be blunt then: historians cannot possibly know the nature of the past because of the aesthetic properties they deploy for discovering it.

This sounds worrying and it is. Knowing the 'reality', 'nature', and 'meaning' of the past is a pursuit on a par with the famous, infamous, and worrying hunting of the Snark that turns out to be a Boojum as Lewis Carroll (famously) suggested. Now, professional historians very rarely worry about being historians because they are trained to be historians and hence they are (trained to be) insulated against silly or pernicious histories. However, as I have suggested, the past is not history and that is why there is a compelling argument for defining history *as* an aesthetic realist undertaking. So, when 'historying the past', historians should understand that when engaging with the past they are engaging with history rather than the past.

Of course, it may seem an odd approach to the past, but all too often historians create histories that they believe are explications, representations, and exemplifications of possible pasts. The first and last problem for historians whether or not they realize it is that 'the past' is only accessible as a construal of aesthetic experience. Of course historians, like everyone else, can learn much of what happened in the past and what it meant or means. However, the ontology of history remains what it is. All histories are 'worked' as aesthetic forms, books, lectures, TV programmes, biographies, seminars, as news reports, denotations, paintings, music, and so forth. Nevertheless, expressing the reality of the past as the historian hears it, sees it, and writes it or 'imagined what it meant' remains an expression of evocation.

So to conclude then, it should not be surprising that when engaging with the past there are no 'ready-made histories lying about awaiting to be discovered' by historians or anyone else. The notion of there being 'the history' in 'the past' is nonsense of course. Of course, only our knowledge of the past will secure 'the reality' of the future past. As I noted before, then, the *factional, factitious, fabricated, factious, factitive, factive, factualist, fictitious, fictive,* and *figurative* authorial engagement with 'the historical past' cannot make sense of the past. So then, the most awkward problem with history is evidently its intersubjectivity. Most historians, then, insist that their consumers must surely believe what historians believe. However, then, and rather than trusting what we already know about the past, historians rely on the security of the hypothetico-deductive method which is founded on observation and plain simple common sense. So, enjoy your history while its lasts.

Index

'actuality' 25–26, 49, 60, 71, 81, 97, 112, 160
'aestheticised historied past' 49–50
aesthetics: 'history aesthetics' 79, 124, 172; influences on 190; influences on past 2, 3, 15, 64; literary 13; of representations of the past 138 ; use by historians 16, 36, 52, 59, 77, 85, 129, 133, 151, 187
'analogy' 164
Ankersmit, Frank 63, 99, 173
'appearance' 26, 152
Aristotle 86–88
'artifice' 31, 44, 49, 60, 115, 179
'authenticity' 35, 100, 113–114, 136, 149, 155, 171, 174–176

Barthes, Roland 106
Baudrillard, Jean 40–41, 43–44, 162, 172, 189
Becker, Carl 29

Carr, E.H. 155
Carroll, Lewis 191
causality 91, 95, 102, 183
chronology 27, 95, 103–104, 114
cogency 68, 174–175
cognitive value 59–60
coherence 18, 20–21, 35, 68, 104, 155
Collingwood, Robin George 10, 35–36, 54, 104, 151–152, 157, 166–167
comedy 59
'composition and decomposition' principles 23
consensus 20–21, 35, 49, 68, 142–143
constancy 111

constructivism 142–143
continuity 104
correlation 20–21, 35, 68, 142–143
correspondence 20–21, 34–35, 49, 57, 68, 142–143, 164, 173
'covering laws' 76

Danto, Arthur 76
Dead Certainties (Unwarranted Speculations) (Schama) 184
deconstructionism 41, 48
'deletion and supplementation' principles 23
Deleuze, Gilles 40
Derrida, Jacques 27, 143, 173, 187
descriptions 6, 8, 12, 47–48, 55, 97–98, 111–113, 116, 156
Doctorow, E.L. 183
'doing history': aesthetics of 59; fabrication of facts in 60–61; *factional* nature of 16, 18, 23, 26, 28–29; *factious* nature of 67–68, 72, 80; *factitious* nature of 31; *factitious* nature *of* 37, 39; *factitive* nature of 87–88; *factualist* nature of 120–121; failure of 107; *fictitious* nature of 135; *fictive* nature of 151; irony in 28, 31, 186; literal renditions and 8; making a living out of 140; mechanics of 12–13, 15–16; perpetual problem with 47; process of 39, 42, 44, 53–54; as re-enactment of the past 157, 166; representation in 129–131; rethinking 132–133; significance of epistemology to 127–128; stress test for 117; through 'historical imagination' 151–154

Index

emplotments 7, 93, 118, 168–169, 174, 178
'epistemic' 2–3, 15
epistemology 74–75, 119, 127–128, 135, 176
evidence: 'authenticity' of 35; discovery of 75, 78, 112–113; *figurative* 174; historical truth and 67; interpretation 18, 20, 27, 50, 56, 84, 100–102, 104, 111, 117, 165; selection of 9, 11–13, 27, 31, 39, 75, 118–121, 126, 140, 153, 173; telling lies about 151–152, 166–168; verified 65

fabricated: concept of 47–63, 186, 188, 191; facts 60–61; history 61–62; historying 21, 51, 54–56, 61; 'story creations' 49–50
fabrications 48–50, 55, 60–61, 184
factional: arguments 18; concept of 14–29, 186, 188, 191; forms 14–17; historical truth 18–21; historying 16–17, 19–22, 24, 26–28
factious: concept of 64–80, 186, 188, 191; dissent 72–73; hindsight 78; historical truth 65–69; historying 64–70, 73–74, 75–76, 78–80; mind-set 72; truth 65–68
factitious: concept of 30–46, 186, 188, 191; 'correspondence truth' 34–35; historying 21, 31–33, 39, 42, 44; truth 34, 39
factitive: concept of 81–96, 186, 188, 191; effect 102–103; historical truth 89, 100, 104; historying 81, 90–91; processing 82–84; truth 89–90, 100; verbs 85–87, 91, 97
factive: concept of 97–114, 186, 188, 191; historying 97, 101–102, 105, 107, 109; reality 106–110, 113–114
facts 2, 3, 25, 48, 54–55, 57, 60, 97–98, 100, 121–123, 155, 170, 172, 181
factualist: concept of 115–131, 186, 188, 191; facts 121–123; 'historical facts school' 121–123; historying 116, 124, 129; imagination 117, 120; language 127–128;
relationship between and *fictitious* 133, 140–141
'fake news' 132
fiction 61, 74, 77, 88, 142, 156, 161, 176, 182–183
fictitious: concept of 132–147, 186, 188, 191; historying 133–135, 137–139, 141; 'reality effect' 135; relationship between and *factualist* 133, 140–141
fictive: concept of 148–163, 186, 188, 191; deploying 154–155; 'historical imagination' 10–12; historying 149, 151; realities 153–154
fidelity 189
figurative: concept of 164–179, 186, 188, 191; deploying 170–171; figurative language 7, 111–112, 128–129, 155, 164–165, 170–171, 178; 'figurative truth' 9, 172; gap 178; 'historical imagination' 10–12; historying 166, 171–172, 177; 'imaginative historical in(ter)vention' 167; realities 168–169
Frye, Northrop 157

Goodman, Nelson 22, 60, 156

Hegel, Georg W.F. 177
hermeneutics 50–51, 57–58, 159, 187–188
Herodotus 28
hindsight 78
historians: authorial concepts 83; 'discovering the history' of the past 2–5, 13, 15–16, 21, 23–24, 26, 30, 35, 49–50, 56–57, 62, 77, 85, 88–89, 112–113, 115–119, 134, 137–138, 146, 150–154, 157–163, 165, 181–185, 190–191; engagement with the past 2–4, 24–26, 31, 36–38, 47–63, 68, 81, 84, 93–96, 106, 113, 120, 132–140, 146–150, 182–186, 189–191; 'extra-diegetic' author 169; *factional* condition 23; *factious* condition 64–65; *factitive* structuring of the past 81–96; *figurative* creations of 164–179; foundational beliefs of 4–5; 'historical imagination' 8–11, 73–75, 98, 104–106, 117, 120, 133–134, 148, 151–154, 156,

166–168, 170, 188; influences on 2–3, 15–17, 27, 38, 64–65, 79, 130, 172, 190; 'intra-diegetic' author 169; narrative creation of the past 1–4, 14–16, 24–25; preferred history 1, 7–8, 13, 15–16, 40, 45–46, 48, 51–54, 58–62, 67–71, 76–77, 82–90, 94–95, 112–113, 118, 120, 135, 139, 145–146, 157–160, 166, 177–179, 180, 186–187; reconstructionist 104; 'transfiguration process' 45
'historical authenticity' 149–150
'historical descriptions' 31–32
historical experience 111, 124–126
'historical fact' 25, 71, 121–123
'historical imagination' 8–11, 73–75, 98, 104–106, 117, 120, 133–134, 148, 151–154, 156, 166–168, 170, 188
'historical interpretation' 20
historical knowledge 35, 89
'historical meaning' 92–93, 116, 124
'historical mind' 176
'historical reality' 106–109, 114, 160–161
'historical situations' 176
historical sources 21, 24, 34, 68, 98, 104, 150–151, 182
historical thinking 167
historical truth: *correspondence* and 57; *factional* 18–21; *factious* 65–68; *factitious* 34–35, 39; *factitive* 89–90, 100, 104; *factualist* 121; *fictitious* 144; nature of 18–21, 49, 67–68
'historical view' 190
'historiographical metafiction' 183
'history aesthetic, the' 6, 28, 35–36, 79, 124
History and Tropology (Ankersmit) 99
historying: accessing 'the past' through 139, 191; aesthetic of 26–27; descriptions 6, 8, 12, 47–48, 55, 97–98, 111–113, 116, 156; *fabricated* 51, 54–56, 61; *factional* 16–17, 19–22, 24, 26–28; *factious* 64–73, 75–76, 79–80; *factitious* 31–36, 39, 42, 44; *factitive* 81, 86–87, 90–91; *factive* 97, 101–102, 105, 107, 109; *factualist* 116, 118–121, 124, 129; *fictitious* 133–135, 137–139, 141;

fictive 149, 151; *figurative* 166, 171–172, 177; as 'historiographic metafiction' 183; influences on 177; as 'a performativity rendezvous with the past' 189; postmodern 22; process of 61, 72, 83
'history reality effect' 107–110
'history workshops' 79
holograms 169
Hutcheon, Linda 183
'hyperreality' 40–44, 110, 163

ideology 78, 84, 88
image 58
'imaginative historical in(ter)vention' 152, 167
interpretation: *fabricated* 49–51, 53–57, 62; *factional* 15, 17–18, 20, 24–29, 98; *factious* 65, 67, 70–71, 73, 78–79; *factitious* 32, 34–35, 38–39, 45; *factitive* 82–83, 85–89, 91–92, 94–95; *factive* 98–99, 100, 103–104, 112–114; *factualist* 117–118, 120–121, 123, 127, 130; *fictitious* 132, 135, 137–138, 147; *fictive* 149, 150, 152–153, 155–156, 159, 161; *figurative* 164–165, 167–168, 170, 176, 178–179; ideological 79; interpretation of American history 10–11; literal 8; preferred 6–7, 9, 94–95, 181–182, 187–188, 190
irony 1–2, 28, 31, 62, 137, 177, 186

Jameson, Frederic 43
Jenkins, Keith 27–28

Kennedy, John F. 44, 81

language: control of 8–9, 31; *factualist* 127–128; *fictitious* 133–134; figurative language 7, 111–112, 128–129, 155, 164–165, 170–171, 178; inadequacy of 34–35
'likeness' 164
literature 136–138, 141–142, 157–158, 177, 186
Lyotard, Jean-François 173

McLuhan, Marshall 42
memory 159–160

Memory, History and Forgetting (Ricoeur) 159
Metahistory (White) 79, 127
'metanarratives' 133
Midnight's Children (Rushdie) 183
mimesis 130, 173–174

non-*factive* mental states 99–100
nostalgia 110

Oakeshott, Michael 145
'ontic' 2–3, 15
ontology 119, 178–179
'ordering' principle 23

'past-*as*-history, the-': central problem with 33–34; common sense logic of 49–50; constitution of 7–8; *fabricated* 49–50, 52, 54–56; *factional* 19, 23–24; *factious* 66–70, 72–73, 75, 78; *factitious* 33–34, 36–37; *factitive* 82, 91–92; *fictitious* 135–137, 143–144; *figurative* 169–171, 176, 179; form of 1; forms 117; 'historical imagination' 10–12; irony in 45; ontology of 190; as product of the historian's personality 159; writing of 112
phenomenology 57–58, 122, 124–126
post hoc ergo propter hoc fallacy 79–80, 92
postmodernism 8, 22, 43–45, 69, 109, 114, 133, 150, 165, 184
'practical past' 161
primary sources 21, 68, 150–151
Propp, Vladimir 94

Ragtime (Doctorow) 183
Ranke, Leopold von 121
realism 178
'reality effect, the' 99–101, 106–110, 113–114, 135
re-enactment 157, 167
'reference' 61, 101–102
'reformation' principle 23
representation: crisis of 40; descriptions 6; *fabricated* 47, 51, 57–60, 62; *factious* 66, 75; *factitious* 40–42, 45; *factitive* 85, 98; *factive* 101, 103, 105, 107–108, 110–111, 113–114;

factualist 115, 120, 122–124, 129–131; *fictitious* 133–134, 138, 140–141, 144; *fictive* 149–150, 154–158; *figurative* 164–165, 169–178; preferred 189–191; preferred style of 19, 33–34, 66; rhetorical models for 7; symbolic 9, 11
'resemblance' 164, 169
Rethinking History (Jenkins) 27–28
'rhetorical models' 59
Ricoeur, Paul 158, 159, 174
romance 59
Rosenstone, Robert A. 184
Rushdie, Salman 183

satire 59
Schama, Simon 184
secondary sources 21, 68, 150–151
'Significance of the Frontier in American History, The'(Turner) 10
similitude 58
simulacra 45
Simulacra and Simulation (Baudrillard) 41, 43, 172
simulacrum 37, 43, 162–163
'simulation' 40, 42–45
Stevens, Wallace 156
'stock characters' 94
succession 83, 95
symbolism 7

Time and Narrative (Ricoeur) 174
tragedy 59
truth: *factious* 65–68; *factitious* 34, 39; *factitive* 89–90, 100; 'figurative truth' 9, 172; forms of 12, 18–21, 23, 34–35, 66–68, 142–143, 144, 172–173; historical truth 18–21, 34–35, 39, 49, 57, 65–68, 89–90, 100, 104, 121
Turner, Frederick Jackson 10–11

Ways of Worldmaking (Goodman) 60, 156
'weighting' principle 23
White, Hayden 6, 7, 27, 78–79, 109, 127, 145, 147, 153, 157–158, 160, 168, 173
Wilde, Oscar 178
Wittgenstein, Ludwig 111
'writing reality effect' 155, 171